Virtuous
Leaders

Virtuous Leaders

Strategy, Character,
and Influence in the 21st Century

Richard R. Kilburg

American Psychological Association • Washington, DC

Copyright © 2012 by the American Psychological Association. All rights reserved. Except as permitted under the United States Copyright Act of 1976, no part of this publication may be reproduced or distributed in any form or by any means, including, but not limited to, the process of scanning and digitization, or stored in a database or retrieval system, without the prior written permission of the publisher.

Published by
American Psychological Association
750 First Street, NE
Washington, DC 20002
www.apa.org

To order
APA Order Department
P.O. Box 92984
Washington, DC 20090-2984
Tel: (800) 374-2721; Direct: (202) 336-5510
Fax: (202) 336-5502; TDD/TTY: (202) 336-6123
Online: www.apa.org/pubs/books
E-mail: order@apa.org

In the U.K., Europe, Africa, and the Middle East, copies may be ordered from
American Psychological Association
3 Henrietta Street
Covent Garden, London
WC2E 8LU England

Typeset in Goudy by Circle Graphics, Inc., Columbia, MD

Printer: Maple-Vail Books, York, PA
Cover Designer: Mercury Publishing Services, Rockville, MD

The opinions and statements published are the responsibility of the authors, and such opinions and statements do not necessarily represent the policies of the American Psychological Association.

Library of Congress Cataloging-in-Publication Data

Kilburg, Richard R., 1946-
  Virtuous leaders: strategy, character, and influence in the 21st century/Richard R. Kilburg.
      p. cm.
  Includes bibliographical references and index.
  ISBN-13: 978-1-4338-1096-1
  ISBN-10: 1-4338-1096-4
  1. Leadership. 2. Executive ability. 3. Strategic planning. I. Title
  HD57.7.K524 2012
  303.3'4—dc23
                                        2011036424

British Library Cataloguing-in-Publication Data

A CIP record is available from the British Library.

Printed in the United States of America
First Edition

DOI: 10.1037/13494-000

To my wife, Joy, an everlasting blessing in my life and without whom this book would have been very difficult to produce.

CONTENTS

PREFACE

During the past 4 decades, I have been a leader in a variety of organizations; a follower of several dozen other practitioners of leadership; a student of the concepts, skills, and processes involved; and a consultant, educator, and coach to more than 1,000 managers and senior executives. I have watched the conceptual and practice literature evolve from the early developments in humanistic and management-by-objectives approaches, through the systems revolutions, to the quality and reengineering revolutions, into and out of learning organizations, and now into the disquiet and distemper of globalization and highly networked, virtual organizations. In a recent effort to review this literature, my colleague Marc Donohue and I plowed through a small mountain of articles and books. The American Psychological Association's (APA's) PsycINFO database now lists more than 11,400 entries on the topic of executive leadership. The field of study and practice is now well beyond the ability of any single person to comprehend completely. Indeed, humanity has come to know a great deal about this most complex, interesting, and important topic.

As concepts and practice emphases have waxed and waned over this period of time, I have consistently been interested in what remains steady—in what seems to be of permanent value for practitioners, teachers, and scientists to know about leadership. Can we say that there is anything fundamentally true about this human process and the people who seek these positions? Over the course of my career, I have contributed dozens of articles and chapters and five books related to this topic in one way or another. Since 2000, I have published three books with the APA on the subjects of executive coaching and leadership (Kilburg, 2000, 2006; Kilburg & Diedrich, 2007). These efforts have led me to the conclusion that yes, there are a variety of seemingly timeless or enduring characteristics of effective leadership.

In 2006, I defined *executive wisdom* as the process of doing the right thing, in the right way, at the right time, and for the right reasons (Kilburg, 2006). Effective leaders can be seen in the struggle to engage in the effort to enact wisdom daily, but is there a way to understand the essentials even more clearly? In this book, my answer is yes, it is possible to discern at least three components of effective leadership that endure across time and human history: strategy, character, and influence. Another way to comprehend these essentials involves framing them as the core components of the what and the how of leader performance. *Strategy*, broadly defined as setting the direction for an organization or organizational unit, can be understood as the answer to the question, What is the most important thing that leaders do? *Character*, described in this book as the consistent exercise of virtuous behavior in the face of constant turmoil, permanent change, frequent provocation, and demanding conditions, is the second enduring element of effective leadership that I have found. *Influence*, the ability to create meaningful relationships with others through which the work of an enterprise is accomplished, is the third component that transcends human history and time. Together, character and influence answer the question, how can leaders best accomplish the strategy that they have established for their organizations? No matter how far back one explores in history, philosophy, psychology, sociology, anthropology, or the other management-oriented sciences and related disciplines, variations of these three elements are always described as being present when individuals succeed at leadership. When there is a failure of leadership, one or more of them is always seen as being deficient or absent.

As I explore more fully in Chapter 1, as we penetrate deeper into the 21st century, leaders will experience the continued evolution of greater challenges than previous generations have encountered. The rise of market states and the importance of the global business corporation, with its emphasis on transnational markets, flexible labor supplies, fluid capital, and complete commitment to profits over virtually every other organizational concern, will be a centerpiece of this era. Sennet (1998) suggested that the peculiar type of uncertainty that people living through and in these types of organizations will experience routinely "exists without any looming historical disaster; instead it is woven into the everyday practices of a vigorous capitalism, instability is meant to be normal, Schumpeter's entrepreneur served up as an ideal Everyman" (p. 31).

For Sennet (1998), the central effect on lives lived embedded in global capitalism and its organizations is often the corrosion of character that he described in graphic narratives of men and women who struggled to survive economically, psychologically, physically, and spiritually in response to the never-ending demands of their employers and the ever-present threat of unemployment because of corporate commitments to seek the best prices for labor as it has increasingly become just another globally available commodity. Against such uncertainty and with the absence of permanence and of simple human commitment and trust more and more visible in corporations of all types, Sennet described the increasing difficulty humans have with defining and living lives of value, creating believable and meaningful identity narratives for themselves and their families, managing the constant taint and taste of failure and shame in their daily experience, and struggling to develop and live in communities that can provide shreds of support against these onslaughts.

Leaders of these global corporations and of their regional and local cousins, as well as elected and selected officials of governments worldwide, will be coping with these phenomena through much of this new century. At present, most of the answers they have produced have simply added to the array of longer term problems humanity faces. This does not mean that they are not trying or that they do not care in an emotional or even moral sense. It simply reflects that humans have not yet invented workable solutions for these problems and processes. In such ambiguous, dangerous, and difficult times, how can we prepare and support the individuals who possess the motivation and ability to provide leadership for our enterprises? The only answer I have found to this question is that we must continue to emphasize the importance of strategy, character, and influence. We must be able to describe the essentials of these core characteristics of effective leadership and continuously teach them to executives. We must hold our leaders accountable not only for defining and executing effective organizational strategy but also for consistently behaving in a virtuous manner and for using methods and approaches to building human relationships and influencing others in ways that consistently treat them with justice and reverence. Without careful and sustained attention to these core elements of leadership in the coming decades, I believe that all of humanity is increasingly likely to experience much more pain, suffering, and disruption than would otherwise be required.

This book would not have been possible without the extensive support of a number of people. Significant recognition and gratitude are owed first to my wife, Joy, who centers my life and supports me in every way imaginable. My friends and colleagues Paul Winum and Harry Levinson have consistently helped me think about and refine my approaches to these issues and participated in a series of programs at the APA and the Society of Consulting Psychologists annual meetings, where the essentials of this book were first presented and critiqued. Cate Kiefe of the Johns Hopkins School of Medicine has provided more of her graphics magic in the development of the figures and tables that appear throughout the text. The acquisitions and production editors of APA Books were up to their traditional high standards of professionalism and guidance. Finally, the clients, supervisors, instructors, executives, and participants in thousands of classes and programs over the course of a 4-decade career, who consistently taught me to pay attention to what is of central and enduring importance in the practice of leadership, deserve my deepest admiration and appreciation,

One final note is in order. All of the cases described in this book that come from my own practice experience have been appropriately disguised to maintain the privacy and confidentiality of the clients. Substantial changes have been made to these descriptions to ensure privacy, yet the essential teaching elements of the material have been retained.

Virtuous Leaders

1

THE TIMELESS NEED FOR LEADERS

THE RECENT ROAD BEHIND

In 1910, merely a century ago, leaders around the globe faced a world that was much different from that of their predecessors in 1810. Although some things had remained the same, many, many changes had accumulated, and it was clear that the pace of those shifts was also accelerating. Geopolitically, imperialism was still the predominant framework for great power interactions. The British, Ottoman, and German Empires stretched across continents. Russia was still ruled by a czar. The nation-states in the Americas had not yet emerged as significant influential agents on the world stage. China was a faded and challenged empire on its last emperor, and Japan had just begun to awaken as a latent power in Asia.

The population of the world was approximately 1.75 billion, and in the United States, it hovered at 92 million. Immigration to the Americas was still a major influence in Europe and Asia as the growing demand and associated economic opportunities across the Atlantic and Pacific drew the commitment of the dreamers and the desperate alike. It took days to cross the United States via steam-powered trains, and mail was the primary means of communication. The telegraph offered an electric alternative but was used by only a very few.

Most people still traveled locally by horse-and-carriage or horse-drawn trolleys. William Howard Taft was in the middle of a 4-year term as president, having succeeded the activist and charismatic Teddy Roosevelt. Federal antitrust laws passed at the end of the 19th century were continuing to have an impact on the emergence of large businesses and competitive markets in the country.

Technologically, the age of electricity was gathering momentum as barriers to generation and transmission were surmounted. Human flight was in its infancy. Automobiles and trucks, the most common form of transportation in the 20th century, had started their eventual conquest of horses and wagons. The Standard Oil Trust had been broken into pieces, but the successors were avidly building a nationwide industry that would power much of the commercial growth of the world during the next 100 years. Particle accelerators had yet to be invented, but Einstein had published the theory of special relativity, which was turning science on its head. The biological revolution had not started, and the majority of physicians in the United States were still being trained in barber schools. Radios and telephones were in their infancy.

Democracy had established itself as a worthy competitor to the remaining kingly states, principalities, empires, and autocratically ruled nation-states, but the debate on the appropriate forms of governance for human activity had hardly reached a fever pitch. The philosophy of Karl Marx had not yet taken hold of any country, but arguments about ownership, the rights of workers, exploitation of labor, and other social and economic issues were widespread. Terrorism was largely confined to efforts to take apart the remaining kingly states (Bobbitt, 2002). Although there was a general sense of the extent of the human world and its diversity, transnational interconnectivity was largely a concern of small governing elites in the major capitals of Europe.

In short, it was a smaller, narrower, slower, yet rapidly accelerating time. In 1910, leaders had no way of anticipating the changes that would soon sweep the world and alter nearly everything. Indeed, there were no formal disciplines devoted to looking forward or to helping human enterprises make systematic change. Scientific psychology was just emerging and, as a discipline, had not yet had a significant effect on humanity or human behavior. Formal approaches to the development of leaders were largely confined to a few military academies around the world. Most executives learned what they needed on the job. They coped with change the best they could with the means at hand. For the majority of managers in private industry and in emerging government bureaucracies, command and control methods predominated. Carlyle's (1849/1907) exposition of the great man–heroic leader hypothesis and the work of Aristotle (1908), Plato (1999), and Confucius (1989) were still the best explanations of how effective executives could be identified and educated. The scientific and conceptual work devoted to understanding leadership in more detail had hardly begun.

By the second decade of the 21st century, the population of the world has increased more than three times to nearly 7 billion. The human community has borne the burden of a century of virtually endless warfare as conflicts of various sizes ebbed and flowed across the face of the planet. Science and technology have literally revolutionized time, space, communication, transportation, medicine, productivity, manufacturing, agriculture, and virtually every other domain of human activity. The Internet, invented in the defense laboratories of the United States and unleashed as a commercial enterprise in the mid-1990s, has been transforming everything it touches. Billions of people are now connected into, for all purposes, an infinitely complex, global web of technical, psychosocial, cultural, and commercial exchanges. Telephones are rapidly being replaced by handheld computers capable of doing unimaginably complex tasks, including allowing instant video calls via microwave connections to the Internet to people with access to similar devices and accessing real-time, computer-aided directions in most cities around the world.

The periodic table of elements has been completely deciphered, and the scientific community is on the verge of simultaneously verifying its beloved standard model of particle physics and opening up the possibility of the first empirical demonstrations of the validity of string theory, which hypothesizes that the fundamental building blocks of nature are not particles and forces but unimaginably small entities that vibrate in seen and unseen dimensions to create all matter and energy (Randall, 2005). The biological revolution has engineered new forms of grain and methods of agriculture that now feed many more people than had been thought possible. The secrets of life are being unwound in laboratories around the world, and humans have taken many steps along the road that will enable them to create and modify biological entities at will, including themselves (Frenay, 2006). Transportation and telecommunication systems are now global in nature. Humans can travel quickly by air to virtually any city on the planet. In many countries, cars and trucks have displaced trains as the main vehicles for carrying people and products locally and regionally.

Geopolitically, we have seen the nearly complete unraveling of the empires of the 19th century. The world's 20th-century courtships with communism and fascism as forms of government have been largely rejected. We now have 195 countries in the world, with 192 belonging to the United Nations. The annual measured global output of goods and services, or global economic product (GEP), now stands well in excess of $60 trillion. Europe has been united into a political and economic union that is the single largest power bloc in the world, annually producing more than $16 trillion in goods and services. Japan, China, Russia, India, and Brazil are the other most significant contributors to the GEP. The predominant forms of government are various types of democracies, but dictatorships, kingdoms, autocracies, tyrannies, and a few diehard adherents to communism also remain. The global fear of weapons of mass destruction has greatly inhibited major wars between nation-states, but internal conflicts over nationalistic ambitions, territory, and ethnic identities; minor wars over access to minerals and other economic assets; and organized terrorist campaigns in support of various political, ethnic, religious, cultural, territorial, and geopolitical objectives are a common feature of global life.

Virtually none of these developments were foreseen by the leaders of nations and large businesses a century ago. The evolution of these phenomena and their impact on humans around the world have required executives in governments and the private sector to educate themselves and to modify significantly their approaches to leadership. Without effective leadership at many levels of human affairs and in many places throughout the world, the developments and outcomes of the past century could have produced a much grimmer picture than the one humanity faces today. Science has taken a significant interest in leadership and its development, and after 70 years of study, we now know a lot more about the components and processes of leadership and how to measure it. Nevertheless, leadership remains an enigma, and what constitutes effective leadership is still a matter of considerable debate.

A GLANCE AHEAD

I need to be clear that I do not believe anyone can truly see the future with any degree of clarity. The number of variables involved in the daily connections and exchanges of a globally wired and competitive economy is by now infinite for all intent and purposes. Furthermore, as we know from relatively recent developments in complexity science (Stacey, 2007), despite our best efforts to ascertain the course of developments in human activities, their very nature enables them to emerge and to change unpredictably. Nevertheless, humanity has developed many new tools with and through which leaders try to do a better job of anticipation. Forecasting techniques, computer simulations, modeling and scenario methods, strategy formation, trend analysis, and even whole genres of fiction writing, film, and television productions are now all commonly being used to support the efforts of leaders to look around the bend in the road and see what is ahead for them, their organizations, and the world as a whole. So as we begin to take this journey together to examine the issue of how we might better think about preparing humans for positions of leadership in our complex world, let us briefly explore what some authors have described as several primary challenges with which we are already coping and that may well present both current and future leaders with extraordinarily difficult times.

First, Bobbitt (2002, 2009), Bremmer (2010), and others have described the radical transformation that the world's geopolitical and economic systems have undergone since the end of World War II. In brief, we have experienced the end of the Cold War (what Bobbitt called the Long War), the near complete death of command-and-control-style economic planning in communist countries, the successful rise of globally competitive private enterprises, a commitment to the principles of free trade through the establishment of the World Trade Organization, and the relatively recent creation of new forms of state capitalism that are providing substantial and sustained challenges to free-market-based economies and the companies that compete in them. Bremmer foresaw a continuing set of problems and conflicts arising as the free-market-based democracies of Europe, the Americas, and Asia try to contend with the variants of state capitalism being practiced by Russia, Brazil, India, Saudi Arabia, and particularly China. He stated clearly that the goals of private enterprise to make returns for investors by driving ever-increasing, efficient methods of capital formation and production into their businesses will increasingly be in complex forms of conflict with state capitalism. Governments that support market approaches anxiously and ambivalently accept the negative aspects of this approach, including the realities of market excesses, severe business reversals, significant displacement and reconfigurations of labor markets, less than predictable business cycles, and ebbs and flows of tax revenue in exchange for the increased efficiencies of markets, effective use of capital and labor, and overall economic growth that come with private enterprise. They use regulatory, judicial, and legal authority to level playing fields and avoid distortions that monopolies, speculation bubbles in markets, and other forms of corruption and misalignment produce. They also work to create social welfare infrastructures to support their citizens who may well be harmed by the unpredictable disruptions and destructive aspects of free market capitalism.

Bremmer (2010) also suggested that state capitalism as practiced in Russia, Saudi Arabia, China, and other countries has fundamentally different goals from its free-market sibling. Capitalist methods and markets in these countries are directed toward supporting the political needs and goals of the power elites that rigorously defend access to governmental authority. Manipulation of currencies; access to customers; and the flow of natural resources, labor, and capital are largely driven not by the desire to maintain functional markets but instead by the elites' desire to remain in power and to support those citizens who in turn keep them in their positions. These elites work hard to avoid severe social disruption and unrest that can challenge their authority and the stability of the state itself. Although most of these states belong to the World Trade Organization and thus accept some of its principles and processes, they have become quite adept at using large, global corporations to further their domestic ends. Bremmer foresaw an extensive period of complex economic and geopolitical competition in which free-market countries and private companies will struggle to stay open to collaboration with these state capitalism countries. The will also have to cope with the further diminution of economic and political power that will probably accompany the vast wealth and new forms of global competition that state capitalism will produce.

Second, as I stated briefly earlier, technology, particularly in the information and telecommunications industries, continues to evolve rapidly. Kurzweil (1999) has tracked the evolution of these disciplines and markets for decades. A decade ago, he wrote that he saw no immediate end for Moore's Law, which states that the number of transistors that can be put onto a given physical substrate (microchip) doubles approximately every 18 months. The inevitable consequences of this rise in capacity, and the associated creation of software programs to take advantage of it, according to Kurzweil, will lead to staggering changes in the world—and in humanity itself. The realities of his vision are with us every day; consider Apple Corporation's 2010 release of an iPhone that enables people to have two-way video conversations. That device is supported by nearly a quarter of a million downloadable software applications that can do extraordinary tasks in a package that fits easily into the palm of a person's hand.

Just as stunning has been the rapid emergence of social networking technologies such as Facebook, which now connects more than half a billion people worldwide and is creating new ways for people to interact. Facebook influences people's private lives, the marketplace, and geopolitics—consider the recent uprisings in many Middle Eastern countries in which protestors reached out to the population via social media and the Internet. E-commerce now makes it possible for people to shop globally for a diverse array of goods and services online. Vast volumes of information flow around the world at the speed of light, enabling accountants, consultants, designers, physicians, and other professionals to work across the globe, creating serious challenges to traditional methods of state-sponsored regulation. Kurzweil (1999) predicted that by 2020, for approximately $1,000 in 1990-equivalent U.S. currency, humans will be able to purchase the computing power of an average human brain. Workstations for home use now routinely have the processing capacity of the supercomputers of the early 1990s. What will humanity do with all of this technological horsepower besides play ever-more-realistic games? Kurzweil suggested several other scenarios—simultaneously intriguing and threatening—and hypothesized that increasingly more types of labor will be done by machines. In essence, he said that if any type of work can be made to fit into an algorithm—that is, an if–then proposition—eventually a machine will be able to perform it.

Third, humanity is approximately 200 years into the technological revolution created by the theoretical understanding of electromagnetism (the first electricity-based telegraph device was invented in 1809) and what we could call early-20th-century physics. We have passed the 50th anniversary of Watson and Crick's publication of the discovery of the structure of DNA (Frenay, 2006; Watson & Crick, 1953). Earlier this decade, the entire human genome was decoded, and nearly every day, new scientific findings are published that describe the functions of various genes and their combinations in humans, animals, and plants. The first artificial biological organism was created in a laboratory run by Craig Vintner and his team, who also contributed significantly to the human genome project. Animals have been cloned, and medical interventions using genetic manipulations are now underway in a number of settings. Algae are being engineered to create synthetic fuels. Bacteria that eat oil and digest plastic in landfills have been deployed in a number of states and countries. The real promises—and the very real challenges—are just beginning, however.

It seems clear to many that within a foreseeable period, humanity will face staggering new opportunities, but also problems, based on this accelerating biological revolution. For example, laboratories around the world are in intense, competitive, commercial races to develop and deploy replacement organs for those that humans wear out. Medical technology now allows the replacement of major joints as well as the transplantation of major organs, but both are extraordinarily expensive and unavailable to many who need them. Later in this century, people may very well be able to order replacements for hearts, livers, lungs, kidneys, eyes, and anything else that fails. Even more promising—and threatening—parents may be able to go to a clinic and design the characteristics of the child or children they want to create. This sounds like science fiction, but the reality is that deeper into this century, human life spans may extend on average beyond 100 years. If that happens, pressures on the resources of the entire planet will increase astronomically. Now let's briefly look at a fourth challenge facing leaders in the 21st century.

Goleman (2009) described a world in which our technology readily produces thousands of new chemicals every year, many of which are then used in commercial products and manufacturing processes with little to no testing on their long-term effects on ecological systems and plant and animal biology. He described the complete lack of a global approach to analyzing these problems or to regulate their impacts. As the situation stands now, it is more or less every nation-state for itself; product formulations, information about ingredients and their histories, and toxicity and safety data are widely available in some places and completely hidden in others. Goleman called for vigorous investments in life-cycle assessments and industrial ecology that would be capable of providing the detailed histories of the production of every ingredient used in products consumed by humans and animals. He advocated for forms of what he called "radical transparency" through which people anywhere on Earth could go online to access comprehensible data about what is in the products they want to buy. He contended that if such information were widely available, consumers could use their purchasing power to influence manufacturers dramatically, ultimately leading to products that are more effective, economical, and ecologically and biologically safer.

What is surely the largest, most potentially devastating, and most controversial ecological issue leaders face as we move deeper into the century is the inexorable rise in the volume of greenhouse gases emitted by humans and the consequent rise in global temperatures. Glacial melting, the annual disappearance of the ice cap in the North Pole and Arctic Ocean, and the progressive rise of carbon dioxide, methane, and other gases that help to hold in infrared solar radiation are now well documented scientifically. Global sea levels and mean daily temperatures have been rising steadily for the past century. They are forecast using complex weather simulations to rise much more, with the potential for devastating impact on human habitat and biological diversity (Archer, 2006). Although these phenomena have attracted other explanations (Spencer, 2010), leaders of nation-states have been struggling for nearly a decade to determine what to do about these problems and to agree on common pathways to ameliorate the damage. If the worst aspects of the dire forecasts are proved accurate, leaders of governments and private organizations will be forced to deal with the myriad effects of such large-scale changes, and to date few have done much short of argue about the issues.

The final issue I want to frame in this introduction focuses on the clearly discernible shifts in global demographic patterns that leaders are now facing and will increasingly confront in the coming decades. Birth rates have been rising in some countries and declining in others over the past 30 years. When left unaddressed, these types of changes can produce radical consequences for local, regional, and national populations. As I write in 2010, birth rates have declined significantly in Russia, Japan, and many European nations. Their populations are aging rapidly, creating significant challenges for the governments and private enterprises that must cope with these patterns. Significantly larger expenditures for health care, severe labor shortages in many industries, the need to import guest workers from more populous nations and the consequent political–social strains that arise in heretofore culturally and even racially coherent societies, as well as declining economic expectations are merely some of the difficulties with which these countries are beginning to struggle.

Other countries, such as India, China, Malaysia, most of Central America and South America, and some in the Middle East are managing the reverse trend, as tens of millions of young people are coming of age with the expectation of becoming full participants and consumers in the global economy. Indeed, it is projected that the world will add some 3 billion new citizens over the next 40 years. In just one illustration of the challenges facing these growing nations, Bremmer (2010) suggested that China will need to continue to add some 10 to 12 million new jobs each year to its domestic economy simply to stay even with the population growth. A mere 300 million people out of a population of 1.4 billion have achieved middle-class status in China. One can readily understand the concerns of the nation's political leadership when hundreds of millions of their current citizens continue to live below China's poverty line. The political, economic, and psychosocial challenges facing nations and their leaders who are and will be coping with the effects of these large-scale demographic trends are amazing. In July 2010, the world witnessed violent mobs taking to the streets in Greece when its government announced a set of stringent economic restrictions in response to a set of extraordinary financial problems that decades of poor leadership had produced.

So here humanity sits, having crossed the threshold of the 21st century in relative safety and prosperity, the global recession of 2008–2009 aside. One could also say this transition has been made with the creation of enormous potential for the whole world. As an entire species, we are better informed and educated, have more sophisticated technologies, and have access to global troves of human and natural resources on scales never imagined by previous generations. Although our challenges may seem daunting, our opportunities are even more spectacular if we can realize them. What will it take for us to arrive at even better global security and opportunity in 2110? I believe that the answer is the same as it has always been. Only if we can produce generation after generation of highly virtuous and effective leaders in every domain of human endeavor are we likely to succeed.

THE WHAT AND HOW OF EFFECTIVE LEADERSHIP

This book attempts to examine what I consider the two essential questions that leaders of any government or public or private enterprise must answer for themselves and everyone connected to the endeavors that the organization seeks to undertake. First, what are we to do? This is a deceptively simple inquiry, but in reality, it takes the executive who asks it immediately into the most critical and difficult types of mysteries, puzzles, and investigations. For the answers to this question lie in determining the identity of an organization and the strategic direction it will pursue. Identity and direction create purpose for everyone associated with the enterprise. When people are asked to identify themselves, they often give their names first and then go on to explain what they do and for whom they work. Names are subsumed in occupations, and these in turn are most often attached to some form of human organization. Working adults around the world spend most of their waking hours supporting structured group efforts to compete effectively in the global marketplace. In individual terms, success means employment, growth in opportunities and security, and the capacity to feed and nurture oneself and a family. In organizational terms, success in defining identity and direction means that the enterprise can continue to support all of the individuals associated with it and that it has the possibility of a long life. Stacey (2007) reported that the average commercial business has an approximately 40-year life span. However, governments, churches, universities, and in fact all forms of human organizations have demonstrated the capacity to survive for centuries and even millennia with their core identities and directions intact. They do so for a wide variety of reasons but most importantly because the leaders of each successive generation are at least able to maintain their operations. Without effective leadership, enterprises quickly wither and die. We explore these issues in more depth in Chapter 2, which focuses on developing and implementing strategy.

The second question is this: How should we go about achieving our organizational goals? This is an even more difficult question to answer simply because what individuals do to lead effectively varies widely. A quick examination of any recent textbook on leadership (Northouse, 2010; Yukl, 2010) reveals the complexity of these issues. Although psychological and managerial science have given the world an enormous array of concepts, skills, methods, and explanatory frameworks to describe and differentiate effective from ineffective leadership, it can be said that there is as yet no universally accepted theory to guide either leadership research or leadership practice (Bennis, 2007). Nevertheless, anyone who accepts the responsibility to lead a human organization and then takes on the authority vested in an executive position will immediately face the problems associated with the question of how to get the work of the enterprise accomplished. Most important, any such individual will in fact face that question in miniature forms dozens if not hundreds of times every day.

The core purposes of this book are to provide leaders of all types of organizations and the development professionals who work with them with some concrete and practical answers to both of these questions. Although the cases and examples that illustrate the principles we explore are drawn largely from business organizations, the issues involved readily generalize to the challenges leaders face in not-for-profit enterprises and governments as well. The following chapters are based on a lifetime of study and practice on my part. For more than 40 years, I have worked in managerial positions, studied and taught management concepts and skills, and consulted to leaders in a wide variety of organizations and industries. The material in the chapters that follow comes from a wide variety of sources that I have either discovered in the profoundly stimulating work of others or have developed myself. The essential theme of the book represents a fusion of ancient ideas with contemporary science, experience, methods, and concerns.

The fundamental position I have come to embrace with regard to leadership is that the initial conceptualizations of the roles, functions, and characteristics of effective executives developed by the ancient Chinese and Greeks and as they have continued to be handed down to us in the manuscripts of Confucius and Plato are as relevant today as in the past. Those formulations stated clearly that to be effective on behalf of citizens (and in the modern sense, this can be extended to all classes of organizational stakeholders), leaders must be virtuous human beings. Confucius and Socrates went to great lengths to describe both effective leadership and the individuals who could provide that function to their respective societies. For both of them, leaders had to possess courage, temperance, justice, and wisdom because these characteristics were required of them every day. Confucius founded and Plato was part of schools devoted to the development of people to provide such leadership. In the case of Confucius, that school continued to provide leaders who served the Chinese empire for millennia and can still be seen in the philosophical roots supporting many 21st-century Chinese organizations. In the case of Socrates, his ideas and ideology continue to permeate nearly every contemporary educational program in leadership regardless of whether those foundations are publicly acknowledged.

This book tries to demonstrate that those ancient foundations are still the best for 21st-century leaders and constitute the fundamentals of how they can do their jobs well on a daily basis. It also tries to provide a contemporary view of how those ancient virtues can be developed and enacted by leaders of our current organizations and how educators, consultants, and coaches can understand and use them in their work with clients. I believe that if development professionals do not aspire to virtue themselves, they will be hard-pressed to help anyone grow in these most important ways. Finally, a successful leader exhibits virtue across the three core components of executive leadership that are investigated in this book: strategy, character, and influence.

PLAN OF THE BOOK

In the six chapters that follow, I pursue these questions in some depth. In Chapter 2, we explore succinctly the issues of what executives should do to lead their enterprises effectively. The associated issues of identity and direction have been largely subsumed in the study and practice of organizational strategy and the processes of developing it.

Chapter 3 opens with a case study based in my coaching practice and examines the typical problems and issues that most commonly lead to the failure and derailment of leaders. These challenges are examined in the rubric of seven deadly management errors. These in turn are contrasted with the human virtues identified earlier and most closely associated with Socrates, Confucius, Plato, and Aristotle.

Chapter 4 also opens with a case study and then provides an overview of a variety of competency-based approaches to defining and developing leaders that are in common use throughout the world. These competency models are discussed within the context of human virtue and the emerging emphasis on that subject within the subdiscipline of positive psychology.

In Chapter 5, we dive into the development and practice of the virtues of temperance and reverence. Two case studies provide a practical framework for describing and understanding how the presence or absence of these types of character traits helps or hurts leaders.

Chapter 6 provides contrasting examples of moral—just and immoral—unjust leadership as a background for the exploration of how leaders create relationships and organizations in which members experience fair or unfair treatment. A conceptual framework for the examination of ethical and moral issues is explored, along with a brief overview of the extensive psychosocial research available on distributive, procedural, and interpersonal justice in organizations.

The seventh and final chapter considers the skills involved in influencing others. An analysis of contemporary research findings and a conceptual model for assessing influencing processes are provided. A variety of methods and skills to influence others are also explored, and suggestions are made to help leaders improve their ability to work with and through their key relationships.

If you are a professional who either aspires to a position of leadership responsibility or currently has one and is searching for ideas and methods that will help you perform your duties more effectively, you will find the material in this book of great use to you. It provides gateways to most of the classic literature in leadership and management, succinct conceptual frameworks within which you can study and improve your approaches to your job, and a significant number of exercises and tools that you can explore and use on your own or with the assistance of a coach. From ways to improve your thinking and approaches to strategy and influence, to how to decrease the likelihood that you will suffer from career derailment, to the exploration of methods to increase the frequency with which you respond to the demands of your job virtuously, each chapter in this book offers an interesting combination of abstract and concrete materials to stimulate your development.

Similarly, for coaches and teachers, the material in the book provides access to scientific, philosophical, and historical literature that can extend the ways in which you think about leadership and its development. The case studies, exercises, tables, and methods that populate each chapter have been created in and through my own work with clients and students. You may find that these specific aspects of the book are of unique value to you in enhancing the approaches you take in your classrooms and practices.

This book attempts to provide a blend of the theoretical ideas and practical applications. Depending on your interests, your attention may flow naturally to different sections of each chapter. The headings and subheads provide guidance on the contents so that the journey made by everyone can be as individualized as one likes. I only hope that each of you is able to take away both interesting ideas and practical applications to improve the work that you have chosen to do.

2

ESTABLISHING STRATEGY AND SETTING DIRECTION: WHAT IS EXPECTED FROM EXECUTIVES

LOUIS GERSTNER AND IBM

On Friday, March 26, 1993, the board of directors at IBM announced that Louis Gerstner would replace John Akers as the CEO and chairman of that venerable company (Gerstner, 2002). It had been a wild, 2-month courtship during which Gerstner had turned down the position numerous times. Initially, he believed strongly that the job demanded someone who was industry-savvy and could understand the technological issues and choices that faced the organization. After careful, preliminary examination of the situation in which the enterprise found itself and intense lobbying by key members of the board of directors, he changed his mind because he came to view the position increasingly as a leadership job, for which he felt more suitably qualified. In the book he wrote describing this chapter of his executive life, Gerstner said, "the challenge for the next leader would begin with driving the kind of strategic and cultural change that had characterized what I'd done at American Express and RJR" (Gerstner, 2002, p. 13). He also stated,

> In hindsight, it's interesting that both Burke and Murphy [the board members who had recruited him so intensely] were operating under

the assumption of IBM that a strategy of breaking up the company into independent units was the right one to pursue. What would they have said if they realized that not only was the company in financial trouble and had lost touch with its customers, but that it was also barreling toward a strategy of disaster? (p. 17)

Gerstner's decision began a 9-year process in which he and his colleagues undertook a series of steps to turn IBM around. When he became CEO, analysts, critics, owners, and competitors universally agreed that the business was on its last legs, struggling with the smaller and more nimble technology competitors emerging around the globe, and could not earn enough from services to replace revenues in the mainframe business, which at the time were in free fall. When he retired 9 years later, he was universally hailed as a business genius of the first rank. Not only was IBM still the dominant player in the global mainframe market, it also held a commanding position in the much more lucrative and rapidly growing services sector of the technology industry.

Conventional approaches to strategy formation (Peng, 2009; Wheelen & Hunger, 2008) emphasize a careful examination of the external conditions facing organizations in this increasingly globalized world and an equally thoughtful review of the internal capacities of their firms. After such analyses, leaders are then expected to establish a vision for their enterprises and a specific and understandable mission. These components, along with accompanying policies and systematic investments, are conventionally thought to constitute the strategy of the organization. Without a clear-eyed view of the strategy that a business is to pursue, organizations are most often believed to be headed for significant trouble.

Lou Gerstner's first 3 months were chaotic at best. He discovered just how badly IBM was doing in the marketplace against competitors and with customers. He uncovered aspects of an organizational culture that had become ossified and so dysfunctional that it was nearly impossible to make a decision for the entire company. He learned about the truly precarious financial situation the enterprise faced. At the end of those 3 months, he was ready to make four core decisions:

- Keep the company together
- Change our fundamental economic model
- Reengineer how we did business
- Sell underproductive assets in order to raise cash. (Gerstner, 2002, p. 57)

On July 27, 1993, he held his first major news conference during which he described the direction the company would be taking. The most memorable statement he made at that event was this:

What I'd like to do now is put these announcements in some sort of perspective for you. There's been a lot of speculation as to when I'm going to deliver a vision of IBM, and what I'd like to say to all of you is that the last thing IBM needs right now is a vision. (Gerstner, 2002, p. 68)

That comment made major headlines around the world. Gerstner was viewed as iconoclastic and going against the direction that analysts and others had set for him and the company. However, to produce a turnaround in time, he had to create a sense of urgency throughout the entire organization that emphasized execution not vision. He needed everyone throughout the company to start to focus on how they were operating the business. As he looked back on those months, he saw the key elements as follows:

- Not spinning off the pieces of the company
- Reinvesting in the mainframe
- Remaining in the core semiconductor technology business
- Protecting the fundamental R & D Budget
- Drive all we did from the customer back and turn IBM into a market-driven rather than an internally focused, process-driven enterprise. (Gerstner, 2002, p. 72)

When reading books and articles on businesses and organizations, one has a sense that what is required to articulate strategy is a succinct statement that can be made by almost anyone in the enterprise. Indeed, it is often suggested that the vision and mission of a company be printed on laminated cards and attached to the necks of all employees so that they can be constantly reminded of what the enterprise is doing and the direction in which it is headed. For Gerstner, the reality of where IBM was headed was anything but simple, and the execution of that reality was even more complex. In his book, Gerstner identified more than five dozen steps or actions that he and his leadership team undertook during the 9 years of the turnaround. Where in such a complex web of actions can we find a simple statement of the "what" of the strategy? Where in a maze of activity is the "what" of direction? Just what would Lou Gerstner have chosen to hang around the necks of IBM employees to achieve such clarity in 1993? It is often argued that strategy and direction separate the true leaders from all of the pretending contenders (Porter, 1980a, 1980b, 1990a, 1990b, 1996, 2008; Prahalad & Hamel, 1990; Strebel & Ohlsson, 2006).

Gerstner's (2002) book did a beautiful job of exploding the myth of strategy simplicity. It turns out that in reality, the "what" of strategy and direction in 21st-century enterprises is complex indeed. It would seem that the clarity of direction quickly runs into the murky muck of execution. In the real world of leaders and leadership, the "what" and the "how" are the two sides of a coin, forever fused, eternally interacting, endlessly fascinating, and sometimes nearly impossible either to understand or to do.

Gerstner (2002) attempted to draw together the major lessons he had learned during his 9 years as CEO of IBM. Although his analysis was much more detailed, he stated that the

> fundamentals that characterize successful enterprises and successful executives are:
> - They are focused
> - They are superb at execution
> - They abound with personal leadership. (p. 217)

Gerstner and the team he assembled around him personally demonstrated these characteristics, and they restructured their company around them. The results were astounding: a 25% increase in company revenue; a move from a loss of $8.1 billion in 1993 to an annual average profit of $7.9 billion when he left; earnings per share in 1993 at −3.55 to +4.35 in 2001; return on stockholder equity in 1993 at −35.2% to +35.1% in 2001; and after the initial restructuring layoffs, a rebounding of total global employment to higher levels than when he started. In short, the traditional financial indices of corporate performance all told the tale of the success of that team. Gerstner and his colleagues not only talked about what they would do, they demonstrated publicly that they could do it.

Yet at the end of his story, Lou Gerstner looked forward, not back. Instead of simply saying, "This is what we did and you can learn from these experiences," he speculated what the future would demand from executives. He stated,

> This next generation of leaders—in both the public and private sectors—will have to expand its thinking around a set of economic, political, and social considerations. These leaders will be:
> - Much more able to deal with the relentless, discontinuous change that this technology is creating.
> - Much more global in outlook and practice.
> - Much more able to strike an appropriate balance between the instinct for cultural preservation and the promise of regional or global cooperation.
> - Much more able to embrace the fact that the world is moving to a model in which the "default" in every endeavor will be openness and integration, not isolation. (Gerstner, 2002, p. 276)

We can readily see that the "what" of leadership—setting direction and establishing strategy—is in reality a complex proposition that even an experienced and successful executive like Lou Gerstner described as a moving target, and the pace of change of this target is accelerating rapidly and in directions relatively unanticipated by the experiences, educational models, and research findings of the past. Although we do have a set of technologies and a group of professionals who use them to try to improve our understanding of what might be coming (Bobbitt, 2002, 2009; Bremmer, 2010; Ralston & Wilson, 2006), leaders of individual institutions will still be responsible for deciding what they should be doing. If these authors and others are correct, we know that humanity in the 21st century will face unprecedented challenges in demographics, biotechnology, information and telecommunications technologies, conflicts and competition between the types of capitalism that have been emerging since the late 1990s, and ecological problems on a scale only anticipated in science fiction. Let's look a little more closely at direction and strategy to learn some essentials that leaders and those who help them develop should understand.

STRATEGY AND DIRECTION—WHERE, WHY, AND WHAT

Direction and strategy address three fundamental aspects of human and organizational life. Where are we going? Why are we going there? What are we doing to get there? In the most practical sense, any journey must answer these core questions as it starts. Even at the most elemental, intuitive level, "we need to head there as opposed to that other place" is an essential issue with which nearly every individual person and certainly every human group has struggled. Children are asked at very young ages, "What do you want to be when you grow up?" They answer with confidence: doctor, police officer, nurse, teacher, rock star, actor—or in the case of one 11-year-old boy I worked with decades ago, pimp. Depending on the child, some of these early ambitions come true, but only after years of preparation and work. The same is true for organizations.

Buss (2005) and Kaiser, Hogan, and Craig (2008) described interspecies work demonstrating that the core functions of leaders are choosing the line of march for foraging; defending collective welfare; managing intergroup conflict; maintaining the structure of the relationships in the troupe, tribe, herd, or organization; and allocating critical resources. Heifetz (1994) made an articulate case for this framework as applied to human enterprises. He also differentiated the nature of the work in those organizations as focused on technical and adaptive tasks. Technical work involves problems for which the definition is easy to understand, the potential solutions are reasonably straightforward and usually require little or minimal learning, and the responsibility for implementing a solution is reasonably clear between leaders and followers. Adaptive work involves problems that require learning by leaders, subordinates, and other stakeholders to define them and to create and implement solutions to them. The leader and his or her subordinates and partners share the responsibility for adaptive work. Executives must address the questions of where, why, and what for both the technical and adaptive components of organizational performance.

A wide variety of definitions have been developed to describe *strategy*. For example,

> The art of a commander-in-chief; the art of projecting and directing the larger movements and operations of a military campaign. . . . Usually distinguished from tactics, which is the art of handling forces in battle or in the immediate presence of the enemy. . . . In circumstances of competition, as in the theory of games, decision theory, or business administration, etc.; a plan for successful action based on the rationality and interdependence of the moves of the opposing participants. . . . To force a person into a position as by strategy. (*Oxford Dictionary of English*, 1998, p. 1992)

This is a classic definition of the term based on the art of human warfare. Strategy in this sense involves the maneuvering of the largest elements of military campaigns, which were usually thought of as part of the geopolitical strategies of leaders who were organizing to expand or defend their territory or other resources. The application of these ideas to the global business world was articulated clearly by Porter (1996):

> Strategy is the creation of a unique and valuable position, involving a different set of activities. If there were only one ideal position, there would be no need for strategy. Companies would face a simple imperative—win the race to discover and preempt it. The essence of strategic positioning is to choose activities that are different from rivals. (p. 68)

In Porter's (1996) now-classic article, he used the case of Southwest Airlines to describe a focused business strategy. Southwest, he contended, organized a significant number of elements in constructing its strategy: short-haul flights, low cost, point-to-point service, midsized cities, secondary airports in larger cities, price sensitive customers, convenience, frequent flights, fast gate turn around, standardized fleet of planes, fewer planes in the fleet, more flights per plane, open seating, and flexible and friendly staff.

From this complex list, we see that Porter's (1996) strategic positioning definition and approach to business strategy comprises a unique set of choices made by the senior leaders of that airline that end up representing its direction. In keeping with our IBM case example, it is doubtful one could fit all of these elements into a simple, easy-to-remember statement on a laminated card. Yet any air traveler who has flown Southwest would be able to describe clearly how that experience is different from those he or she has on other airlines and therefore articulate key aspects of that organization's strategy.

Peng (2009) defined strategy more succinctly, stating that it is "a firm's theory about how to compete successfully" (p. 10). He emphasized the increasingly global nature of business in the 21st century and discussed in detail such approaches as foreign markets, strategic alliances, mergers and acquisitions, corporate restructuring, diversification, and governance. If all of these types of approaches and differing definitions can be applied to answer the questions executives answer of the where, why, and what of their organizations, how can we hope to develop a conceptual grasp on this extremely complicated and slippery set of issues?

Figure 2.1 attempts to pull together fundamental attributes of strategy into a conceptual framework that can help us orient to the various domains and issues that are involved. In this framework, the foundations for strategy rest on global economic and business and geopolitical cycles, demographic patterns and shifts, and increasingly on environmental and ecological changes and constraints. As I write this in August 2010, the world is in the early stages of recovery from the worst economic recession since the 1930s. Unemployment worldwide is significantly higher than in 2007–2008 when the recession began. Hundreds, if not thousands of major businesses have failed around the world. If we agree with Bobbitt (2002, 2009), for the past 10 years, we have been consistently involved in the opening phases of the next epochal war with the conflicts in Iraq, Afghanistan, and now in Pakistan, illustrating that wide discrepancies and extremely hostile reactions to the proper way for humans to govern themselves still cause people to take up arms against each other. In addition, the United States has just experienced the single worst episode of oil-based environmental degradation in global history with the blowout of the British Petroleum well in the Gulf of Mexico. Figure 2.1 demonstrates that executives in human organizations must understand that these forces inevitably have major, and at times catastrophic, consequences for their enterprises and leadership. Failure to attend to these parameters can be deadly for businesses and careers alike.

On top of this foundation of basic parameters, Figure 2.1 displays another cube that attempts to describe a generic organization and its various dimensions. On the vertical axis or face of the cube, the stages of the life cycle of organizations are depicted (Adizes, 1988). This framework focuses on the issue that direction and strategy—where the organization is going, why, and what will it do—depend greatly on where an enterprise is in its development. The approaches pursued for the start-up phase of a business are most often very different from those employed for a mature, bureaucratic, global corporation. Leaders then must also have a good diagnostic sense of where their organization is currently in its evolution and where they believe it is going to frame a strategy properly.

Schools of Strategy

Marketing / sales
Manufacturing / production / operations
Distribution
Research & development / engineering
Internet / IT Technology
Finance / accounting / economics
Human Resources
Legal services
Governance
Ownership
Politics / geopolitics

Stage of Organizational Life Cycle	Positioning	Cognitive	Cultural	Learning	Power	Planning	Design	Entrepreneurial	Environmental	Configuration
Courtship										
Infancy										
Go-go										
Adolescence										
Prime										
Maturity										
Aristocracy										
Early Bureaucracy										
Bureaucracy										
Renewal/ Death										

Global Economic / Business Cycles

Transitions – Chaotic / turbulence – Catastrophic phase shifts

Expansion / Inflation / Employment
– More production of goods and services – More linear / predictable – Catastrophic phase shifts

Contraction / recession / depression / deflation / unemployment
– Less production of goods and services
– More linear / predictable – Dynamic equilibria

Global Geopolitical Cycles

Epochal wars followed by governance / constitutional consolidations – dynamic equilibria, crises and catastrophic phase transitions, chaotic equilibria

Multi-polar, bi-polar, and hegemony solutions in an anarchic international system

Political entities (states / non-state actors) (owners) work to survive and maintain their territorial / market integrity; (national) autonomy, and (domestic) political order; have military / economic capacity to hurt each other; cannot be certain of each other's intentions; and are ultimately rational actors

Environmental/Ecological Changes and Constraints
In regional, national, and global markets that affect the organization positively or negatively.

Demographic Patterns and Shifts
In regional, national, and global markets.

Figure 2.1. A conceptual framework for understanding strategy.

Along the side of the upper cube in Figure 2.1, the major functional domains of most organizations are identified. Marketing, human resources, research and development, manufacturing, distribution, legal services, information technology, governance, finance, and so forth are arrayed in no particular order. Each of these operating areas of an organization demonstrates its own complexities. In large enterprises, these arenas are frequently separate organizational structures that have clear boundaries, policies, procedures, resources, and separate strategies. Microcultures and identifiable histories provide these subunits with identities and developmental paths. In large businesses, universities, and governments, suborganizations such as cabinet-level departments and schools can be found that have histories dating back for many centuries. These identifiable substructures must also be considered in terms of their own life cycles and how their unique characteristics interact with each other to cocreate the interdependent and more macro aspects of the whole entity.

Finally, on the horizontal face of Figure 2.1, we see the 10 schools of strategy identified by Mintzberg, Ahlstrand, and Lampel (1998). They provided an organized approach to examining these schools that allowed comparisons to be made.

Mintzberg and colleagues (1998) suggested that the literature on strategy formation and execution had achieved a series of key agreements, including the following:

- Strategy concerns both the organization and the environment.
- The substance of strategy is complex.
- Strategy affects the overall welfare of the organization.
- Strategy involves structure, process, and content.
- Strategies are not purely deliberate.
- Strategies exist on different levels—what businesses are we in and how do we compete in each?
- Strategy involves both analytic and intuitive thinking.

In addition, they explored some of the more paradoxical characteristics of strategy, demonstrating that it can set the direction for an enterprise and simultaneously put blinders on its members; it can focus the efforts of people but lead to reduced peripheral vision or groupthink; it defines the organization but can do so in an overly narrow way; and, although it can provide consistency across the domains of action of an enterprise, it can severely restrict creativity and the capacity to adapt to changes in the external environment. In essence, they describe strategy as a necessary but extremely complex tool and process that leaders must master for their organizations to thrive.

These authors then presented the essentials of seven descriptive schools and three prescriptive schools as follows:

Descriptive Schools	Prescriptive Schools
Configuration	Planning
Learning	Design
Entrepreneurial	Positioning
Cultural	
Environmental	
Power	
Cognitive	

Each of these schools possesses its own characteristics and, to some degree, its own methodologies. The planning, design, and entrepreneurial schools advocate looking ahead of the current state of the organization. The positioning school tends to look behind to enterprise history and to its current environment, especially at customers and adversaries. The learning and power schools look at the details of the strategy and its implementation. The environmental school tends to try to use powerful methods to anticipate what is and will be happening externally in those ecological domains in which the enterprise competes. The cultural school is organized around the core assumptions and beliefs that drive the leaders and members of an organization. The cognitive school looks inside of the strategy-making process to try to ensure that it is comprehensible and methodologically coherent. Finally, the configurational school tries to examine the strategy itself to ensure that the organization is optimizing what it is doing. One of these schools or combinations of them most often are adopted by leadership teams as they try to set the direction for their business given its stage of development. These approaches can also be used by and within the functional components of organizations to establish their own goals and strategies as part of the entire enterprise.

Thus, the leaders of the marketing, human resources, and research and development functions inside a given company may well have their own planning processes. It is not unusual to see the major organizational silos of organizations undertake strategic planning exercises either as part of an enterprise-wide initiative or on their own. When such efforts are undertaken without collaboration across the internal boundaries of these functional units, a great deal of unnecessary conflict can result, sometimes with tremendously negative results for a business. For example, market forecasts, product design, and inventory planning efforts that occur without the knowledge or participation of engineering, manufacturing, sales, and customer service units can lead to catastrophic oversupply or shortages of products, inability to respond to customer demands, or defective offerings. A central aspect of strategy requires leaders to understand their organizations and then to derive meaning from and for them (Weick, 1995). In this context, Shotter (1993) described the manager's process as not one of choosing but of generating, of generating a clear and adequate formulation of what the problem situation "is," of creating from a set of incoherent and disorderly events a coherent "structure" within which both current actualities and further possibilities can be given an intelligible "place"—and of doing all this, not alone, but in continual conversation with all the others who are involved. . . . To be justified in their authoring, the good manager must give a sharable linguistic formulation to already shared feelings, arising out of shared circumstances—and that is perhaps best done through the use of metaphors rather than by reference to any already existing theories. (pp. 150, 152)

Thayer (1988) suggested that a leader is

one who alters or guides the manner in which his followers "mind" the world by giving it a compelling "face." A leader at work is one who gives others a different form, a different "face" in the same way that a pivotal painter or sculptor, or poet gives those who follow him (or her) a different way of "seeing"—and therefore saying and doing and knowing in the world. A leader does not tell it "as it is"; he tells it as it might be, giving what "is" thereby a different face. . . . The leader is a sense-giver. The leader always embodies the possibilities of escape from what might otherwise appear to us to be incomprehensible, or from what might otherwise appear to us to be a chaotic, indifferent, or incorrigible world—one over which we have no ultimate control. (pp. 250, 254)

It should be clear by now that leadership and strategy formation and execution are inextricably bound together. All stakeholders in an enterprise look to their leaders to set direction and to oversee its implementation. Indeed, the very survival of the institution depends on them doing this responsibly and well.

If strategy formation is done properly, the individuals in organizations are able to structure fundamental aspects of their personal and professional identities around the direction and core activities of the enterprise. Answers to the question "who am I?" become suffused with descriptions of what I do for the company for which I work, where that company is headed, and why it has chosen that path. For many people, the career aspects of their adult identities dwarf all other components. In this sense, strategy can evoke particularly strong emotional responses in the members of an organization, making it even more complex than what is normally involved in choosing a line of march for a troupe of humans to make sure that they survive economically and physically.

Many approaches have been advocated for understanding strategy, and no chapter-length treatment of the subject can come close to doing them justice. For example, Kaplan and Norton (2005) described the importance of developing a balanced scorecard that would provide leadership teams with a methodology through which they could monitor the implementation of strategy and provide themselves with comprehensible and useful data sets to do so. Prahalad and Hamel (1990) argued effectively that businesses do better in their competitive environments by first determining their core competencies and then structuring themselves and their products or services around those aspects of their identities. In assessing the performance of various companies, they demonstrated that those who competed through components that depended on using the same basic knowledge and skills did much better over time than those who simply tried to cobble together groups of companies that may not have much in common. Treacy and Wiersema (1993) advocated that the strategic emphasis of businesses should be driven by their relationships with their customers. They stated that leaders must understand the needs and desires of their clients if they hope to design products or services that they can sell reliably. It seems that the deeper one delves into strategy, the more there is to know about it, and consequently, the easier it is to fail. A variety of tools and methodologies have been developed over the past 50 years or so to help leaders do a better job of understanding, designing, and executing strategy. In other words, how can leaders and those who help develop them learn to create strategy?

TOOLS THAT SUPPORT STRATEGY FORMATION

There has been a lot of creative energy and effort put into the development of methods and techniques that consultants and leadership teams can use in formulating organizational strategies and evaluating corporate performance. An abbreviated list of such tools includes the following:

- Macroeconomic Environment Analysis
- Political–Geopolitical Landscape Assessment
- Strengths, Weaknesses, Opportunities, and Threats (SWOT) Analysis
- Boston Consulting Group Unit Analysis
- Organizational Assessment
- Market Segmentation Analysis
- Competitor Analysis
- Business Scenario Planning
- Product Life-Cycle Assessment
- Environmental Impact Analysis
- Demographic Trend Analysis
- Organizational Economic–Market Performance Dashboard
- Sales Dashboard
- Finance–Accounting Dashboard

- Information Technology Dashboard
- Human Resources Dashboard
- Legal Services Dashboard
- Manufacturing–Production–Operations Dashboard
- Governance Dashboard
- Ownership Dashboard
- Research and Development Dashboard

There is no one place that students, leaders, or consultants can go to find these tools because they are scattered throughout the landscape of subspecialization theory and practice. Economists can produce macro- and microeconomic analyses. Market professionals can do competitor and segmentation analyses. Demographers can provide reasonable updates on national, regional, and global patterns. Ecologists and environmental scientists and engineers can do impact and product life-cycle assessments. Consulting psychologists and organization development professionals can provide organizational assessments. There is a subset of the consulting community that specializes in helping leadership teams do scenario planning and future trend analyses. Text after text written on the specialized subdisciplines of business provide the essentials necessary to construct performance dashboards for the various functional silos of institutions, but there is no comprehensive overview of these approaches and methods with which I am familiar. Nevertheless, senior leaders of organizations and their teams need to cocreate and construct a set of common understandings and tools through which they can make decisions about strategy and its execution. Let's look at a couple of them in a little more detail as a way of providing at least an introduction to the how of strategy formation and execution.

Exhibit 2.1 presents a list of 151 questions and issues that consultants and leaders can use to help orient them to the strategy-formation process as well as to lead or conduct them. This list frames perhaps the most widely adopted and well-understood method used to help organizations decide their direction, the SWOT analysis (Kaufman, Oakley-Browne, Watkins, & Leigh, 2003; J. A. Pearce & Robinson, 1998; Wheelen, & Hunger, 2008). As noted earlier, SWOT stands for strengths, weaknesses, opportunities, and threats. It is based on the core ideas that leaders need to understand simultaneously the inside of their enterprises and the outside. The four core questions to be addressed are the following: What are our strengths? What are our weaknesses? What opportunities exist in our external environment(s)? What threats dwell there? Each of these inquiries can generate extensive reviews of the various components of a business, as was delineated in the IBM case example. SWOT is more or less, and for better or worse, the default methodology for enterprise strategy development worldwide. In the hands of skilled and experienced leaders and

EXHIBIT 2.1
Questions and Issues for Strategy Formation

1. How are directions and strategies formed in and for the organization?
2. Who, if anyone, is responsible for setting the direction and the formulation of strategy for the organization? Does s/he or the group have the final authority to say yes or no?
3. For what time frame is the direction being set and the strategy formulated—1, 3, 5, 10, 20, 50, 100 years?
4. Does the organization have a chief strategist and if yes, who is it?
5. Does the strategist really understand the organization, its industry, and the environment in which it competes?
6. What are the underlying motives of the chief strategist and those responsible for setting the direction of the organization—achievement, power, economic rewards, and contribution to society?
7. Are the chief strategist and those responsible for setting the direction of the organization virtuous or corrupt leaders?
8. Does the chief strategist have a true vision for what s/he wants the organization to pursue/become/accomplish? Who has the business idea? What is the idea that the chief strategist conveys?
9. What mental models or concepts does the strategist have and share to express the vision/direction/strategy?
10. How do the people involved in direction setting and strategy formation learn as individuals and as a group?
11. How do the people involved in direction setting and strategy formation create and use knowledge, skill, ability, and experience for themselves?
12. How does the strategist/leader see reality? The future? Is it a rigid or flexible view?
13. What is the strategic intent of the strategist/leader or strategy group?
14. How does the strategist/leader or group actually think? What methods and approaches do they use as they think individually or together?
15. How does the strategist/leader or group manage the emotions associated with setting direction and strategy—anxiety, ambiguity, shame, frustration, anger, sadness, competitive strivings, joy, curiosity, guilt, greed, power hunger, etc.?
16. Can the strategist/leader or strategy group be characterized as generally virtuous or generally corrupt in their characters and behavior—demonstrate courage, temperance, justice, wisdom and reverence or cowardice, intemperance, injustice, stupidity, and irreverence?
17. Do the people involved in direction setting and strategy formation have a true operational understanding of the organization?
18. Do the people involved in direction setting and strategy formation have the reflective capacity and skills necessary to see the organization, its industry, and the environment, and create useful alternative views of what the future might be?
19. Is the strategist or strategic group professionally and personally committed to the organization? If yes, over what time frame? If no, when and how will they exit?
20. Does the organization have a succession process in place for the strategist and strategy group?
21. Does/will the organization use a formal planning process to set its direction and establish its strategy?
22. Who controls the processes of formulating strategy?
23. What roles do/will staff and other stakeholders play in the process compared to strategy formulators?
24. What theories, concepts, methods, and technologies are/will be employed to establish direction and strategy? How old are they? Are they relevant to and for the current organization and its leadership?

EXHIBIT 2.1
Questions and Issues for Strategy Formation   *(Continued)*

25. Is the leadership team involved in setting direction and strategy formation still learning and interested in learning or does it rely on the tried and true or received wisdom from the elders of the past?
26. Does the planning process overwhelm the management team? Does it focus on the right things, in the right way, at the right time, with the right level of resources devoted to it?
27. Does the planning process produce true and clear choices for the leaders and the organization?
28. Does the decision making process allow for a true dialogue among those that participate?
29. What approaches to decision making are followed by those who are involved in setting direction and strategy formation?
30. How is conflict managed by followed by those who are involved in setting direction and strategy formation?
31. Who can say no or stop a direction or strategy from being established or enacted?
32. Is the strategist/strategy group aware of and does it actively manage tendencies to overanalyze, overrely on the intuition of key members, decision biases, and pattern recognition preferences?
33. Is the strategist/strategy group aware of optimizing and satisficing tendencies in decision-making?
34. Does the strategist/strategy group have a sufficient grasp of organizational and group dynamics such that they can manage their own structures and processes creatively and effectively and avoid group and organizational dysfunction in the direction setting, strategy formation, and strategy implementation processes—group think, dependency, fight/flight, subgroup dynamics, dysfunctional diversity, inclusion, control, collusion, and privilege patterns, and so on?
35. What are the historical and current strengths of this organization?
36. What are the historical and current weaknesses of this organization?
37. What are the historical and current threats facing this organization?
38. What are the historical and current opportunities facing this organization?
39. In what stage of evolution is the organization—courtship—renewal/death, and so on?
40. What resources does the organization need?
41. Where will it find those resources and how will it obtain them?
42. What stage of evolution are the major products and services of the organization—dogs, cash cows, problem children, and stars?
43. What is the organization's value chain?
44. What are the core competencies of the organization?
45. What margins are present in the various elements of the organization's value chain and from its core competencies?
46. How is the organization financed—debt (private, public), equity (private, public), and government?
47. What expectations for financial returns are held by the financial participants—EBIDTA, margins, cash, dividends, and stock values?
48. Are the financial participants invested for the short or long term?
49. Into what group(s) does your organization and its subcomponents fall (niche player, pioneer, local producer, dominant producer, copycat producer, global replicator/chain/franchise, professional services, focused producer, global integrated suppliers, diversified developer, national or global conglomerate)?

(continues)

EXHIBIT 2.1
Questions and Issues for Strategy Formation   *(Continued)*

50. What is the underlying structure of the industry in which the organization competes?
    a. Describe the rivalry among the competitors.
    b. Describe the bargaining power of suppliers.
    c. Describe the bargaining power of buyers.
    d. Describe the threat of new entrants.
    e. Describe the threat of substitute products or services.
51. Are these underlying forces compatible with actual or long run profitability?
52. Are there likely to be significant changes in the industry and its basic forces in the next year, three years, five years?
53. What products and services are unique to the industry?
54. What products and services are also found in other industries?
55. In what geographic arenas is competition found—local, regional, national, and/or global?
56. Identify the buyers and buying groups.
57. Identify the suppliers and supplier groups.
58. Identify the competitors.
59. Identify the substitutes for products and services from other organizations.
60. Identify potential organizational entrants to the industry/market.
61. What is the average level of profitability and why is it there?
62. What major forces control the average level of profitability?
63. Who are the most profitable players and how are they positioned against their competitors?
64. What changes in the political, geopolitical, social, technological, or macroeconomic environments affect the industry or the organization? What is changing?
    a. customer preferences
    b. technologies
    c. demographics
    d. legislation
    e. regulations
    f. case law, court rulings, law suits
    g. interest rates
    h. exchange rates
    i. personal income
    j. consumer confidence
    k. war
    l. terrorism
    m. new political forces, parties, alliances
    n. political coups
    o. elections
    p. environmental changes and disasters
65. What is the overall picture of the structure of the industry in which the organization competes?
66. Is the organization about to enter a competitive battle with one or more adversaries?
67. Is the organization currently in a competitive battle with one or more adversaries?
68. Is the organization ready for a battle? What is it bringing to the contest? What is missing? What do the adversaries bring? How will they attack their adversaries? How will adversaries attack them? How will they limit their adversaries' impact on their organization?

EXHIBIT 2.1
Questions and Issues for Strategy Formation   *(Continued)*

69. Does the organization face a formal takeover threat? If yes, from whom, when, why?
70. What strategic approach is the takeover organization using—friendly, hostile, merger, and acquisition?
71. Is leadership open to the approach or hostile to it?
72. Is governance/ownership open to the approach or hostile to it?
73. What processes are being used to manage the takeover process?
74. Who is leading the takeover processes?
75. What external resources—legal, financial, other consulting services—are being used to help manage the response to the takeover process?
76. Is the organization actively pursuing acquisitions/mergers as part of its strategy?
77. What experience and expertise does the leadership team have in structuring and integrating acquisitions and mergers?
78. What is the organization's experience with cultural integration of mergers or acquisitions?
79. Are there lingering economic, organizational, managerial, or cultural issues with past mergers or acquisitions and if yes, what are they?
80. What data and analytic procedures are being used to make the assessments that support the strategy formation process? How reliable and valid are the sources of the data and procedures?
81. Has any accuracy or objective data been lost during the process of formulating the strategy?
82. What is the level of uncertainty in the various components of the environment and industry?
83. Does the organization use empirical data to create scenarios to understand the organization, competitors, industry, and environment?
84. Does the organization use leadership intuition to create scenarios to understand the organization, industry, and environment?
85. Are the scenarios and data and analyses review processes successful in challenging and widening the perceptions of the strategy formulators?
86. Does the organization use economic, marketing, operational, human resources, or other forms of analysis to test its strategies/scenarios? (Examples: return on invested capital; improvements in book value; margins on products and services; cash flow analyses; increases in market share. How will the value of the strategy to the organization be measured?). If yes, what does it use and why? If no, why does the organization not formally test its strategies with formal analyses?
87. Describe the culture of the organization and its effects on how the organization competes.
88. Does the culture of the organization support strategy formulation and execution?
89. Describe the approach to leadership taken in the organization and its effects on how it competes.
90. Does the approach to leadership taken in the organization support strategy formulation and execution?
91. Describe the leadership and followership dynamics in the organization and their effects on how it competes.
92. Do the leadership and followership dynamics taken in the organization support strategy formulation and execution?
93. Describe the executive team dynamics and processes in the organization and their effects on how it competes.

(continues)

EXHIBIT 2.1
Questions and Issues for Strategy Formation *(Continued)*

94. Do the executive team dynamics and processes in the organization and their effects support strategy formulation and execution?
95. How simple or complex is the strategy of the organization? Can everyone in the organization describe it?
96. Does the strategy tell the members of the organization and its stakeholders the direction in which they are heading, their anticipated destination, and desired objectives/outcomes?
97. Does the strategy address the competitive advantages of the organization—cost and differentiation of the products and services—and the competitive scope that will be pursued—broad or narrow; focus of the products and services?
98. Is the time frame of the direction and strategy wise? Is it mired in the past—focuses on what it has done? Anchored in the present—keeps to its knitting? Flexing into the future—makes new patterns? Imagining what is possible—shatters current reality in favor of something radically different?
99. Does the direction and strategy adequately test the realities that face the organization?
100. Does/will the direction and strategy of the organization actually improve its competitive position and capacities?
101. Does the strategy set identifiable goals for the organization?
102. Are the goals SMART—specific, measurable, ambitious, realistic, timelines clarified?
103. How will the members of the organization and its stakeholders know that they have reached the destination (goals) their strategy set for them? (Examples: return on invested capital; improvements in book value; increases in market share, EBIDTA increases, cash position. How will the value of the strategy to the organization be measured?)
104. Who is responsible for implementing the strategy of the organization?
105. Through what organizational structures and processes will the strategy be implemented and evaluated?
106. Are the implementers different from the strategists?
107. Do they have the requisite knowledge, skill, ability, experience, and resources to implement the strategy fully and successfully?
108. How will the strategists and implementers respond to challenges and changes as the action processes unfold—manage discernment, problem solving, decision making, conflict, communication?
109. Does the direction and strategy fire the imagination, ignite the passions, cement the commitments, and solidify the motivations of the members of the organization?
110. What are the competencies of the organization and are any of them unique in the industry?
111. Does the organization test its theory/understanding of the industry and of itself; if yes how; if no, why not?
112. What are the explicit risks in the strategy of the organization? Have they been assessed and contingency plans put in place?
113. What are the implicit risks in the strategy of the organization? Have they been assessed and contingency plans put in place?
114. Has there been an assessment of why, when, where, and how these risks might change?
115. How does a/the revised strategy relate to its predecessor? Does it substitute for it? Does it expand it? Does it contradict it?
116. Is the strategy unique to the organization?

EXHIBIT 2.1
Questions and Issues for Strategy Formation *(Continued)*

117. Are the leaders, subordinates, and other stakeholders supportive of the strategy? If not, why and how does that lack of support manifest?
118. How is the strategy related to the budget process of the organization? Do budgets reflect the commitments of the strategy?
119. How are budget priorities set? How does the budget process relate to the strategy formation process?
120. When and if directions and strategies fail, how does the organization manage that outcome and its processes—shoot messengers, play the shame blame game, try to learn from mistakes?
121. What approaches does the organization take to learning—muddling through, incrementalism, bottom-up/grassroots, professional formulations, deliberate or retrospective sense making, break it and learn, adapt or die, chaos and complexity?
122. What is the current geopolitical landscape faced by the organization—multipolar, bipolar, hegemony?
123. In what country does the organization make its primary home?
124. What approach does that home country take to the regulation and taxation of organizations?
125. What approaches does that country take to global economic competition?
126. What approaches does that country take to supporting or discouraging imports and exports?
127. In what phase is the global economic system—expansion, transition, recession?
128. In what phase is the domestic economic system—expansion, transition, recession?
129. In what countries is the organization competing economically?
130. What success or failure is the organization having in these countries?
131. What legal resources are routinely available to the organization—external counsel; internal legal staffs?
132. What legal strategies is the organization pursuing—torts, patents, copyrights, regulation reform, tax reform, antitrust complaints, anticompetitive complaints, foreign dumping complaints, and so on?
133. Is the organization defending itself against legal attacks by other enterprises?
134. If yes, how and with what success or failure?
135. Is the organization defending itself against state legal attacks in its home country or internationally?
136. If yes, with what success or failure?
137. Does the organization have effective legal, political, and regulatory representation in the national capitols of the countries in which it competes?
138. Does the organization's legal and representative team understand its business strategies and its roles in implementing those strategies?
139. Do the organization's legal and representative teams need to be changed in any way? If yes, how, when, why, and so on?
140. What legal form does the organization take—corporation; government, non-profit; for profit?
141. Who owns the organization—family business, partners, limited stockholders, private equity, and public ownership—wide base of stockholders?
142. How is the organization governed—board of directors?
143. Who represents the owners or stakeholders in the governance structure?
144. How is governance structured—board, committees, size, meeting frequency, goals, roles, relationship to the leadership team?
145. How well does the governance structure operate as a group?

(continues)

EXHIBIT 2.1
Questions and Issues for Strategy Formation   *(Continued)*

146. How well does the governance structure work with the leadership team?
147. If there are significant conflicts within the governance structure or between governance and leadership, how are they being managed? Are the approaches to conflict management successful?
148. How does the governance structure review and authorize organizational strategy?
149. Is there an executive compensation plan tied to the organization's strategy?
150. How is the executive compensation plan managed between governance and the leadership team?
151. How effective is the compensation plan in supporting the organization's short- and long-term performance?

consultants, it can lead to refined analyses and nuanced choices. However, in many organizations, it is used in a perfunctory fashion and creates little more than an annual forecast based on the previous year's experience. Although such uses may well be appropriate for organizations in relatively stable external environments, using a SWOT analysis in this way in highly turbulent situations can be life-threatening for the enterprise and career-ending for the leaders who do so.

Exhibit 2.1 contains subsets of questions and issues pertaining to most of the major categories represented in Figure 2.1. As such, it is an extended and extensive version of the kind of inquiry that usually drives a SWOT analysis. Over time, for-profit businesses have become much more attuned to the needs, desires, and changes that their customers display (Cateora, Gilly, & Graham, 2009; Farris, Bendle, Pfeifer, & Reibstein, 2006; Hussey & Jenster, 2000; Lehmann & Winer, 1994; Stevens, Sherwood, Dunn, & Loudon, 2006) and have created a variety of tools to help them monitor the current and changing status of those who purchase their products and services. Although there is insufficient space in this chapter to review these methods in any detail, it is helpful to have a succinct understanding of some of these basic frameworks.

In a market-demand analysis, leaders must pay attention to a core set of issues, including identifying a market, identifying market factors, estimating market potential, and estimating anticipated revenues from a particular venture. From there, leadership teams, sometimes in conjunction with external marketing firms, move to consider related variables, such as specific environments, countries, and populations; the needs and desires of people in these large groupings; how these demographic groups can be segmented into coherent entities for whom specific marketing approaches might work; and the industries in which the enterprise is choosing to compete. Segmentation analyses are driven by consideration of the geographic, demographic, and other dimensions of diversity of the population being studied; their product or service usage; and the benefits and expectations of and for customers upon purchase and over the life of the product or service. The results of such studies drive two major inquiries for leaders. What product or service are we analyzing or wanting to offer to customers or clients? How do we assess the needs, size, economics, and psychosocial characteristics of the potential customers or clients? Answers derived from these demand analyses and segmentation studies are used to structure product and service offerings, research and development activities, engineering and manufacturing processes, and means and messaging of advertising and sales campaigns.

In competitor–adversary analyses, leadership teams are faced with the job of trying to assess the major organizations with whom they compete with as much skill, intensity, and detail as they do with their own enterprises. The questions and issues identified in Exhibit 2.1 can be used to drive these types of inquiry just as effectively as those used for the home organization. The end result of a competitor analysis leads to a direct comparison of the relative strengths and weaknesses of themselves as businesses with these most threatening and dangerous companies. After the competitive landscape is sufficiently understood, executives can craft more specific strategies with and through which to attack others or defend themselves. Without a careful assessment of this aspect of the external landscape, leaders can push their institutions in directions that may well be ineffective at best and life-threatening at worst with the best of intentions. As Gerstner (2002) put it,

> At the end of the day, a successful, focused enterprise is one that has developed a deep understanding of its customers' needs, its competitive environment, and its economic realities. This comprehensive analysis must then form the basis for specific strategies that are translated into day-to-day execution. . . . Good strategies start with massive amounts of quantitative analysis—hard difficult analysis that is blended with wisdom, insight, and risk taking. . . . Products have to be torn down and examined for cost, features, and functionality. Each element of the income statement and balance sheet has to be examined with total objectivity vis-à-vis competitors. What are their distribution costs? How many sales people do they have? How are their sales people paid? What do distributors think about them vs. us? . . . Truly great companies lay out strategies that are believable and executable. (pp. 222–225)

As early as the 1970s, some practitioners, scholars, and leaders began to question the usefulness of traditional strategy and planning methods such as those just described (Ralston & Wilson, 2006; Wack, 1985a, 1985b). The major concern expressed was that the external technological, competitive, and economic environments of businesses were becoming increasingly fragmented, chaotic, and even more unpredictable. The methodological answer that a group of people constructed is called *scenario planning* (Lindgren & Bandhold, 2009; Van der Heijden, 2005). Instead of the more conventional methods described earlier, the planning and futures communities, in conjunction with executives from various types of organizations, began to believe that they needed to push their thinking in more creative and radical directions. Their environments were outrunning their imaginations, and as a result, their organizations were often caught unprepared to manage the challenges that arose. Rather than depending on SWOT analyses, conventional marketing studies, demographic trends, and macroeconomic assessments, they began to create ideas about what the future could possibly hold for them. Creativity came to be combined with analytics to offer them better ideas about what might be in their futures.

Ralston and Wilson (2006) described a multistage process for scenario planning that involves forming both internal and external teams for an organization. For them, the single most important feature of the exercise is to have the senior executives establish as much clarity as possible on the decisions they need to make. Decisions then come to form the foundation on which all of the other activity rests. Once the teams are created and the decision focus is established, data are collected on all of the relevant issues, views, and projections. The data are organized and presented in a series of workshops in which the teams' forces and drivers in the arenas under exploration are examined carefully. Large numbers of variables and alternatives are considered as possible pathways through which key decisions must be threaded. Then the groups work to define essential story lines that will frame the scenarios.

Members of the external team then draft the scenarios in succinct formats that are readily understood and provide the appropriate range of possibilities thought by the participants to reflect their potential futures. The cases are reviewed and refined to check them against the analytic information that was collected as well as the most creative ideas from the teams. In another workshop, the senior leaders are brought together with the scenario teams to examine and discuss the products. The scenarios and decision frameworks are examined carefully, especially by the senior team. In the cases in which scenarios have been optimally useful, they provide a profound set of guideposts for the organization. Leaders then need to communicate the results of the exercises to the relevant members of the enterprise to ensure both understanding and alignment. In the final stage of the process, the leadership team must execute on the decisions that they made within the chosen scenarios and assess the correctness and success of their actions and activities. Through such processes, organizations that have used scenarios have been able to better anticipate radical shifts in geopolitics, macro- and microeconomics, demographic trends, technological developments, and market movements. The absence of surprise and the creation of more nimble corporate capacities to take advantage of such significant changes have given some of the institutions using these methods strong competitive advantages in their respective marketplaces.

SUMMARY

I hope that this and the previous chapter have given readers a sense of the challenges facing leaders today. The world as we know it has grown substantially more complex and, in many respects, both threatening and potentially more rewarding. Executives must decide what their organizations will do to manage and survive this complexity. Further, as we have seen both in the case study in this chapter and the more technical material describing strategy and its formation, the answer to that most important question lies in a series of other complex and challenging questions. Although there are more methodologies and resources available to leaders than ever before to help them with these decisions, in the end, they alone have the authority and the responsibility to set direction and manage execution.

However, if we assume for the moment that leaders can get the "what" taken care of, including the "how" of the "what," they are still left with the extensive and exceedingly important task of safely steering their institutions through this complexity. In other words, they constantly need to manage the "how" of strategic implementation. As the IBM case study clearly reveals, this activity always plays out over time, and it presents consistent and pervasive challenges to leaders and their teams. Lou Gerstner's record at IBM over nearly a decade demonstrates that there are always major problems to be addressed and that any leader will be severely tested during his or her term of office. How do we reasonably ensure that executives will be able to pass these tests? What characteristics, skills, and resources do they need to assist them with such burdens? In the following chapters, we examine a series of ideas based on both ancient concepts and modern research that I have come to believe can offer true organizing principles for leaders and those who help them develop. In essence, it is my contention that our organizations must be directed by people of virtue if they are to survive and thrive deeper into the 21st century. Ironically, those beliefs and contentions are shared with scholars, practitioners, and educators who have asked the same questions for thousands of years.

In the next chapter, we begin this exploration with a deeper dive into some of the things that often go wrong for leaders and their organizations. I call them the seven deadly management errors.

3

THE PSYCHODYNAMIC ORIGINS OF SEVEN DEADLY MANAGEMENT ERRORS

THE CASE OF THE JALAPEÑO PEPPERS

"I can believe that some of the other people in this organization have problems with my style, but I can't believe that my staff is saying this crap about me," Tom Withers complained to me in a coaching session in which we were reviewing some of the data I had collected from a sample of the nearly two dozen people who reported to him.

Tom was a tall, lanky, eloquent African American who had risen to become a regional sales manager of a medium-sized packaged goods company. Impeccably dressed in corporate pinstripes and sitting behind a huge mahogany desk in his corner office, he lit up the space with his enthusiasm, energy, and intensity. Tom had started as a salesman soon after graduating from a state university, and he had thrived. Handsome, easygoing with and very attentive to customers, and obsessively concerned with the service provided to him and his territory, he had formed excellent relationships with his accounts, and from the start of his career, his numbers dwarfed those of every other salesperson in the company. After 5 years in the field, he was promoted to manage a small sales team. On the strength of his own individual performance and his constant pounding on his colleagues to improve their own numbers, he was promoted a second time to head a major region for the company.

Two years after that, Paul Hendrickson, the president of the company, called me to express grave concerns about Tom's leadership abilities. Paul explained that Tom continued to be the top-performing salesperson in the entire organization. He consistently made his numbers, and his customers raved about his attention to their every need. As far as Paul was concerned, he wanted an entire sales force of people like Tom Withers. The problem that had led him to call me focused on the stream of complaints that he had received about Tom from many people in company. Everyone understood that Tom was a top salesperson and on the rise within the company. However, virtually everyone who worked directly with him eventually found themselves frustrated and angry with him. Although his concern for his customers and attention to their needs had become legendary within the organization, he was even more well known for being hypercritical of anyone who did not display his commitment to work, customer relationships, and increasing sales volumes. He was as hard on the members of his sales team as he was on himself, and despite his visible success, he continued to maintain viciously demanding expectations for his own performance.

Paul explained that it was neither a matter of race nor gender; everyone complained about Tom. He said that it seemed to him that Tom enjoyed the process of criticizing others, and his assertive, articulate, and extraverted approach to life made him particularly effective at it. Tom had an especially poor reputation with the leaders and staff members of the customer service, credit management, and distribution departments, who came in for heavy bombardments when he believed that one of his customers was being ill served or that something should be improved in their operations. Paul explained that Tom seemed almost like two different people. With customers, he was warm, funny, relaxed, and quite caring. All of his customers idolized him. However, with his staff and colleagues, he appeared to be caustically critical and judgmental in the extreme. No one escaped his barbed complaints and endless, toxic suggestions for improvements. People ranted that Tom was arrogant, cold, uncaring, and often cruel. Paul was worried that he might face a decision that would require him to take Tom's management responsibilities away from him. He feared what that would do to the sales numbers for the whole organization because he doubted that Tom would stay if he lost his leadership position.

Paul and I spent some time considering the approach to Tom with the suggestion that he work with a coach. In the end, Paul simply told Tom that he and others in the organization were going to be given the opportunity to further develop their management and leadership skills and that coaching would be a part of the plan. To Paul's surprise, Tom quickly embraced the idea and acted immediately to set up our first appointment.

Initially, I found Tom to be surprisingly easy to relate to and open to learning more about leadership and management. It turned out that he had played both basketball and football in high school, and he was an avid golfer and skier as well. He was constantly looking to improve his performance in everything that he did and often went to well-known schools for golf and skiing lessons. We negotiated an assessment phase for the coaching, and he was supportive of me meeting with his staff and others in the organization to get their impressions of him as a leader.

"Do you think that your employees were all lying to me?" I asked, in answering Tom's complaint on hearing some of their comments.

"No, it's just that I really go out of my way to try to help people around here, and this is the thanks that I get."

"So, this information comes as a surprise to you."

"Boy, I'll say. Paul told me a couple of times to ease up on people, but I had no idea that so many people think I'm such a hard-ass."

"Tom, the data are consistent. Everyone I spoke to on the list that you gave me reported having critical exchanges with you that left them frustrated and nervous. Some of them expressed a lot of bitterness over how they felt you had treated them."

Tom's hands clenched the edge of his desk, and he pushed back away from me. His face showed a mixture of anger; frustration; and even more, surprise.

"I just can't believe this," he said again.

"Can you think of anything that you are doing that might be producing these results? Everyone is so clear about it, and they are equally clear that all of your customers simply love you. It is a very confusing picture for me as well."

Tom leaned back in his chair for a moment and brought his large, well-manicured hands up to rub his face. His eyes searched the room, and silence stretched between us.

"Look, I am incredibly busy. No other sales manager services their own customers like I do. I'm in the trenches with my people. Their problems and frustrations are my mine, too. Sure, I ride them hard on numbers, but I ride myself even harder. Their only legitimate complaint is that I simply don't have much time for them individually."

"How much time do you spend with them?" I asked.

"Well, we have our weekly sales meetings for a couple of hours but other than that, I just see them whenever I pass them in the office or I need to talk to them about their numbers or customer problems," he answered.

"How would you characterize those interactions?"

Tom paused again in silence, then said, "I think I'm very careful with my people. I know I don't have much time with them, so I try to make each moment, every time count. I think a lot before my meetings with the group and with them as individuals. I try my very best to always give them something useful, so I usually think of something that I can criticize in their performance. I think I owe them my best, and teaching is the biggest gift I can give them. I do the same thing with my wife and kids."

Now, it was my turn to pause. Tom's description of his behavior and his rationale for it fit the data I had collected perfectly. Everyone I had spoken to complained about how critical and negative he was. He rarely said a good word about anything or anyone in the organization, and yet everyone acknowledged that he was always trying to improve things, to make them better for customers and for the sales units.

"Can I ask you a question?"

"Sure," Tom answered.

"When you read through the critical remarks that I've summarized for you, how did it make you feel?"

"Lousy."

"Can you be more specific?"

"It's embarrassing and makes me mad. Don't they realize how hard I work?"

"I'm sure they do realize that, but let's concentrate on these feelings for a moment. What's it like for you to feel embarrassed?"

"It feels miserable. I hate it. I work as hard as I can so I don't feel that way."

"When someone criticizes your performance, it makes you feel embarrassed and miserable; you hate it, and work harder to avoid it. Yet there seems to be a paradox because you just finished telling me that because you don't have much time to spend with your people, you make sure that you say something critical whenever you talk to them. Can we conclude that a key component of your management strategy appears to be to routinely embarrass your people and make them feel angry and miserable?"

"Well, no . . . I'd never want that . . . of course."

"Yet, it seems to be precisely what you are doing. Now, here's something for you to think about. Criticism most often produces shame in people. That's the feeling of embarrassment you had when you read my summary. Shame is probably the most difficult feeling for people to handle. Small doses of it go a long way."

"But I'm only giving them my best," Tom argued with a small whine in his voice.

"Perhaps you are giving them your best criticism, but surely there are other things you could give them as well. When was the last time you complimented someone?"

Tom stopped cold, his face frozen in a question mark. He seemed to search his memory desperately for some example that would put me off or mitigate my point.

"I can't remember," he said with wonder and chagrin in his voice.

"Tom, have you ever had jalapeño peppers in your food?"

"Yeah, I love Mexican food, but the peppers give me indigestion."

"Have you ever had really hot jalapeños?"

"A couple of times."

"What was it like to eat them?"

"I couldn't eat much. They burned my mouth. It was crazy," he laughed.

"Well, here's what I would suggest you consider in the future when you meet with your staff members or talk with others in the organization. Any time you insert criticism into a conversation with a person, you raise the potential that they will feel embarrassed or ashamed. For most humans, that's the emotional equivalent of eating the hottest peppers on the planet. I think one thing that may have been happening to you and your team is that with the best of intentions, you've been feeding them almost nothing but very hot jalapeños, and they all have chronic indigestion."

Tom laughed at this metaphor and we went on to discuss the implications for his relationships with his wife and children. It was easy to draw comparisons with how he treated his customers with whom he nearly always inhibited his criticism. We also talked about other approaches to his meetings with staff and colleagues, and he seemed eager to try to behave a little differently. Coaching sessions over a multiyear time period focused on increasing flexibility in his approach to staff and colleagues. Tom improved significantly, and Paul later told me that he felt no need to take disciplinary action against him. When I return to that client company, I still check in with Tom periodically. His reputation in the organization is much improved, although far from perfect. He can still behave as that expert and caustic critic. Recently, Tom applied for and got into final consideration for a vice presidential position in the company. He was not selected, but he surprised everyone with his presentations and how he handled himself. Tom was simultaneously pleased with how close he came and disappointed that he did not win the position. He remains determined to advance himself and to continue to improve on his performance.

EXECUTIVE DERAILMENT

The problems that lead to executive derailment are well documented in the literature (Finkelstein, 2003; Hogan, Curphy, & Hogan, 1994; Hyatt & Gottlieb, 1987). Although leadership and management development programs have sprouted from many schools of business and in governments throughout the country, it seems that the pages of newspapers and magazines bleed profusely with stories of leadership gone astray with sometimes catastrophic results for organizations, markets, and world society as a whole. Executive coaching has developed since the 1990s to become an increasingly well-defined subdiscipline within the field of consulting aimed at improving leadership performance (Diedrich & Kilburg, 2001; Hargrove, 1995; Kilburg, 2000, 2004, 2006; Kilburg & Diedrich, 2007). Early efforts to create coaching services arose because of the perceptions of participants in executive development programs that classroom-based learning was simply not enough. The rise of 360-degree assessment processes combined with this pent-up demand to fuel the initial experiments with more formal coaching in the 1980s and 1990s (Kilburg, 1996).

The subdiscipline of executive coaching has continued to evolve with the creation of coaching training programs; certification efforts; and, more recently, the recognition and specific inclusion of individually focused interventions into the knowledge and skill portfolio of consulting psychologists (Kilburg, 1997, 2002). Despite the best efforts of the entire field of consulting psychology to address the problems of executive derailment, as the case study that opens this chapter suggests, many leaders continue to sow the seeds of their own demise, often with the best of executive intentions. The fundamental paradox that arises all too often when individuals in leadership positions work extraordinarily hard to perform well and yet sometimes destroy themselves in their organizations is the focus of this chapter.

What follows is an effort to tie the problem of leadership derailment to the ancient Judeo-Christian conflict between virtue and vice. Following the metaphor of the seven deadly sins, seven deadly errors in leadership performance are identified and then traced to what are seen as their roots in traumatic and nontraumatic human learning. This is put into a framework for understanding leadership as an emergent process that is cocreated through and with all of the major elements involved in organizations. A structural model of the components of behavior underlying these forms of learning is presented. The psychodynamic patterns of behavior underlying the worst forms of poor leadership behavior are described, with special attention given to the problems of severe neurotic behavior, sadomasochism, and personality disorders. The chapter finishes with an effort to describe steps coaches and leadership teams can take to develop executive virtues as a specific set of antidotes for the toxic effects of the seven deadly errors.

SEEDS OF DESTRUCTION

In the history and culture of Western civilization, the most powerful method that developed to describe and define problematic human behavior was embedded in the Judeo-Christian religious tradition of identifying it as "sin" (Pieper, 1966). Gergen (1999) summarized and described the phenomenal cultural and organizational power that the ability to signify or label a behavior gives to the person who creates the capacity for such symbolization in a society. Thus priests, ministers, rabbis, imams, and other religious leaders, along with government officials, for many centuries had the ability and the power to set norms and expectations for behavior in any given society by defining sin.

Historically, the best-known sins have been defined as the *seven deadly sins* in the Judeo-Christian-Islamic religious traditions: pride, covetousness, lust, envy, gluttony/drunkenness, anger, and sloth. These cover a range of human behaviors and emotional states, and defining these as sins has traditionally framed them in the context of social–spiritual control. Individuals identified as behaving in these ways or having these characteristics were and still are expected to confess to being "sinners" and to make acts of contrition, penance, or healing to be forgiven and welcomed back as full partners in the community.

Even as humanity was creating these adversarial agencies of social and behavioral control, they were simultaneously engaging in the exercise of raising the expectations for behavior in positive ways. As early as the dialogues of Plato, the analects of Confucius, and other works of Western and Eastern writing, we see major evidence of the effort to identify positive images, ideas, and models for how people should behave. In Plato's *Republic* (trans. 1999), he formally recorded Socrates' efforts to specify what have become known as the *four cardinal virtues* (prudence, courage, temperance, and justice). Later, Christians added faith, hope, charity, and mercy to complete the positive base of their teachings. When taken together as a whole, the sins as behaviors to be avoided and the virtues as patterns of behavior to be pursued provide ample guidance for how an average citizen of the world should behave. However, modernism and postmodernism have challenged this traditional way of thinking about behavior (Gergen, 1999).

Religious and philosophical systems of regulating behavior are now in direct competition with those of science; social convention; and, increasingly, the mass media. The newer forms of control are reinforced by structures in nation-states, modern organizations, and technologies of mass communication. Inappropriate behavior is now defined in laws, regulations, organizational policies, in the social and behaviorally based classification system of the psychiatric profession (American Psychiatric Association, 1994) for mental illnesses, and in the headlines of the tabloid press and television. Increasingly, behavioral science tells us what works, what does not work, and what is disordered or normal. In the literature on executive derailment, case studies, surveys, and other scientific methodologies have been employed to describe what happens when executives fail.

The findings of derailment studies led me to identify what I call the *seven deadly leadership errors*. Modeled on the traditional theme of seven major human sins, the literature suggests that seven types of behavior get leaders into significant trouble. The most frequent error that leaders make is the failure to execute well (how they get work done; Bossidy & Charan, 2002). When you look inside these execution errors, the absence of wise leadership is what most often is on display. In my 2006 book *Executive Wisdom: Coaching and the Emergence of Virtuous Leaders,* I defined *executive wisdom* as the ability to do the right thing, in the right way, against the right time frame. The dark side of execution is leadership action undertaken in deliberate ignorance of the appropriate issues, activities, and time frames. The second error that is often made and has been quite visibly on display in myriad cases of executive misconduct being prosecuted around the country, now including the infamous Bernie Madoff Ponzi scheme, involves failures of integrity. Acts of injustice, discrimination, and simple lawlessness often put leaders and their organizations into deep trouble.

The third error arises when leaders prove themselves incapable of taking the appropriate action at the right time. This error can take many forms, but they most often can be described as acts of cowardice when the leader cannot step up to his or her responsibilities and take the steps necessary to protect an organization or nation. The fourth error is what I call *emotional incontinence*. This is perhaps an extreme way of phrasing the problem, but it is serious and frequently on display in many if not most organizations. There seems to be something about having a position of authority and power that frequently stimulates people to lose emotional control. Most often this occurs when leaders act poorly toward those who are subordinate to them in the organization. This is not simply the lack of emotional intelligence described so well by Goleman (1995); Goleman, Boyatzis, and McKee (2002); and others but involves more extreme forms of bad behavior that are sometimes displayed by leaders in many kinds of organizations.

The fifth error, *domination dynamics,* describes the extreme forms and abuses of managerial relationships and supervision. As Hogan, Curphy, and Hogan (1994) described, leaders who either micromanage or abandon their staff are at high risk for failure. Similarly, patterns of bullying behavior can create significant problems for anyone who works with a leader who displays them. The sixth error focuses on the problem of inflated expectations. Virtually every vision statement and strategic plan crafted by leadership teams these days focuses on words and phrases such as *best in class, market leader, number one,* or *excellence.* Peters (1992), Bossidy and Charan (2002), Maccoby (2003), and others have exhorted everyone and every organization to be the best, and yet it is a simple statistical impossibility for every enterprise to reach these levels of performance. Indeed, many organizations survive nicely and for long periods of time by simply doing well. Leaders who stand in front of organizations and suggest that the only well-performing organization is the best in class are often setting themselves up for tremendous problems. Human beings respond well to goal setting, support, and challenge (Heifetz, 1994). When these aren't properly communicated, greed, hubris, and impossible ideals often follow. Thus, the failure to test reality often leads executives into deep trouble. Finally, the seventh error occurs when leaders engage in unnecessary and unbridled secrecy and dishonesty; bad performance is the usual result. Living in organizations in which leaders lie, cheat, steal, and expect subordinates to collude with them and cover up the problems create an impossible dilemma for effective and ethical people and has the potential to sink the entire organization in a legal morass (Argyris, 1990, 1993).

Executives who make these mistakes are not necessarily completely venal, corrupt, or ineffective people. Indeed, most of them had to have performed well for long periods of time in organizations to gain the opportunity to lead. In today's enterprises, anyone who obtains a position of leadership has in the past and will in future face a host of vulnerabilities, any one of which can create the conditions in which one or more of the deadly errors will be made.

Exhibit 3.1 presents a list of 13 types of vulnerabilities that can have a dramatic impact on how well a leader performs and whether any of the deadly errors will be committed. Bradford and Cohen (1998) described the expectation many organizations and individuals create that the leader of any enterprise will in fact be a hero of mythic proportions. Heroic executives always have the right answers and the right ideas. They get along well with everyone and seem to be able to intuitively ascertain what will come in the future. The

EXHIBIT 3.1
The Vulnerabilities of Leaders

1. The Expectation of Knowing Everything
2. The Speed of Business
3. The Fog of Uncertainty
4. Being in the Public Eye
5. The Capriciousness of Markets
6. The Challenges of Competition, Being a Competitor, and Creative Destructionism
7. The Perpetual Trauma and Conflict in Executive Life
8. The Limitations of Individual, Group, and Organizational Performance and the Expectations of Perfection
9. The Realities of Limited Power and Control
10. The Experiences of Helplessness, Hopelessness, Powerlessness, and Human Frailty
11. The Power of Human Emotions
12. The Complexities of Human Defensiveness
13. The Temptations of Omnipotent Fantasy

expectation that our leaders will know everything is a key problem because it often prevents them from harnessing the true power of well-developed and well-differentiated human organizations. In such organizations, knowledge and skill are spread throughout the enterprise, and truly excellent leaders know how to identify and act on it. In the example provided in Chapter 2, Lou Gerstner demonstrated this kind of ability when he avoided the constant pressure applied to him to provide the heroic answers and instead consistently and quickly reached out to others inside and outside of IBM to help him craft solutions. Nevertheless, individuals and their subordinates all too often engage in the fatal game of "the boss should know everything."

A related problem involves the speed at which business can be conducted. For example, in the world of securities trading and financial deal making, transactions literally take place at the speed of light. Financial markets now work 24/7. The volume of business is too great, and its pace is too fast, for any one person to keep up. The pace demands that information be gathered quickly and processed thoroughly and that decisions be made incredibly fast. Executive reputations and futures in industry now seem to be decided every 90 days, and this produces a mind-set in leaders that almost forces them to exclude any but the most immediate needs from consideration. The expectation of knowing everything in a world in which knowledge is expanding exponentially and the speed at which organizations and markets can act produces the third vulnerability for leaders. They often experience a cognitive and emotional fog of uncertainty in which the amount of information, the alternatives available for action, the timelines against which they are operating, and complexity of their organizations can overwhelm their individual information-processing capacities. This can push leaders to stick close to what they know how to do, to lead from their and their organization's all-too-familiar strengths, and not to take the risks that are often necessary for long-term survival.

These vulnerabilities play on a stage where the modern leader seems to stand naked and exposed. People at the tops of organizations are seen by everyone, and CEOs and presidents of major enterprises are often the subjects of systematic media coverage. This can artificially inflate individuals' sense of self-importance to the point that they actually believe that they, as individuals, are synonymous with their organizations and all successes and failures. Simultaneously, we know well that markets are extraordinarily capricious. What was once a stable and reliable source of revenue for an organization can disappear overnight as tastes, technology, and public opinion change. The effects of the mass media only tend to exacerbate these issues. Leaders who wake up in the morning knowing that everything is going fine for their enterprises can never rest easy because they know the media may report that day that another enterprise, an economic or political problem, or a better idea can literally destroy part or all of their organizations in incredibly short periods of time (Schumpeter, 2009).

This is related directly to the sixth challenge—namely, that to be the leader of an organization is almost automatically to be in a competitive war. We now live in an era in which businesses and organizations of all sorts and sizes vie for market share in their portion of the global marketplace. The trend to competitive markets now extends to education; health care; and even religion, in which a shrinking base of church members can now lead to a minister, priest, rabbi, or imam being replaced for poor performance. As Schumpeter (2009) described, organizations and markets now deliberately sow the seeds of their own destruction, and leaders who fail to understand and cope with such forces are not long for their positions.

These demands create lives for leaders in which they are perpetually in conflict and in which they are constantly forced to manage the traumas that face the individuals that comprise their organizations and those that confront the organization as a whole. The conflicts and traumas play out in the real world of institutions that comprise all-too-limited individuals carrying the challenges and celebrations of their personal lives alongside the responsibilities of their positions. In fact, I have begun to think of leaders as the "chief trauma officers" of their organizations as they respond to the pressures, stresses, demands, problems, threats, and opportunities.

Every leader has strengths and weaknesses based on his or her knowledge, skill, education, socialization, psychological makeup, and genetic endowment. Each person in an organization, including leaders at the very top, occupies a role with limited power and control. Every leader, no matter how effective he or she might be, can face situations and circumstances that will produce feelings if not actual experiences of powerlessness, hopelessness, and helplessness. In addition, at each turn along the competitive road, the power of human emotion threatens to overwhelm leaders and must be harnessed for the good of the enterprise (Goleman et al., 2002). In this complex, demanding, and sometimes overwhelming world, leaders, like everyone else, are forced to defend themselves and their psychic integrity. Such defensive operations are difficult enough to manage in the personal lives of executives, but when they manifest in their working lives, as they inevitably must, these defenses can lead individuals to make poor decisions, choose improper directions, and commit one or more of the deadly errors.

The final vulnerability emphasizes the temptation that has probably most often led leaders and their organizations to ruination. When individual leaders cope with the array of problems that assail them by engaging in omnipotent fantasies, only the worst kinds of outcomes can be expected. Once an executive routinely enters into a world in which reality has little real hold on what is felt, thought, or believed, glorious and grand visions can be seen. However, the major problem is that such leaders then force those around them to report reality in accordance with their grandiose visions and then everyone may begin to live in a false world of dreams, wishful expectations, fantasies, deceit, and imaginary information. History has borne witness to leader after leader who has succumbed to this final vulnerability.

In the case study that opened this chapter, Tom Withers was widely viewed within his organization as a sales star who was soon to self-destruct as an executive within the company. His subordinates experienced him as someone who was completely out of control emotionally, spewing shame-laced criticism in every interaction, and who drove himself and his team members to sales volumes that never felt based in reality. Tom literally pushed himself and his teams to be number one in the organization, and he never stopped thinking about ways to sell even more. Peers and subordinates alike in the organization saw his expectations as expansive at best and grandiose at worst. They often experienced his criticism as a kind of oafish bullying that could get Tom much of what he wanted but cost him enormous amounts of interpersonal and political capital. His bosses, long aware of these patterns, largely left him alone because he did get financial results. For years, they had been uniformly reluctant to tamper with a sales leadership formula that was working for them and the company. Applying the framework of the deadly errors, we can see that Tom was routinely committing versions of three of them. When confronted with the reality-based consequences of his behavior, Tom surprised me by stating that his behavior was part of his own deliberate and courageously enacted strategy. The courage and integrity that he displayed in executing his strategy were as breathtaking as the long-term failure that it was producing for him in his organization.

In Tom's behavior, I saw difficulties with emotional incontinence or intemperance, domination dynamics, and inflated expectations. Despite producing impressive sales volumes over a long period of time in this organization and obtaining promotions to the second level of management, Tom had virtually stalled out in his leadership career. As is typical in many organizations, Tom had no true idea that he was really in trouble. When I provided the feedback to him, especially from the CEO of the company, he was quite surprised. He incorporated the information rapidly. I came to see this as a testament to his ability, his willingness to learn, and his reality-based perceptions of his own personal and professional vulnerability based in his long history of managing racially based discrimination throughout his life. Initially, he seemed unconcerned that he had been nearly completely blind to the problems that his personality and chosen style of interacting had produced for him. Without conscious awareness, Tom was on the verge of being judged as a total failure as a leader in this organization. Such a failure of execution in someone who thought of himself as on a fast track to an executive leadership position would probably have permanently crippled his long-term potential for promotion. His use of feedback and subsequent coaching work for the most part eliminated his knowledge and communication deficits with peers and subordinates and helped him develop new and more effective ways to lead his sales teams. This in turn restored the long-term possibility that he might rise to the level of vice president within his company.

FERTILE SOIL: SOME PSYCHODYNAMIC FOUNDATIONS OF THE LEADERSHIP ERRORS

If we allow ourselves to think of the errors and vulnerabilities that we have discussed so far as the surface manifestations of many of the major problems that modern leaders face in their roles, then it is logical to ask what challenges, issues, or patterns of behavior might connect what is on the surface with what might be going on in the unconscious worlds of leaders who commit one or more of these errors (Kilburg, 2000). As I have thought about these issues on the basis of my professional experience and understanding of some of the literature that I believe is relevant to these problems, I have come to believe that several major, interrelated components must be examined for the contribution that they make to the likelihood that a leader will commit these errors.

First, we can look at the patterns of learning that can lead to the errors. Historical, traumatically based patterns of learning as well as more obvious experiential and nontraumatic patterns can produce these difficult problems. Second, I have often seen these errors made by individual leaders who struggled with one or more of the behavioral characteristics of what Wurmser (2000, 2007) described as severe neurotic behavior. Third, within the dense and sometimes difficult-to-comprehend neurotic patterns of individual leaders' behaviors, the problem of sadomasochism plays a particularly significant—and as far as I can currently see, nearly constant—role in many of the complex pathways that lead to the deadly errors. Finally, severe neurotic behavior combined with sadomasochism form much of the foundation of each of the major personality disorders (American Psychiatric Association, 1994). Leaders who operate psychologically on a consistent basis from one of the personality disorders are most often at severe risk to make these errors. Let us explore these issues in more depth.

One of the pillars upon which modern psychology rests can be succinctly stated as follows: The vast majority of human behavior is in fact learned (Kimble, 1961). Despite the knowledge that *Homo sapiens*, like virtually all other biological species on the planet, carries some capacities or potentials for genetically regulated behavioral sequences (Zhang & Meaney, 2010), there appears to be a broad consensus that learning is one of the true fundamentals of psychological science. Exhibit 3.2 describes the core elements

EXHIBIT 3.2
Primary Features of Traumatic- and Nontraumatic-Based Learning

Traumatic learning	Nontraumatic learning
1. Experience of significant traumatic stimulation—physical, sexual, or emotional abuse in childhood or adolescence, soul blindness, soul murder, abandonment, invasiveness and enmeshment, hypercompetitiveness, loyalty challenges, control fights at all ages	1. Experience of stimulus conditions, initial learning challenges, and environmental conditions
2. Hyperphysical or emotional arousal—severe acute or chronic states of fear, shame, sadness, anger, guilt, sexuality, physical or emotional pain	2. If role models are present: demonstrations, modeling, identification, internalization, practice and reinforcements for success and failure
3. Distortions of thinking ability—regressive patterns of cognition; failures of objectification, categorical thinking, overgeneralization, catastrophizing, inability to think systemically or deconstructively	3. If role models are absent: trial and error behavior, use of intuition, reinforcement schedules—variation, selection, and retention
4. Primitive defensive efforts to reduce pain and stress—Denial, Splitting, Repression, Projection, Depersonalization, Detachment, Derealization, Dissociation, Reversal	4. Construction of schemas, scripts, routines, patterns, habits, internal models, and meta models
5. Emergence and reinforcement of complex conflict dynamics and compulsively driven compromise formations	5. Recognition primed and formal decision making in routine, novel, or threatening situations
6. Creation of convoluted patterns of behavior, character traits, and in the most severe cases, personality disorders	6. Reflective practices applied to consolidate knowledge and experience or produce adaptive variants based on situational changes or challenges
7. Severe distortions of behavior, personality, and ability to function in life—neuroses of varying complexity and severity	7. Reinforcement, extinction, and punishment schedules applied or experienced
8. Short term reinforcements of maladaptive patterns of behavior—secondary gains	
9. Repeated trials of compulsive, dysfunctional patterns with aperiodic reinforcement (primarily the short-term reduction of anxiety)	

of two major forms that such human learning can take. Traumatically based learning was illuminated by Freud (1923/1973d, 1916/1973e, 1933/1973f) and his inner circle and has been the subject of more than 100 years of scientific and clinical study. Today's understanding of posttraumatic stress disorder (American Psychiatric Association, 1994) and its severe manifestations is a descendant of the original psychoanalytic ideas that humans can be profoundly and permanently injured by psychic trauma. Bach (1994), Gray (1994), Herman, (1992), Wurmser (2000, 2007), and others have adequately described the primary features of traumatically based learning, and these are summarized on the left-hand side of Exhibit 3.2. Among other things, trauma can include physical, sexual, or emotional abuse and overstimulation; abandonment; overinvolvement; competitiveness; control battles; and loyalty challenges within families of origin. For an individual person, even a mundane event such as a failure in school or a rejection within a love relationship can serve as a traumatizing stimulus.

The effects of warfare on human psychology are extreme examples of what can happen to people when physical deprivation, pain, fear, loss of control, and overwhelming emotional states are experienced. Such states lead to conditions of physiological and psychological hyperarousal and can then be connected or associated with feelings of terror, rage, humiliation, sadness, guilt, or other forms of psychic pain. These stimuli and states can also create major distortions in human information processing and patterns of thinking. Left uncorrected, such distortions can become nearly permanent features of the inner landscapes of people. Similarly, primitive defensive operations that consist largely of efforts to deny or significantly distort the overwhelmingly painful aspects of the traumatic events can also assume major and largely permanent roles in the unconscious lives of people. In turn, major conflict states and patterns of behavior are created and come to be associated with behavioral compromises that most often produce short-term reductions in the amount of psychic pain endured but offer no real long-term hope of coping with the original problems.

These conflicts, defenses, emotions, and forms of distorted cognition merge into complex and convoluted patterns of behavior that often look mysterious yet strangely recognizable to people who see them with some degree of objectivity. In the worst cases, severe, prolonged, and sometimes permanent distortions of personality and human capacities result. In a paradox of the grandest proportions, these distortions are most often self-maintaining because of the power of short-term reinforcement provided by the rapid reduction of the psychic pain they can create. Because the reinforcements do not challenge the fundamental structures and processes underlying the patterns of behavior, the traumatically learned sequences can reappear in compulsive, dysfunctional cycles.

The right-hand side of Exhibit 3.2 lists major characteristics of learned behavior that apply to nontraumatic conditions that humans face. In nontraumatic, or what we could call "normal" learning (Kimble, 1961), experiences of stimulus conditions, environmental events, and learning challenges are encountered by any person. When role models are present (Bandura, 1977, 1982), individuals have the opportunity to witness demonstrations of coping or adaptation to the learning challenges. Such role-modeling behaviors can lead to identifications, internalization, practice, and social reinforcement of the patterns in those who try to execute them. In the absence of role models, trial and error, exploratory and sensation-seeking behavior, the use of intuition, and other learning routines are initiated. In the sense of evolutionary psychology, successful behaviors result from variation of efforts to cope, selection of winning methods, and retention of those patterns with some potential for long-term improvement in the lives of the individuals who learn. Findings in cognitive–behavioral psychology (Beck, Rush, Shaw, & Emery, 1979) have demonstrated that internal schemas, scripts, routines, habits, and meta-models are constructed from such adaptive efforts and are used both symbolically and in reality to cope with future challenges. Klein (1999, 2003) suggested that the results of such learning lead to two major forms of human decision making: recognition primed and formal decision approaches that enable individuals to respond to routine, novel, or threatening stimulus conditions. Argyris (1993), Schön (1987), and Siebert and Daudelin (1999) showed that some humans also resort to reflective practices that help them enhance the learning they obtain in responding to the challenges in their lives. Finally, the traditional learning processes of practice, reinforcement, extinction, and punishment will often determine whether a behavioral pattern continues to be used or expressed or whether it disappears into the morass of history or the past life of a person.

When applied to the situation involving executives who infrequently, periodically, or rather consistently commit the seven deadly errors, I believe that both traumatic and nontraumatic forms of learning can lead to these actions. In the case of traumatically learned behaviors, significantly disturbed patterns of behavior can be produced in individual leaders, some of which can be highly valued by their organizations. For Tom Withers, his compulsive need to set extraordinarily high goals and to pursue them with relentless energy and intensity provided the leadership of his organization with many reasons to value, reward, and promote him. When he began to apply those patterns of behavior to his subordinates and colleagues, interpersonal and intraorganizational conflicts erupted that began to detract from the positive effects of the compulsive patterns. When they combined with the severely corrosive effects of his chronic, emotionally laden criticisms, the toxic combination eventually shifted the balance of the evaluation in the eyes of the leaders of the organization. The previously valued behaviors, as extreme as they were, became major burdens for the CEO and his colleagues. Eventually, they tried to mitigate the negative effects and reduce the frequency of the errors.

As I discovered in the course of my coaching work with Tom, his rather extreme and compulsively high achievement needs were directly related to early circumstances of poverty, parental abandonment, racism, and his determination to never be in a position of powerlessness again. As he came to understand and appreciate that there were other forms of leadership behavior that he could display and use to achieve the goals and outcomes he sought as well as some of the underlying dynamic forces that motivated his behavior, he was able to bring the worst aspects of his interpersonal relationships and leadership behavior under better control. His reputation in the company was resurrected and his possible future as a marketing and sales executive restored.

Similar examples abound in the lore and literature of modern organizations (Tedlow, 2001). However, we also have examples in which normal, nontrauma-based learning patterns can adequately describe the commission of the deadly errors. One need look only to the leadership decisions and executive group processes involved in the Enron, Tyco, Adelphia, Arthur Andersen, or WorldCom debacles of the early 2000s to understand that modeling and social reinforcement can have disastrous consequences.

Figure 3.1 illustrates many of the major components of the adaptive world of individual leaders and helps us to understand much about the complexity that faces executives in their daily lives. The figure contains seven interpenetrating domains to, in, and from which a person must initiate his or her efforts to succeed as a leader. Traditionally, the easiest elements to describe and focus on are the adaptive situation in the external world the executive faces and the general status of the home organization. Indeed, most business and organizational case studies tend to start and stop their analytic efforts with objective views of the largely strategic questions related to organization–environment fit. The keystone of organizational strategy centers on the niche an executive wishes his or her enterprise to occupy in the global marketplace, and the majority of leaders' time and attention tends to focus on this question. However, the world of the individual executive is much more complex, as Figure 3.1 demonstrates. First, the leader cannot organize and operate a large enterprise alone. The primary purpose of leadership is to extend the adaptive capacity of individuals through the organized efforts of others. Leaders of any organization need and want to create an executive group through which they direct the operations of the enterprise. The capacities of the individual leader are multiplied enormously through the time, energies, and talents of his or her direct subordinates. However, the creation and operation of an executive team take huge amounts of a leader's time and attention. The challenges of leading such groups are well documented (Katzenbach, 1998; Katzenbach & Smith, 1994), for they

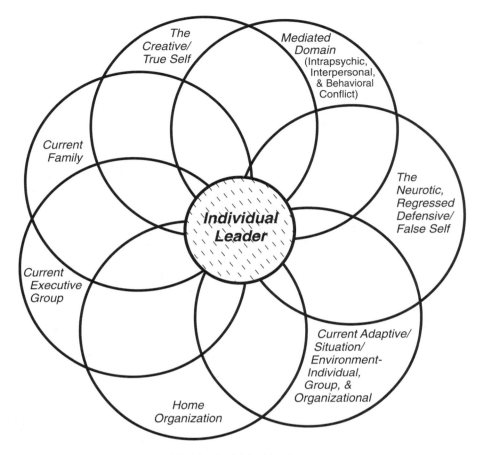

Figure 3.1. The adaptive world of the individual leader.

do not create or maintain themselves. Second, leaders have their own personal lives to manage outside of the organization itself. If their personal lives are successful, well run, and supportive, leaders will usually experience little except time and energy demands. If things go astray in their families, executives can become preoccupied and distressed in the extreme, even to the point where their capacities to lead can be impaired.

Finally, we must look inside the mind of the leader (Kilburg, 1997, 2000, 2002, 2004, 2006). Figure 3.1 provides three additional domains to examine. Following traditional ideas about the formation of intrapsychic structures (Freud, 1923/1973d, 1916/1973e, 1933/1973f; Wurmser, 2000, 2007), the figure depicts the Creative or True Self; the Neurotic, Regressed, Defensive Self; and a Mediated Domain that rides between the two. In the True Self, we find the traditional elements of the observing ego (Hartmann, 1958) and those expressive components of the mind and body that are largely unafflicted by psychological or behavioral symptomatology. In the Neurotic, Regressed, Defensive Self, we find those elements of an individual that were created in response to traumas of various types, intensities, and durations. Defensive patterns of thoughts, emotions, and behaviors occupy this domain. The relative size, strength, and contribution that these two domains of internal psychic functions make to the adaptive efforts of an individual leader can vary widely and wildly from person to person and even within a single person from situation to situation. The seventh element, the Mediated Domain, is provided to illustrate that these other six elements of the adaptive world of a leader produce intrapsychic, interpersonal, and behavioral conflicts. Managing these various conflicts creatively and effectively are the sum and substance of the lives of leaders.

In the center of Figure 3.1, we see a circle depicting an individual leader. Executives nest in the interlocking network of these elements. He or she brings to the job and to life all of the knowledge, skill, ability, and experience that are possible to cope with the complex adaptive world confronting the home organization. Executive attention flows from one domain to another during any single moment, day, week, or even year in the effort to collect information, discern critical patterns, make wise choices, and direct personal and organizational actions in response to challenges, threats, and opportunities. The trauma- and non-trauma-based learning foundations of any executive operate in and through these various structural domains and can have both direct and indirect impacts on the performance of a leader. The commission of any one of the deadly errors usually comes about as a result of an interaction between several of these structural domains, for it is to this interaction between intrapsychic, interpersonal, organizational, and environmental pressures and variables that leaders must direct their attention to discern what is critical, to make wise choices, and to take effective executive action. Whether they succeed or fail is often a matter of very public scrutiny.

For the general purposes of this book, I believe it is important to place the components of the individual executive's adaptive world into a broader conceptual model of the key elements of leadership. Kilburg and Donohue (2011) have developed an approach that integrates many of the currently understood and well-researched aspects of leadership theory into the 21st-century concept of emergence.

Figure 3.2 provides a flow diagram that attempts to depict the principle known elements that contribute to the emergence of leadership in any given organization. In this model, the external environment including the ecological, geopolitical, social, geographic, and economic niches in which an enterprise operates establishes the basic context for leadership to emerge in an organization. The personal characteristics and capacities of the leader,

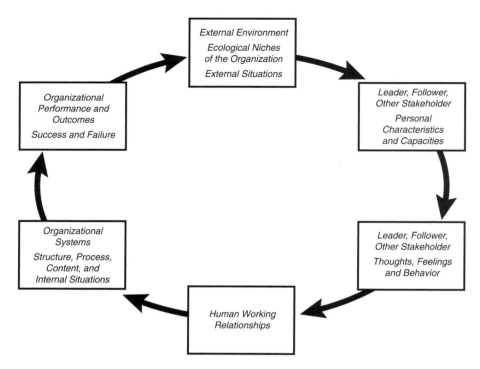

Figure 3.2. The basic leadership model.

followers, and other stakeholders in the organization including the histories, personalities, other elements of diversity, knowledge, skills, abilities, and experience bases of those involved establish fundamental building blocks of leadership within that specific environmental situation. These include the components of the adaptive world of an executive described in conjunction with Figure 3.1

Leaders, followers, and other stakeholders then produce thoughts, feelings, and observable behaviors that comprise the moment-to-moment and day-to-day exchanges within which leadership processes occur. As a result of those exchanges, the members of the organization form human attachments and relationships within and through which they do the work of the enterprise. They create, maintain, and, when necessary, change structures, processes, and functions within their organizational systems and between their enterprise and the external environments with which they interact. Over time, those organizational systems produce performance and outcomes that can be detected and evaluated in the external environment, and those results are most often characterized as leadership and organizational failures or successes. Those successes and failures then modify the external environments of the enterprise and affect how they engage and interact with the leader, followers, and other stakeholders.

This flow diagram suggests that these fundamental elements of leadership are enacted in a circular fashion with each component leading logically to the next in an overarching feedback loop. Thus, characteristics give rise to thoughts, feelings, and behaviors, which in turn create structured human relationships. Those relationships are enacted within the systems of the organization and produce successes and failures in the adaptation and ecological fit of the enterprise. The exchanges that occur between the organization and its ecological environment are dynamic in nature and result in a process of co-modification or mutual adaptation. These adaptations then impact the leaders, followers, and other stakeholders in the organization.

In reality, this kind of circular flow model represents a simplistic view of how leadership arises in an ecologically active enterprise. Figure 3.3 goes on to representationally connect each of the six major elements with two-way arrows that demonstrate that the model is not linear or even circular. Each of the six major elements of the model can and often does engage simultaneously in some dynamic way with every other element. For example, exchanges like this often occur when external consultants or market analysts interact

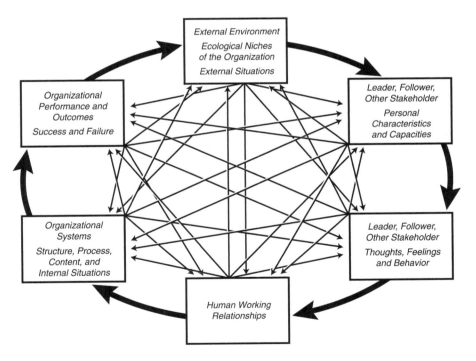

Figure 3.3. The basic leadership model fully connected.

with members of the board of directors of a business. These types of interactions can and do change the nature of the relationships that members of the board have with each other and with the executives of a firm. Finally, changes in the inputs, throughputs, and outputs of the psychosocial and technical systems of the enterprise can simultaneously involve the thoughts, feelings, behaviors, and relationships of key members of a leadership team and those of competitors, investors, vendors, and customers in the ecological environment of the organization. The extensive and often unpredictable nature of these dynamic exchanges makes leadership an enormously challenging process and creates much of the technical and conceptual difficulty in doing effective research on leadership.

Figure 3.3 demonstrates that leadership is indeed an emergent property of all of these dynamic exchanges between the complex subsystems involved in the adaptive processes of psychosocial–technical organizations in competitive ecological environments (Stacey 1992, 1996, 2007). Leadership cannot be successfully divorced from any of these complex subsystems. Indeed, it is explicitly and inherently part of each and every one of these elements. Scholarly efforts that focus on particular parts or subprocesses that comprise elements of the emergent property identified as leadership can be extremely useful. They help to illuminate and clarify the nature of many of the dynamic exchanges that Figure 3.3 suggests are occurring all of the time. However, micromodels of leadership run the risk of not engaging all the other dynamically interacting components of these ecological systems.

We have briefly discussed some of the learning, interpersonal, organizational, structural, and generic psychological issues, providing an overarching approach to understanding the adaptive world of executives and an emergent model of leadership within which they can be understood to practice that can create the circumstances for the commission of the deadly errors. We now turn to the sometimes difficult-to-understand world of psychopathology for additional insight into what can put senior people in organizations into such dangerous territory. Wurmser (2000, 2007) provided a detailed and chillingly complicated picture of the inner structures and dynamic processes and patterns of severe neurotic behavior. I have tried to capture the key components of his descriptions in Exhibit 3.3. Understanding such distorted patterns of human behavior begins with an appreciation of the toxically corrosive effects of traumatically based learning on individual people, families, groups, and organizations.

Wurmser (2000, 2007), in his revision of classical psychoanalytic principles, suggested that trauma(s) are internalized by individuals along with learned patterns of emotion, cognition, defense, and conflict and result in endlessly compulsive efforts to cope with the impacts of the trauma. These distorted patterns of behavior, originally created to help a person cope with the pain and suffering of the trauma, come to have even more permanently

EXHIBIT 3.3
Some Characteristics of Severe Neuroses

1. Internalization of the trauma—insatiably, endlessly, and compulsively repeating it in order to master the overwhelming affects and turning of the aggression against the self.
2. Magical reversal of the affects involved in the trauma and the denial of perception of the trauma.
3. Splitting and the polarization of opposites—the creation of two realities one which contains the trauma and its related experiences and one which does not; the world becomes divided between good and evil, love and hate, God and the Devil.
4. Globalization and absoluteness of a value, belief, behavior, emotion, or thought and absolute exclusion or denial of anything that does not coincide with it.
5. Sexualization as a defense against helpless rage and anxiety—the centralization and eroticization of power in human emotion and behavior (the erotic allure of the deal).
6. Painful touch or relatedness as defense against being separate and isolated— pain is better than nothing.
7. Counterfantasy: idealization of invulnerability and sexual completeness; the repetitive experience of attempts at omnipotent resolutions to human problems.
8. Pervasive guilt founded in omnipotent responsibility. If I am omnipotent, I am responsible for everything that goes wrong in my life.
9. Isolation, deanimation, dehumanization—the compulsive reversal of overwhelming feelings of powerlessness, helplessness, and hopelessness by being unaffected by them.
10. Layers of conflicts, underlying and supporting the severely compulsive and dysfunctional patterns of behavior.
11. Conflicts between and about global affects—shame, anxiety, guilt, sadness, anger, sexuality.
12. Conflicts between and about union and separateness.
13. Conflicts about control of one's body, mind, and relationships.
14. Triangular conflicts in relationships.
15. Conscience conflicts—rescue missions; loyalty conflicts; value and moral conflicts.
16. The nobility of suffering—I choose to suffer because to do anything else generates intolerable anxiety.
17. The sacrifice—I sacrifice my well-being for others and for preserving the status quo.
18. Eyes that looked at her without seeing her—"Soulblindness" and "Soulmurder"— pervasive patterns of being unable or unwilling to see what is happening, to test reality, to acknowledge the problems that exist based upon developmental experiences in which others treated the person as a "thing" or worse actively attempted to destroy the person's spirit (Shengold, 1989).

corrosive and destructive effects on him or her simply because of the consequences of the complex sequences of symptoms and behaviors and the energy expenditures required to both produce and recover from them. Exhibit 3.3 provides examples of these patterns and consequences. The energy involved in trying to ensure that the true nature of the trauma and its effects are denied is most often one of the most significant problems produced in these situations. In a sense, people who struggle with these patterns can be captured in prisons of their own creation. Behaviors that were so carefully discovered, invented, and assembled into a self-protective system designed to help them escape the consequences of the original wounds and suffering become in themselves a source of perpetual torture for these people. In the behavior of leaders so trapped, we see primitive defenses; global and extreme expressions of emotion; patterns of response in which pain can seem to be the only purpose of living; enormously inflated expectations of the self and others; the absolute denial of many of the realities of life; and, in the most lethal examples of these forms of severe problems, institutional and ritualized forms of homicide being conducted in the service of political, religious, or organizational ideologies.

The 20th and now 21st centuries are replete with examples of people afflicted with such troubled behavior coming to power in countries and organizations and using their considerable genius for organization and leadership to commit some of the most horrendous crimes in human history. Hitler, Stalin, Mao, Pol Pot, the leaders of the Rwandan minorities, the Serbs in Yugoslavia, Saddam Hussein, Japanese military leaders in their actions in Korea and China—the extensive list goes on. If we ask what these examples have to do with modern business and not-for-profit organizations, the simple answer is that these behaviors can be linked to the underlying patterns of severely neurotic human behavior that traumatic learning and adaptation can produce. These patterns can frequently be found in the leaders of any type of organization.

Human conflict can manifest overtly in triangulated communications; immoral and unethical decision making; discrimination; and the nearly endless forms in which prejudice, intolerance, racism, sexism, ageism, heterosexism, and homosexism can be expressed. Inside these complex examples are core equations in which humans choose one form of suffering over another simply because the short-term effects of the often exotic symptoms are unconsciously experienced as usually less costly and easier to tolerate than the sometimes massive anxiety, shame, guilt, rage, and sadness that are associated with more direct connection to the internalized trauma. The leader who struggles with such forms of behavior often sacrifices his or her well-being to preserve that of others or, as is more often the case, simply to preserve the status quo in his or her inner world.

In a final and shatteringly destructive component of neurotic behavior, leaders can blind themselves to what is happening inside themselves and to what their decisions, behaviors, attitudes, and values can create in the lives of others. As Kilborne (2002) described in his careful examination of Oedipus Rex, leaders afflicted in these ways can deliberately blind themselves in order not to witness the consequences of what they are doing. As Oedipus the King tore out his own eyes to avoid looking at what he had done, so modern leaders often ignore the short- and long-term consequences of their acts, choosing instead to spin stories that attempt to shape public perceptions in ways that belie the true purposes or true impacts of their actions. We need only to watch the evening news to reaffirm that these largely unconscious and extremely powerful forces have and probably always will have a hand in shaping human destiny.

Similarly, Exhibit 3.4 presents a summary of 12 of the major components of sadomasochistic patterns of unconscious adaptation. Novick and Novick (1996) thoroughly explored and provided terrific insight into the complexity of these dynamics in a series of papers about their psychoanalytic studies of severely disturbed children. Along with Freud (1937/1973a, 1919/1973b, 1924/1973c), they suggested that a major underlying component of sadomasochism is the presence of beating fantasies that take different forms for boys and girls and men and women. It is common to watch many young children go through a period of time in which they struggle to relate to and control others through hitting or other forms of aggression. Over time, these patterns migrate into games or interpersonal routines in which aggression forms the core of how children relate. Hitting, teasing, chasing, and dodging are the sources of endless hours of play. In the worst cases, these "games" end in targeting one or more of the most vulnerable of the children who participate, with sometimes traumatizing results. Perhaps one of the best examples of this pattern in modern fiction occurs in *Lord of the Flies* when the shipwrecked boys turn themselves into a hunting band that targets and kills two of its scapegoated members (Golding, 1954).

According to Novick and Novick (1996), these patterns of behavior start in the complex exchanges that occur between parents and their children. An absence of accurate empathy, understanding, or other parenting skills can create repeated experiences for children in which they feel helpless, hopeless, and powerless to change their worlds. They learn that effective relationships and effectiveness in relationships arises primarily from primitive forms of power and control in which their behavior gives them the ability to at least periodically move adults to act on their behalf. In the worst cases, children learn that security, safety, and pleasure reside in ineffective relationships with parents who often produce significant suffering and pain. These relationships can become synonymous with suffering, and children can appear as if they deliberately seek pain with and through others. In reality, they are acting out what they have learned—namely, to get pleasure or security in life, they must endure a certain measure of trouble.

Left unaltered, these patterns continue to evolve into adulthood and can come to be seen in complex, compulsive cycles of relating to others in and through the experience of pain. Because such suffering is often unbearable, the individuals make repetitive efforts to change themselves, their relationships, or their surroundings or to reach out to others for help. All too often, there is a built-in subroutine in the pattern in which the efforts to

EXHIBIT 3.4
Components of the Shadow Structure
of Sadomasochistic Patterns of Adaptation

1. Beating wishes—normal and fixed or neurotic wishes founded in the period of development . . . "in which almost all children form their concepts of relationships in terms of power and control. Hitting and being hit is a major avenue of discharge for aggressive and hostile impulses . . . "—with normal gender based differences in the patterns (Novick & Novick, 1996, p. 6).
2. Hitting, chasing, teasing, and catching games in childhood—doctor, tag, monkey in the middle, cops and robbers, scapegoat—children as perpetrators and victims (*Lord of the Flies,* Golding, 1954).
3. Insufficient empathic resonance and attunement between caregiver and child producing disturbances in the pleasure economy between parent and child.
4. Parent-child mismatches produce disturbances in effectance—children begin to understand very early, even preverbally, that something is wrong in their ability to exert influence in the social world to help them control pleasure and pain.
5. Normal effectance in children translates to a primitive form of power and control, in essence omnipotence. My cries, smiles, and behaviors can get me what I want and need.
6. Safety, security, and pleasure come to reside in an ineffective or periodically effective relationship with a parent or parents.
7. In worst cases, parental relationships come to be synonymous with pain and chronically high anxiety and seemingly can produce a personality that appears to be centered on a need for pain.
8. In adulthood, the appearance of compulsive, repetitive, complex patterns of behavior in which unusual amounts of pain are induced and experienced in relationships, adaptive challenges, and the activities of daily living with the concomitant experience of psychological, social, organizational, physical, or spiritual suffering.
9. Compulsive, repetitive efforts to change the pattern(s) of behavior or solicit help in changing with the consistent, unconscious defeat of those change attempts.
10. The development of and reliance upon defensive operations based primarily in projection and externalization or finding both fault in and explanations for problems experienced in life in the attitudes, emotions, behaviors, or values of others.
11. An underlying, largely unconscious delusion of omnipotence made manifest overtly or covertly in inflated or grandiose wishes, needs, drives, goals, choices, communications, competitions, and other complex patterns of behavior—I am the best, the greatest, the strongest, the smartest . . .
12. Patterns of relationships characterized by one of two underlying themes or schemas in which "The pain of suffering defends against the greater pain of loss" (Bach, 1991, p. 86).
    a. "I can do anything to you and you won't/can't leave me."
    b. "You can do anything to me but don't leave me" (Wurmser, 2007).

change or obtain help are systematically defeated in the twisted expectation that it is only the completion of the neurotically compulsive pattern that will yield true relief. The internalized efforts of these people to protect themselves concentrate on projection and externalization, in which the problems and difficulties of their lives must ultimately find explanations in the motives, actions, thoughts, and feelings of others. Most important, Novick and Novick (1996) suggested that the inner core of this pattern comprises a delusion of omnipotence. Inside the delusion, the individual wraps oneself in a type of false security and self-esteem. The surface manifestations can best be seen in variations of the theme of "I am the best, the greatest, the strongest, the smartest." Grandiose expectations of life and of relationships are common and come to replace the more realistic experience of simply living a life with other humans in which one struggles, succeeds, and fails but is ultimately judged simply as a decent person and not the best.

Finally, according to Bach (1994) and Wurmser (2007), sadomasochistic forms of relating are characterized by two symbiotic psychological schemas or themes, both of which reflect the inner experience of these people in which the suffering that comes from the painful relationship is used to defend or protect against the even greater perceived pain of loss. These two themes Wurmser described eloquently as "I can do anything to you and you won't or can't leave me" (the essence of the sadistic form of relating) and "You can do anything to me but don't leave me" (the core of the masochistic type of relating).

One might ask how such traditional psychoanalytic and psychodynamic ideas can be reasonably applied to the challenges of understanding and helping leaders steer their organizations and develop themselves. If we return to the opening case example, we can quickly see that Tom Withers exhibited many of these characteristics in the way he related to his colleagues and in the way he treated himself. Over decades, he created a pattern in which he delivered searing psychological, interpersonal, and organizational pain to others through his chronic, caustic criticism. He defended his behavior by explaining that he was doing his best for them. He resisted others' efforts to push him to change his behavior. Indeed, the coaching intervention itself was viewed by the CEO as a last-ditch, high-risk effort in which he had little hope of success.

As coaching uncovered, Tom struggled with the core sense of omnipotence that Novick and Novick (1996) described because he saw, promoted, and ritually drove himself to be the best salesman in the organization. He would do anything to maintain his status, and he made sure that everyone around him understood that he was willing to pay any price to do so. His relationships could readily be described as sadistic in their basic form, conforming to Bach's core theme. Tom firmly and largely unconsciously believed that he could do almost anything to people under or around him and that his sales numbers would protect him. He was quite surprised to hear from his boss that this was not the case. He was even more shaken when he saw the written evidence of how others viewed him. It was a testament to Tom's inner resilience and commitment to being effective in the world that he was able both to hear the information that the evaluation process brought to him and then go on to change many of the worst forms of behavior he had developed.

So, we see in this case material that Novick and Novick's (1996) formulations can be readily identified in the ineffective behavior of an executive in an organization. Even more important, we can see that coaching and its core technologies of reality-based feedback and reflective examinations of self, relationships, groups, organizations, and adaptive situations can be helpful in changing at least the work-related manifestations of some significant and troubling psychodynamic patterns.

CORRECTING THE ERRORS

History is replete with examples of individuals such as Adolf Hitler who have led their organizations, including governments, countries, and entire human empires to ruination and destruction, just as we have many examples of people like Lou Gerstner who managed to bring their enterprises back from the brink of extinction or led them to unimagined success. If we accept that the seven deadly errors identified in this chapter represent an ongoing danger to individuals and their organizations, then we should ask what executives can do to try to prevent themselves and others from committing one or more of them. It is not possible to describe everything that individuals or organizations can do to correct these errors when they happen or, even more important, to prevent them from occurring. However, Exhibit 3.5 presents a dozen recommendations that, if implemented by an organization or an individual leader, will significantly decrease the likelihood that the errors will emerge or that permanent damage will occur if they do.

First, I believe that organizations need to recruit, train, reward, and retain leaders who demonstrate the classic virtues described thousands of years ago in Plato's *Republic*. Leaders who work from a foundation that includes wisdom, temperance, courage, and justice are unlikely to behave in the ineffective and destructive ways that the errors represent. Second, leaders can promote and routinely use reflective practices as they direct and manage the affairs of the enterprise. In two previous works (Kilburg, 2000, 2006), I described core practices in awareness that increase the likelihood that leaders will display executive wisdom. In addition, there are a series of what could be considered antidotes to the errors, including leading with imagination, empathy, good communication skills, using human intuition, building effective relationships,

EXHIBIT 3.5
Organizational and Individual Interventions to Buffer Vulnerabilities and Decrease the Probability of the Deadly Errors

1. Develop, recognize, reward, and maintain executive virtues—wisdom, temperance, courage, justice, reverence.
2. Create and follow an ethic of reflective practice—promote the six awarenesses (self, family, executive group, organizational, situational, and moral) and seven antidotes to executive ignorance (imagination—strategic vision, empathy, communication, intuition, effective relationships, good decision making, self-regulation); and mindfulness.
3. Test reality constantly—create an ethic of constructive engagement.
4. Commit to the progressive development of yourself, your team, and your organization—train and educate everyone in the organization; provide mentors and coaches.
5. Create and respect external accountabilities for yourself and your organization.
6. Discover and effectively use external resources.
7. Focus on execution.
8. Nurture and extend executive attention.
9. Respect and explore the role of unconscious behavior in human organizations.
10. Develop and maintain the psychosocial and physical components of your life.
11. If dysfunctional behavioral patterns persist seek consultation.
12. Discipline repeat offenders and if the pattern continues, dismiss them.

making good decisions, and regulating oneself. Finally, the Buddhist practice of mindfulness (Hanh, 1975) can assist leaders in managing themselves and their organizations.

A third core intervention to prevent the errors consists of activities through which leaders thoroughly test reality. Sitting at the top of organizations is a heady yet precarious experience because information and experience are often completely distorted. Virtually anything that a leader does to provide himself or herself with better and richer information about what is happening inside and outside of the organization will result in better decisions and wiser actions. Leaders also need to commit themselves and some of the resources of their organizations to the tasks of lifelong development. Pushing oneself to learn and grow and creating an environment in which others are expected to do so can ensure that new ideas and experiences come into the lives of leaders and their organizations. New paradigms and fresh ideas can help organizations avoid making the deadly errors. Similarly, leaders can systematically create and respect external accountabilities for themselves and their organizations. Calling in audits, asking for external reviews, and conducting performance examinations can help with reality testing and create new learning opportunities. Leaders should also look for resources for themselves and their organizations outside of normal types of contacts and business relationships. Again, people, ideas, experiences, and technologies from the outside are likely to challenge the status quo, the received and tacit knowledge of the leaders in an organization, and push executives to consider other possibilities. Executives must focus on execution (Bossidy & Charan, 2002), and they must also be aware of what they focus on and cherish to help identify potentially destructive patterns. Concentrating on improving individual and organizational execution and deliberately expanding one's ability to pay attention to different sources of information and experience will reduce the likelihood of the errors.

As I have advocated in this chapter, it is important that anyone who leads or works with leaders acknowledge and understand that unconscious manifestations of behavior in individuals, groups, and organizations can produce extraordinarily destructive effects. Respecting the unconscious in human affairs and developing the capacity to intervene effectively when such patterns manifest in the errors of leadership can help reduce the damage that can occur when such unconscious patterns emerge.

Individual leaders also must ensure that they take care of themselves physically, emotionally, and socially. Life at the top of organizations can be grueling and dangerous to the health and well-being of the people who occupy these positions. The level of stress experienced by leaders is well known, and they need to counteract the negative impact through systematic efforts to improve their health.

Finally, if leaders see these errors emerge in their organizations, they must take constructive and effective action. Consulting people with expertise in a wide variety of areas can help diagnose and ameliorate problems as they are detected. However, in the end, leaders must also be prepared to discipline and ultimately discharge those in their organizations who repeatedly commit these deadly errors and especially those who seem incapable of understanding the seriousness of what they have done. Failure to take such decisive and constructive action can endanger the career of the leader and, in some situations, the very life of the organization. In the most serious cases in governments and other organizations involving security, public safety, and public health, many human lives may also be at risk if effective action is not taken.

CONCLUSIONS

In this chapter, I have posited the existence of seven deadly leadership errors that have been repeatedly identified in the literature on executive derailment and examined these errors within several conceptual frameworks. To begin with, they can be understood as what could be considered as managerial sins or the failure or absence of leadership virtues within the philosophical and religious traditions of Western civilization. They also can be understood as arising from an incredibly complex array of vulnerabilities that impinge on all leaders regardless of their exact role and the size of their enterprise. In addition, commission of these errors can occur because of trauma- or non-trauma-based learning that influences leaders through a system of complex interacting social, psychological, organizational, and environmental domains. Finally, in the worst cases, the presence of these errors can be seen as arising from psychodynamically informed patterns of severely neurotic, sadomasochistic, and personality-disordered behavior.

The continued emergence of the subdiscipline of executive coaching demands that practitioners create and use a conceptual foundation and set of intervention skills that encompass not only the easiest, simplest, and most readily transformed clients but also the most difficult and indeed most dangerous of leaders and leadership situations. Human history is replete with examples of leaders who have brought slaughter, destruction, and catastrophes to the world. As coaching practitioners continue to demonstrate their ability to understand how these individuals come to lead in these ways and our willingness to attempt to intervene constructively in increasingly complex and difficult cases expands, the field will offer more opportunities to help leaders cope with the difficulties that they face. It is my own hope that the subdiscipline of executive coaching will continue on a path that tries to incorporate an extraordinarily wide range of ideas and methods to support our efforts. Anything we can do to help individual leaders avoid the initial commission or ameliorate the effects of any one of these deadly errors will be of enormous assistance to them and to their organizations. In the event that some of us begin to work directly with the leaders of governments or governmental agencies, we will eventually be in a position to have even broader impact on the human world. Now let's turn to a more careful and thorough exploration of the major virtues that I believe are the foundation of effective leadership and the avoidance of these deadly errors.

4

WISDOM, COURAGE, TEMPERANCE, JUSTICE, AND REVERENCE: PLATONIC VIRTUES AND LEADERSHIP COMPETENCE

INTRODUCTION

In 2004 and 2005, the world experienced three major disasters: a tsunami in the Indian Ocean Basin, Hurricane Katrina at the southern coast of the United States, and a large earthquake in Pakistan. In 2011, an incredible earthquake and tsunami in Japan crippled parts of its economy and left its national power grid in a shambles. Post hoc assessments demonstrated that leaders of the countries affected by these disasters knew the risks to their people yet took few effective preventative actions. Lest we believe that executive folly is confined to governments, we have the financial disaster of 2008–2011 that bankrupted most major banks in the United States and would have sunk them save for the phenomenally costly intervention of the federal government. Again, post hoc analyses revealed that the leaders of these organizations knew what problems they faced but took inappropriate actions to preserve their enterprises.

Simultaneously, as we have explored in Chapter 2, we have IBM, which faced enterprise-threatening problems in the 1990s, but its leadership team managed to execute strategies that made the company much stronger as it headed into the new millennium. We also have at least one company, General Electric, that has survived and thrived in a globally competitive market-place for more than a century by continuously assessing the nature of its environment and redeveloping its organizational processes, structures, products, and services to ensure its growth. What are the differences between these organizations? Why do some leaders and their executive teams face threats and choose the right strategies whereas others act in ways that bring organizational destruction and, at times, massive human death?

The goal of most talent management programs in corporations is to provide a ceaseless supply of effective leaders who are ready, willing, and able to step into executive assignments as they are needed. Many organizations go to extraordinary lengths to ensure that they have the necessary executive talent to enable them to compete successfully. Talent review processes in most of these organizations focus on past performance, knowledge, skills, abilities, and experience. However, the historically instructive questions that focus on whether a person can lead wisely, courageously, justly, reverently, and with temperance are most often only addressed with and through surrogate forms of data.

The purposes of this chapter are to examine competency models for leadership development through the lens of the four classic Platonic virtues, provide definitions and conceptual approaches to understanding these virtues and their applications to executive functions, and suggest some methods for developing virtuous behavior in leaders. A case study of virtuous leadership will illuminate these ideas through the lenses of courage and executive wisdom. In keeping with the stated thesis of the book, this chapter suggests that the difference between executive teams that are able to preserve their countries or organizations over the long term and those that are not is based largely on the degree to which those leaders possess and enact the Platonic virtues of courage, temperance, justice, and wisdom.

LEADING THROUGH A STORM OF CRITICISM—A CASE STUDY

"So what do you think I should say when they ask?" Sheila Norman, the chief operating officer of a medium-sized service company asked me during our coaching session. She was one of two final candidates being considered for the position of CEO in a larger corporation in the same industry. Sheila had made it through multiple rounds of interviews, credential checks, and reference calls. She was meeting with the search committee of the board of directors, senior members of the organization's executive and management teams, and some of the major stockholders in a matter of days. Her question to me was directed at the fact that Doug Rasmussen, the CEO of her company, had barely survived a vote of no confidence conducted by their major shareholders in the previous month. Sheila and several other members of the executive team had worked behind the scenes to ensure the vote came out the appropriate way. The effort had been monumental and emotionally challenging. Doug had been a charismatic and controversial CEO over the previous 5 years. The board of directors was due to renew his contract in the near future, and a group of stockholders who had been upset with the direction set by Doug and the board had managed to get the vote of confidence on the agenda for the annual stockholders meeting despite all efforts to block them.

"What are you worried about?" I asked her.

"Well, I was talking to the secretary of the board of directors in this company interviewing me, and he asked me about the vote. I asked him if he thought it would be a concern, and there was this pause. Then he said that I should be prepared to address questions about it. I then asked if there could be a problem. There was another pause and he then said that it might be possible that some folks would voice a concern depending on what they heard. Now I'm spooked. So what do I tell them, coach?"

As is frequently the case in these situations, I was somewhat reluctant to simply tell her what to say, so I asked her a few more questions. I typically do this both to see how far a client has pushed his or her thinking along as well as to buy a little time to think about the situation in more depth. I had been working with Sheila for about a year and knew her fairly well, but although we had spent a good bit of time discussing her role in helping Doug manage the vote and the stockholders meeting, we were on new ground now that she had thrown her hat into the competition for her own job as a CEO.

"What do you see as your choices?" I asked.

"Well, that call with the secretary told me that I can't duck the issue completely."

At that point, Sheila sighed and looked out the window of her well-appointed corporate office. We were sitting at the small conference table in a corner of the room.

"Is that what you'd rather do?" I pressed.

"Of course, I don't like the thought one bit that my career as a leader is yoked to the way Doug has handled some of the situations that initiated the vote. George and I have been cleaning up after him for years, and it's so frustrating sometimes."

Sheila was referring to George Geopopos, the long-term CFO of the company. Doug had been controversial from the moment he had taken office. The mandate he had been given was to expand the business and become more strategically involved in new markets. Doug had recruited Sheila in his 1st year in office, and together they had recrafted the organization's strategy and set it on a sharply defined course. They had shed some of the business units that were not likely to produce a lot of new revenue in the future and plowed the money from the sales into the technologically driven edges of the corporation. They had successfully recruited a large number of new professionals who had quickly set about changing a lot of what the enterprise had been doing. Many of their traditional shareholders, who had held their stock for decades and looked forward to dividend checks that came every quarter, became incensed when Doug and the board told them that their dividends would be reduced significantly because of the need to invest in the future of the company. Despite major improvements in performance in the new sectors of their business, their recent revenues fell significantly short of previous years' results. When two successive quarters of dividends were withheld because of investment needs, the rumbles had led to an open rebellion on the part of some long-term stockholders. They had enough clout in the organization to force a vote despite the board support that Doug enjoyed. That group knew the business much more intimately and had calculated along with Doug and his team that it was only a matter of time before the revenues in some of their traditional services would tank. They were happy that they had sold those assets early enough that they had received true value for what they had shed.

Doug had not handled the situation as diplomatically as he could have. Known inside and outside of the company for his candidness, his quick wit, and a sharp tongue when under pressure, he had often allowed both private and public meetings to deteriorate almost to the level of name-calling. He had become so wounded for having his judgment challenged that he more or less asked Sheila to deal directly with the dissidents as well as with the stockholders who did understand the changes in strategy.

"What do you think you can tell them about Doug?" I asked her.

"Well, many of them already know him. The industry is not as large as you would think, and the fact of the vote has already been reported both in the local business pages and in the industry newspapers means the word is out. They also know that we've repositioned the company pretty radically, and as a result, we're being watched closely. In fact, I think that's perhaps the main reason I'm one of the finalists for this job. Some people in the business have started to figure out what we saw 4 years ago and are moving to change now while they still can."

"So, you believe you don't need to start from scratch with at least some of them."

"That's right."

"And you already know that they know the broad outlines of what you've done and the challenges you've had."

Sheila looked directly at me and nodded.

"Is there anything wrong with telling them the truth?" I asked.

"What should I tell them? That Doug has consistently irritated people that he didn't need to? That with a little more grace and reassurance of some of the key players there would never have been a vote? That as talented, smart, and aggressive as he is as a leader, he constantly gets in his own way?"

At that point, I smiled. "He's been a real handful for you, eh?"

"Oh God, don't you know it. I am so ready to get out of here. I can't tell you the number of times he's told me he's going to have to fire me if I don't do this or that. I mean he's absolutely correct on what he has done and our strategy and tactics are really going to pay off, but he can be completely obnoxious. I know I can't say that in the interviews, but the danger is that managing stockholders' meetings has been in my portfolio, and Doug has created enough distance between the two of us on this that if the board did get upset, it would probably be me that took the fall for what has happened."

"And what steps has the board taken?"

"Oh, that was another crisis this week. The chairman of the board, who is even worse than Doug in some ways, drafted a letter to go to the stockholders that all but told them to shut up and sit down. He didn't use the word *idiots*, but he sure came close."

"What happened to the letter?"

"Fortunately, Doug showed it to me and I got our general counsel and George together to review it. We crafted an alternative, and after three more drafts, we sent it out yesterday. It was still a mess, but it was somewhat more conciliatory."

"If we go back to your question, then, why couldn't you focus on the real story?"

"Which is?"

"Well, in my experience of both interviewing people for jobs and being interviewed for them myself, humans learn best through storytelling. Your audience already knows the end of the story and some of the cast of characters. So it's like one of those movies where you see the last scene first but the real story of the film is how did the hero get in that predicament in the first place? If you tell them the truth about how you got there, what you did during that journey, the issues that you have collectively faced in making the changes that you have, you have a tremendous narrative to share. From what you've said to me, they are interested in you because you've been a key player here and they are thinking seriously that they have to make the same journey."

"Yeah, but how do I do that?"

"Well, you said that you are going to be meeting with different audiences during the day you are there, like members of the board, senior staff, and so forth."

Sheila nodded.

"And in light of that, you'll have to tell them versions of the same story because they will talk to each other."

She nodded again.

"Just imagine, then, that you have them drawn up around a campfire and you are going to tell them this story of the very difficult but rewarding journey that you've taken. These are folks who are eager to go on the same journey, and they are worried about what they will encounter along the way. Your story has a beginning, a middle, and a current status. You can concentrate on Doug's positive traits."

"How?"

"Who approved the strategic plan you crafted?"

"The board."

"Who made the decision to shed those business units?"

"Ultimately, the board with our recommendations."

"So this is a story of a courageous board and an intrepid executive team that needed to significantly change the shape and direction of the company. It's a story of what you've done, the resistances you've encountered, and the steps you've taken to manage the whole process. It's also a form of a status report, and from what you've told me over the past few months, everything that you've done has been working well except that the amount that you've had to invest in technology, the rapidity with which you could change over your staff, and the rate of growth in the new lines of business have not exactly matched the projections you made 5 years ago."

"That's right."

"Why can't you tell everyone the truth? It's a heck of a story."

"When you put it that way, it sounds really good. I can sure tell them what has happened without airing out all the company's secrets. But what if someone asks about Doug and my relationship with him?"

"Again, why can't you tell the truth? If both of you are known in your industry, the folks interviewing you may be unconsciously pushing you to betray him, to rat him out, or to scapegoat him. But do you really have to do that? You've said mostly good things about him to me for nearly a year. What if you described all of the good things that your team has done to manage the governance crisis and then also said something like, 'We've also learned some lessons about what we should have done better'?"

"If you put it like that, I could talk for a whole day about what we've learned."

"Why can't you put it like that? It sounds to me like this board of directors is looking for someone who can help them create the kind of storm of change you've already done here and to manage its effects. Isn't your job in the interview to convince them that you've sailed in stormy, criticism-filled seas that your own board created because they knew they had a duty to the future of the company and not just to the present? Can't you tell them the story of what it will take? Don't they need to understand that they will need real wisdom to decide what to do, courage to stick to their strategy in tough circumstances, and the ability to manage their emotions when tempers are lost?"

"Well, aside from managing tempers, we've been pretty wise and courageous here over the past 5 years," Sheila said quietly and with determination.

"Can you tell them that story?"

"Yes, of course I can," she replied and smiled.

We broke out of our coaching session after a few more minutes. I went home insanely curious about what would happen during her interviews. I didn't hear anything from her for a couple of weeks. Finally, I threw in the towel and sent Sheila an e-mail asking her what had happened. She replied quickly that we needed to talk because the other company was getting ready to offer her the job and Doug was whining.

Over the course of the next several weeks, I spent several hours on the telephone with Sheila as she walked through the processes of negotiating her position as the CEO of the new company that had recruited her and her exit from her existing organization. She reported that the interviews had been stressful but that the discussion we had before those meetings had been very helpful to her in preparing for the questions she had been asked. In several portions of the interviewing process, the focus had been almost exclusively on how she had assisted Doug with the strategy formation and execution processes and the resulting political pressures that had erupted at various points. Sheila said that she had addressed these types of inquiries as candidly as she could and also set limits where she thought it was appropriate. She did attempt to cast the vote of confidence in the context of the strategic changes that the leadership team had pushed into the organization and the natural resistance to many of those changes that they had experienced. The feedback she received after the interviews was that her candor and seeming sophistication in speaking to the processes of courageously leading changes in the face of opposition appeared to be the major factor in asking her to join their company.

As soon as she received the offer from the other organization, Sheila approached and confided in Doug. Initially, he seemed hurt, hostile, and opposed to her leaving her position. I heard through Leslie, the vice president for human resources, that Doug was also upset with my coaching activities because they appeared to lead to one of his key executives leaving the company. This was despite the fact that at the outset, Doug acknowledged that this was one of the possible outcomes of coaching and that he himself had stated several times that having Sheila move on was in the best interest of the organization. In our subsequent sessions, Sheila was able to craft an approach to Doug that seemed to reduce both his open hostility to her decision to leave and to take care of the major concrete reasons for his opposition. Together, they decided on the wording and timing of the announcements of her departure, an activity plan that would enable her to complete most of the critical assignments on her plate before she left, and how they would try to relate to each other in the future.

Sheila crafted a deal with her new company that reflected her increased appreciation for the complexities of politics and change processes in corporations. She was careful during those negotiations to explore the positions of the various members of her new board of directors and began to form a set of alliances and positive working relationships with many of them. When it finally occurred, her departure from her position had many paradoxical components to it. Doug was extremely sad to see her go and complimentary about her contributions and support to him. Sheila also experienced an initial wave of true grief in leaving her colleagues behind, including Doug, and in examining those emotions she discovered how attached she had become to them and how proud she was of their achievements. She also began to have a fair amount of performance anxiety as she started to assume her new duties; it rapidly became clear to her that the expectations for the person stepping into the CEO role were extraordinarily high and virtually instantaneous on her signing the agreement. Although she worked hard to set reasonable limits and goals in both organizations, the plain fact was that both of them expected her to be working constantly on their behalf. Despite all of these pressures and tensions, Sheila successfully separated from her existing position and moved on to become the CEO of the new company. She took a phenomenal amount of expertise and experience with her, but she also understood that she had an incredible amount to learn as she took over the senior executive position in the new organization.

CONTEMPORARY COMPETENCY MODELS AND EXECUTIVE PERFORMANCE

Since the 1980s, advanced approaches to the selection and development of executives have involved the creation and use of competency models that describe the nature of successful leadership performance. Bartram, Robertson, and Callinan (2002) defined *competencies* as "sets of behaviors that are instrumental in the delivery of desired results or outcomes" (p. 7). This definition illustrates the extent to which modern leadership theory has become increasingly based on an intimate understanding of the specific behaviors that executives must be able to deploy to perform effectively. Extensive sets of competencies have been developed by a number of organizations, and these have evolved out of empirical efforts to create questionnaires that reliably and validly measure the extent to which individuals demonstrate such behaviors in their leadership roles. These competency models now form the foundation of every major assessment instrument used to conduct 360-degree reviews of executive performance.

Exhibit 4.1 provides a listing of the major elements of the competency models that are currently in use in Personnel Decisions International's (PDI's) Profilor, Lominger's The Leadership Architect, and the SHL Group's Universal Competency Framework. The Profilor has eight factors or major groups of competencies (Personnel Decisions, 1991), The Leadership Architect has six core competencies (Lombardo & Eichinger, 2001), and the SHL Group has eight "great" competencies (Bartram, 2005). Looking across Exhibit 4.1, you can see that each of the models incorporates elements involving strategy formation or critical thinking in organizational contexts, interpersonal skills, the capacity to manage in complex environments, and what could be described as emotional maturity. Although there is some divergence in the models, the degree of similarity between them is striking and is most likely reflective of the core elements of what constitutes effective leadership behavior as well as the most likely common pathway that factor analytic methods of constructing assessment instruments create for such research efforts.

These competency models rest on the assumption that executive performance is best understood as the actions and behaviors that managers undertake in the service of their organizations. For example, Rotundo and Sackett (2002) stated that "job performance is conceptualized as those actions and behaviors that are under the control of the individual and contribute to the goals of the organization" (p. 66). This description is well within the boundaries of modern theories of human performance, which increasingly define it in terms of what people do and what can be observed and measured. Those concepts in turn can be seen as logical extensions of behavioral psychology.

EXHIBIT 4.1
Summary of Three Competency Models

Bartram's Eight Great Competencies	Personnel Decisions International's Profilor: Eight Factors	Lominger's The Leadership Architect: Six Core Competencies
Leading and deciding	Leadership factor	Strategic skills
Supporting and cooperating	Interpersonal factor	Operating skills
Interacting and presenting	Communication factor	Courage
Analyzing and interpreting	Self-management factor	Energy and drive
Creating and conceptualizing	Thinking factor	Organizational positioning skills
Organizing and executing	Organizational knowledge factor	Personal and interpersonal skills
Adapting and coping	Organizational strategy factor	
Enterprising and performing	Administration factor	

Thus, most organizations seeking to assess leadership performance and use modern approaches to measurement almost automatically find themselves adopting a behavioral approach to their assessments. It is also logical to conclude that efforts to design scientific approaches to selecting executives (Campbell, 1990) incorporate this conceptual foundation, as do most leadership development programs that use 360-degree review instruments. Within these approaches, it is probably safe to say that the effective performance of any leader can be judged by what they do, the actions that they take, and the observable skills that they exercise in the conduct of their duties. Executives being evaluated in the competency paradigm are being asked to address the questions, "what do you do?" and "how do those actions make your performance effective as judged by others?"

HUMAN VIRTUE AND EXECUTIVE PERFORMANCE

Since around 2000, a relatively small group of scientists and practitioners has made an effort to move the study and profession of psychology in the direction of what they call *positive psychology*. At its core, this initiative is in response to the century-long study of psychopathology and its traditional emphasis on treating mentally ill people (Seligman & Csikszentmihalyi, 2000). Within the movement, a number of psychologists are examining behavior from the perspective of how to improve positive attributes of people and create excellent performance in various domains of human activity (Ericsson, 1996; Fredrickson, 1998, 2009; Lubinski & Benbow, 2000; Snyder & Lopez, 2002).

Peterson and Seligman (2004) produced a challenging conceptual framework for this approach by offering a classification system for the positive characteristics of human behavior. Their research identified major virtues and character strengths implied or advocated within the principle philosophical, religious, and ethical systems in the world. They also compared these results to classifications of personality traits and behaviors that have been developed within psychology over a 60-year period of time, including those aimed at social competencies (Leffert et al., 1998). The Peterson and Seligman classification includes six core virtues defined in the following ways:

- *Wisdom and knowledge* —cognitive strengths that entail the acquisition and use of knowledge
- *Courage* —emotional strengths that involve the exercise of will to accomplish goals in the face of opposition, external or internal
- *Humanity*—interpersonal strengths that involve tending and befriending others

- *Justice*—strengths that underlie healthy community life
- *Temperance*—strengths that protect against excess
- *Transcendence*—strengths that forge connections to the larger universe and provide meaning (pp. 29–30)

Each of these core virtues possesses a set of other strengths. Twenty-four virtues or character strengths are described in their model, and the philosophical and research base supporting each of them was reviewed in some depth.

In the context of leadership theory and practice, the Peterson and Seligman classification is interesting in that it adopts the core virtues of philosopher kings of Plato, as described in the Socratic dialogues of *The Republic* (trans. 1999). In that work, Socrates stated that the virtuous leader of a Greek city-state should possess courage; temperance; justice; and, above all, wisdom. He went on to suggest that the acquisition of these virtues is a lifelong endeavor that requires periods of reflective contemplation and study, along with periods in which leaders put their virtues to the test in the service of their communities in creating the common good. Socrates also suggested some of the areas of study that he believed would contribute to the development of these virtues.

In an earlier work (Kilburg, 2006), I provided a contemporary update of this classical view of leadership development in which I described the empirical, psychological, and philosophical foundations of *executive wisdom*. I defined this as "an expert system in the fundamental pragmatics of organized human life" in which leaders "discover or create the right thing to do; do the right thing in the right way; and do it against the right time frame" (p. 47). For the purposes of this presentation, I would like to extend my conceptual model of executive wisdom to incorporate the other three classical or cardinal virtues described and advocated by Plato as being essential for effective leadership plus the virtue of reverence.

Figure 4.1 depicts the three core processes of executive work presented in Kilburg (2006). They include *discernment*, in which a leader sees his or her environments in wise ways and perceives the best paths of action for himself or herself and the organization; *decision making*, in which a leader makes wise choices from the alternatives that are available; and *action*, in which a leader ensures that the decisions lead to activity that produces the desired outcomes for the organization and its stakeholders. Executive wisdom is seen as an emergent process arising out a complex set of interacting systems using these three core processes. Each of the three processes is connected by interacting components of evaluation, feedback, and learning that enable a leader to make consistent progress on any given problem or in any given stage of his or her career.

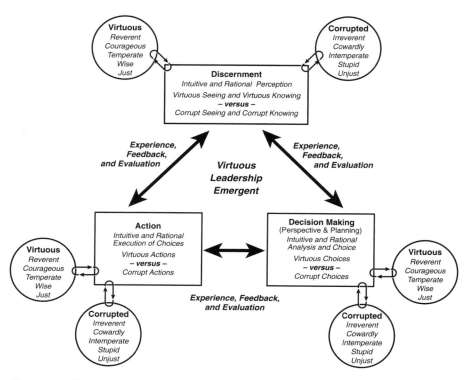

Figure 4.1. Virtuous leadership and the three core processes of executive work.

Figure 4.1 extends the model of executive work with the addition of the other Platonic virtues of courage, temperance, and justice plus the virtue of reverence, which we explore in a subsequent chapter. In addition, each of these virtues is presented as having an antithesis—namely, stupidity, cowardice, intemperance, injustice, and irreverence. In this extended model, "virtuous leadership" incorporates all three core processes of discernment, decision making, and action, and each of them are hopefully conducted in a virtuous way—courageously, temperately, justly, reverently, and wisely. However, the model also allows for the reality that leaders can and all too often do act corruptly. Thus, we see frequent cases involving intemperance, cowardice, injustice, irreverence, and stupidity on the part of leaders, their teams, and their boards. In the case study introducing this chapter, Doug demonstrated corrupt patterns of intemperate, irreverent, and cowardly behavior that undermined the good work he had done.

Within the modern framework of human virtues suggested by Peterson and Seligman (2004), virtuous leaders are seen as possessing and consistently exercising the character strengths that they describe in their classification system. These virtues are primary features of the fundamental character structures of these kinds of leaders. Within these concepts, a virtue-centered approach to understanding leadership can be best characterized not by the competency-based questions of "what do you do?" and "how do those actions make your performance effective usually as judged by others?" Instead, leadership centers on questions of who you are, who you want to be, and how that affects your performance in the areas of discernment, decision making, and action. The latter question moves the discussion of leadership effectiveness beyond the realms of specific behavior and leadership competencies and requires consideration of other factors contributing to performance. *Within this model, we can define virtuous leaders as those who discern, decide, and enact the right things to do, and do them in the right ways, in the right time frames, for the right reasons.*

VIRTUES AND COMPETENCIES IN EXECUTIVE DEVELOPMENT

Comparing the Peterson and Seligman (2004) list of six core virtues with the list of major competencies identified in Exhibit 4.1, we can see that only Lominger's classification system specifically identifies one of the Platonic virtues by name. To be sure, there are surrogates for temperance in competencies such as Lominger's personal and interpersonal skills, Bartram's adapting and coping competency, and PDI's interpersonal and self-management factors. In addition, there are surrogates for wisdom in the items specifying competencies dealing with organizational strategy and positioning and leadership. Digging deeper into the specific skills identified in these models, one can come closer to Socratic virtues. In PDI's Profilor, there are sections that deal with leading courageously, acting with integrity, using sound judgment, thinking strategically, recognizing global implications, listening, fostering teamwork, and promoting corporate citizenship. Lominger's Leadership Architect identifies 67 competencies that include items such as making complex decisions; being open and receptive by demonstrating composure, humor, listening, and patience; and acting with honor and character. The SHL universal framework has 112 competencies that include deciding and initiating action, adhering to principles and values, adapting and coping, and entrepreneurial and commercial thinking. Thus, we can see that modern, behaviorally based, leadership competency models have conceptual and programmatic elements that come close to the Socratic virtues.

The major challenge that can be identified when discussing the traditional philosophical approach to understanding and creating virtuous character and the modern competency-based models of leadership behavior centers on a series of crucial questions. Are virtuous leaders those who consistently exercise the types of competencies that have been identified through empirical research methods? Is it enough to create development programs that ensure that skills are practiced in each of the competencies that these models suggest are important components of effective leadership, or do such models also require that the skills must be routinely and appropriately applied on the job every day? In short, is virtue something that can be learned through behaviorally formulated instruction and practice and acquired in leadership development programs, or is it more innate, a function of life-span human development, and therefore difficult to develop?

For example, there are many case examples in which individual leaders can be said to possess high levels of competency but nevertheless choose to act in corrupt ways. One need look no further than the Enron case to see a chairman of the board, Ken Lay, who was known early in his corporate career as a paragon of personal virtue, who was raised in a professionally religious family, and who obviously possessed all of the appropriate competencies that modern methods of executive and managerial performance can measure. Despite these competencies, he was convicted on multiple charges of fraud and faced the possibility that he could spend most of the rest of his life in prison for what happened during his leadership of Enron. He then died of what some people close to his family suggested was a stress-related heart attack. During his entire trial, Lay maintained that he was completely innocent of all charges. In his testimony in court, he laid most of the responsibility for the disaster at Enron on the shoulders of a few rogue employees while eschewing any culpability for the problems that occurred during his term of office. Can we truly say that his approach to leadership in this disaster was virtuous?

Similar cases abound in the literature, so there appears to me to be a clear difference between developing and possessing requisite leadership competencies and the consistent enactment of human virtue by individuals in executive positions. This paradoxical enigma—between the acquisition of habits, the doing of observable behaviors, and the substructures and processes of human mind and emotion that reliably produce right thought and right action in the inevitably stressful and often chaotic operations of modern organizations—has been in the foreground of philosophical, religious, social, economic, political, and psychological debate for millennia.

THE BEHAVIORAL GEOGRAPHY AND PSYCHOLOGICAL GEOLOGY OF VIRTUOUS LEADERS

Figure 4.2 extends the core model of virtuous leadership by adapting another of the conceptual models introduced in Kilburg (2006). The figure depicts a multilayered, three-dimensional structure. The top of the structure

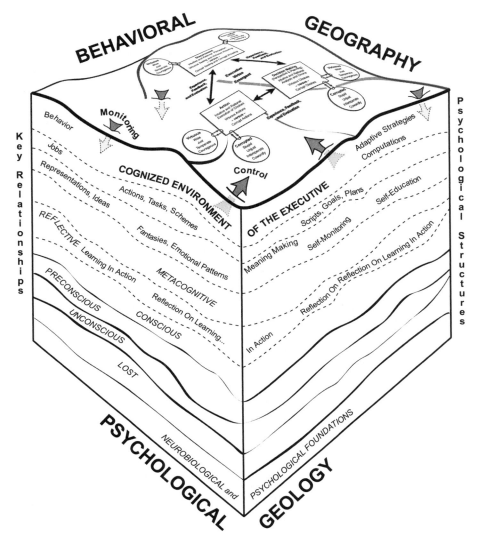

Figure 4.2. Behavioral geography and psychological geology of virtuous leaders.

highlights the observable world of a leader, what is identified as the behavioral geography of the individual. Figure 4.1 is laid on top of a complex topographic map that attempts to demonstrate that the observable world of any executive is complex. If we watch leaders carefully, we can see evidence of what they discern, the decisions they make, and the actions they take. Observing these behaviors over time, we can make judgments of the degree to which we could agree that his or her performance is consistently virtuous, corrupt, or merely human in the sense that sometimes we see evidence of both major patterns—virtue and vice.

However, Figure 4.2 also attempts to depict what I have called the metacognitive and psychodynamic foundations of the behavior (Kilburg, 2006), what is labeled as the psychological geology of the leader's world. In this complex underworld, we can see the levels of the unconscious mind and past experience that interacts with reflective states of awareness and the external, real-world existence of the leader to create a cognized structure through which he or she monitors, interprets, and attempts to exercise a measure of control in the world. In the cognized world of the executive, complex models of understanding and behavior are constructed and used to guide the three core processes of discernment, decision making, and action. The cognized world is influenced by past and present relationships of meaning and importance and by the underlying psychological structures of instinct, ideal self, rational self, and conscience that are built through developmental time (Kilburg, 2000). We can often see manifestations of this cognized world in the plans that leaders make, the scripts that they enact, and the thoughts and feelings that they express. However, Figure 4.2 suggests that both the competency and virtue models of executive performance are influenced by many interacting elements.

We know from systems and chaos theories (Stacey, 2007; von Bertalanffy, 1968) that when complex sets of elements interact, they can produce emergent properties that can manifest themselves with seemingly incomprehensible unpredictability. Thus, a religiously well-developed, churchgoing, and seemingly moral man like Ken Lay can and did preside over the development of a corrupt organizational culture and leadership team and enacted behaviors that in retrospect were viewed by a jury of his peers as both illegal and immoral. The same can be said by groups of Doug's staff and stockholders about the judgment of his behavior. So we see that aspects of virtuous behavior may be relatively easy to measure in the form of the 360-degree ratings based on competency models, and it also can be difficult to produce reliably in the real worlds of executives.

A VIRTUOUS LEADER ON DECK—WISDOM AND COURAGE DURING STORMS OF CRITICISM

Let's examine the case study that introduced this chapter through the question of whether the COO, Sheila Norman, consistently exercised what we have come to understand as executive virtue. If we accept at face value the definitions of wisdom and courage offered by Peterson and Seligman (2004), the definition of executive wisdom provided in Kilburg (2006), and the definition of virtuous leadership described earlier in this chapter, we start with a set of criteria for Sheila's behavior in the adaptive situations that she faced. Wisdom, then, is a collection of cognitive strengths that entail the acquisition and use of knowledge, and executive wisdom is an expert system in the fundamental pragmatics of organized human life in which leaders discover or create the right thing to do, do the right thing in the right way, and do it against the right time frame. Courage is seen as emotional strengths that involve the exercise of will to accomplish goals in the face of opposition.

Hadot (1995), Harris (2001), Hornstein (1986), W. I. Miller (2000), Pury and Lopez (2010), Putman (2004, 2010), and Rorty (1988) have provided extensive examinations of human and managerial courage. Putman (2010) succinctly reviewed the philosophical roots of courage and suggested that there are at least three major types depicted in that tradition. Physical courage involves facing and surmounting fear of death or harm while seeking a noble goal for family, country, and so on. Moral courage is found in the acts of people who retain their ethical integrity in circumstances in which they may be socially rejected or scapegoated. Psychological courage is expressed by facing the potential or real loss of one's identity or psychological death. Putman emphasized the frameworks provided by Aristotle, the Stoics, the Existentialists, and the Confucian and Buddhist Eastern traditions in his analysis. Rate (2010) provided examples of contemporary research on courage as he and his colleagues endeavored to discover a proper, scientifically grounded definition for the virtue. After reviewing dozens of definitions and conducting several types of studies, he concluded that there are seven primary elements that characterize most definitions: characteristic–trait–skill–ability, external circumstances, cognitive processes, motivation toward excellence, behavioral responses, volition, and affect–emotion. In an additional experiment, he concluded that "if an act is courageous, then by definition (a) the action was freely chosen, (b) the actor seeks to bring about a noble purpose, and (c) the act is attempted or accomplished at substantial risk to the actor" (p. 61).

Harris (2001), W. I. Miller (2000), Pury and Lopez (2010), and Rorty (1988) in particular offered detailed models for understanding both the different manifestations that courage can take and the processes through which it is expressed. On the basis of their models, I have come to believe that there are at least four major avenues through which humans behave courageously.

Attack–Persist–Fight—behaviors in and through which people move forward forcefully to encounter a trial, problem, challenge, competitor, or enemy. Most often this is commonly associated with the classical "charge" in battle during war, its metaphoric equivalents in corporate or sports competitions, or in the professional and personal arguments, disagreements, or conflicts typical in organizations and human relationships.

Retreat–Disengage–Flight—behaviors in and through which people reverse direction or move away from a trial, problem, challenge, competitor, or enemy.

Most often this is seen in the classical retreat from a battle during a war or its metaphoric equivalents in competitions, arguments, disagreements, or conflicts in human relationships.

Resist–Freeze—behaviors in and through which people stay involved with a trial, problem, challenge, competitor, or enemy even though they may not make progress, overcome the difficulty, or escape the pain involved with such dilemmas. This is frequently seen in situations in which individuals continue to take punishment while refusing to yield to a competitor either in the hope that the situation will improve or with the determination not to fail or to outlast their enemies. In some situations involving the experience of trauma, humans and other mammals may simply freeze in the face of pain, suffering, or wounding because they perceive correctly or perhaps incorrectly that any other course of action is too dangerous or so anxiety arousing that they cannot pursue it.

Approach–Engage–Relate—behaviors in and through which people move toward a trial, problem, challenge, competitor, or enemy in constructive efforts designed to try to build a relationship through which warfare, competition, and forms of conflict can be turned into other behaviors and beneficial outcomes for all parties. Such courageous actions are often seen when diplomacy is engaged to prevent or end wars or stalemated negotiations.

If we were to ask ourselves what kinds of courageous behavior would we expect to see from virtuous leaders, I think the answer is pretty obvious. We would expect to see all four types of courage exercised in the actions undertaken by these kinds of leaders. Furthermore, we would expect to see such courageous behavior undertaken with high levels of emotional maturity and in the service of just causes. Executives would do so using the core processes of discernment, decision making, and taking action. Finally, we would expect to see courage under the control of the virtue of wisdom at all times as the executive discerns what kind of courage is needed in a given situation, selects the right form of courage behavior, and enacts it in the right way, for the right reasons, and against the right time frames.

Exhibits 4.2 and 4.3 facilitate pushing the assessment of courageous behavior in even further detail. Exhibit 4.2 provides a framework for looking at the four types of courageous behavior arrayed against the four major types of human motivation described in detail by McClelland and Burnham (1976). Thus, we can see attacking, retreating, resisting, and engaging behaviors in motivational states involving achievement, power, attachment, and transcendence, which can be extremely useful when examining the behavior of leaders or executive groups.

Exhibit 4.3 provides an additional framework by arraying the four types of courageous behavior against the six major categories of psychodynamic conflict identified by Wurmser (2000) and discussed by Kilburg (2004) as they

EXHIBIT 4.2
Types of Courage and McClelland's Primary Motivational Needs

	McClelland's primary human needs			
Types of courage	Achievement	Power	Attachment	Transcendence
Attack/Persist/Fight				
Retreat/Disengage/Flight				
Resist/Freeze				
Approach/Engage/Relate				

EXHIBIT 4.3
Types of Courage and Psychodynamic Conflict

	Types of courage			
Types of psychodynamic conflict	Attack/ Fight	Retreat/ Flight	Resist/ Freeze	Approach/ Engage
Emotional management				
Wishes for self-expression and curiosity and fears of intrusion, control, and exposure; empathic mis-alignment				
Human attachment—developing and maintaining an independent/ interdependent/ dependent sense of self or identity				
Wishes for self-control and fears of control or intrusion by others				
Competitive strivings and triangular relationships				
Questions and challenges to loyalty				

apply in leadership settings. This typology allows the examination of situations leaders face and the courageous actions they undertake as examples of managing conflicts involving the expression of emotion, wishes for self-expression and fears of invasion and control, desire for human attachments and maintaining a sense of personal self, wishes for self-control, competitive strivings, and conflicts of loyalty. In this framework, we can ask whether the individual leader of the executive group attacked, retreated, resisted, or engaged in a healthy and effective fashion as each of these types of conflict unfolded.

If we take these core notions of executive wisdom and courage and the broader concepts of executive virtue and apply them to Sheila's case, a number of interesting levels of analysis can be undertaken. Let's briefly explore several of them.

First, the central problem that Sheila faced involved the extensive, long-term consequences of wise strategic choices that had been made by the board of directors and Doug. Although consistently acknowledging the wisdom of their original discernment of the position of their corporation and their courageous determination in deciding to radically restructure their portfolio of services and their organizational processes, Sheila had consistently struggled to help Doug and the board execute their decisions in the right ways and against the right time frames. These are some of the most complex and difficult problems that leaders face. Although the challenges of courageously and wisely seeing the situation in which their organization found itself were difficult and the decision to undertake a radical and expensive transformation of the company was agonizing, the board and Doug completely underestimated the time and effort that it would take to realize their dreams. In my experience, this is routinely one of the most difficult challenges that leaders face.

The quality of courage required to call for and initiate an attack on a problem or obstacle can be quite different from the kind of character-rooted persistence in the face of challenge after challenge after challenge that often arise after the initial call to arms is issued. Furthermore, Doug's struggle to control himself emotionally and interpersonally added fuel to the raging fires of anxiety, sadness, anger, and shame that large organizational or human change efforts inevitably produce. His frequent emotional outbursts and attacks on people only got in the way of them doing their jobs. In addition, change processes always involve one or more of the types of psychodynamic conflict identified in Exhibit 4.3. In this situation, conflicts involving emotional expression, attachment and identity formation, competition, control, and loyalty were extensive. Sheila was explicitly involved in managing all of these types of conflict in herself as she struggled to identify herself as an executive and a person independent of her current organization and job despite her attachments to them. Doug's overt ambivalence about having her as an effective member of his team, his unconscious competitiveness with everyone around him, and his need for constant reassurance and control over everything in his environment were clear.

My coaching efforts had proceeded in two simultaneous directions in light of these issues. First, Sheila clearly needed to separate from the company and pursue her own professional path. Simultaneously, she needed to protect the investments that she had made in the corporation and in its people, including the reputations of her executive colleagues, members of the board, stockholders, other employees, and Doug. So I encouraged her to pursue other positions and simultaneously work hard at protecting Doug, the board, and the company itself from the acting-out behavior of a significant number of the members of the board.

As illuminated in Exhibit 4.2, Sheila was clearly struggling with her own needs to achieve, develop more power in her life and career, and also remain humanly attached to the people in whom she had invested. In the coaching session described earlier, she perceived correctly that she faced a conflict of loyalties (Exhibit 4.3) between her desire to obtain the CEO position in the new organization and the consequent need to tell the people who would be interviewing her the truth about the individuals with whom she had been working and the possibility that in doing so in a courageous fashion, she would betray them. She felt frozen in place as we started that discussion, but my use of inquiry, metaphor, interpretation, and suggestions about appropriate limits in her disclosures enabled her to discern the nature of the conflict, determine that she had choices other than those that she had previously conceived, and then to attack the interview courageously in a tactful, straightforward, and strategic fashion. She found the right thing to do and did it in the right way, at the right time, and for the right reasons as evidenced by the fact that she both received the job offer and negotiated herself out of the relationship with Doug and her existing company in a healthy way.

Sheila had correctly conceived the interviews as a situation in which she would need to attack the problems and was preparing for the inevitable carnage that often happens as a result. Our coaching session was successful in helping her to formulate a way to constructively engage the interviewers without explicitly betraying Doug or the dissident members of the board. In that solution, she was able to attack questions and issues forcefully but in a very human way that maintained her relationships and protected the reputations of everyone involved in the change efforts in her organization. Again, she found the right combination of courage and wisdom that allowed her to succeed in pursuing her need for additional achievement, autonomy, and power without undercutting her colleagues. Having a clear and wise strategy to pursue courageously also enabled her to access and use the virtues of temperance, reverence, and justice. She resisted the many temptations that she was offered during her interviews to criticize Doug, the board, and her other colleagues and thus elevate herself and her performance. In subsequent coaching sessions, Sheila reported that she had maintained an even disposition in the face of intense and hostile questions and treated her colleagues and company justly and reverently during the interviews and in her negotiations for her exit.

Thus, we can see in this relatively short case vignette that executive virtue is a complex phenomenon that has many interacting elements and that can change radically in its course of execution. We can also understand how leaders can be led astray when complex motives and unconscious conflicts arise in their working lives. It would have been all too easy for Sheila to tactfully, artfully, and destructively describe both Doug's leadership of the change efforts and the behavior of the dissidents on the board who forced the vote of no confidence. Her interview then presented as a true test of character and not just an exercise of leadership competencies. To be sure, Sheila needed to use many skills effectively in this situation—determine strategy, communicate clearly, manage conflicts, manage her relationships, and so on. Even more so, she needed to access and consistently use the goodness of her fundamental character and to demonstrate to both the organization trying to find a new leader and her existing company that she was a truly virtuous person capable of acting courageously, temperately, justly, reverently, and wisely. In the end, I believe that the board of her new organization hired Sheila for both her demonstrated executive competencies and because they wanted the kind of person she revealed herself to be during the interviews. The case vignette also illustrates the complexities involved in coaching leaders who face these situations. For even as their characters are tested in such circumstances, so are the professionals who are charged with helping them.

DEVELOPING WISDOM, COURAGE, AND EXECUTIVE VIRTUE

In Plato's *Republic*, Socrates suggested that the development of virtues in leaders involves a lifelong process of study, practice, and reflective learning based on experience. I have suggested (Kilburg, 2006) a lifelong developmental process called *wisdom mapping* to assist leaders in becoming wiser. Figure 4.3 presents a modification of this core approach, which is called *virtue mapping*. This process suggests that leaders need to become much more familiar with the personal and familial roots of their attitudes, beliefs, values, knowledge, skills, abilities, thoughts, emotions, defenses, and conflicts associated with virtuous behavior. Becoming more aware of how virtue did or did not appear in their families and how they themselves are primed to behave either in virtuous or corrupt ways represents the first step in becoming a virtu-

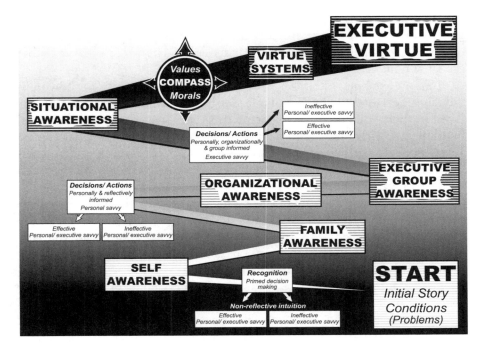

Figure 4.3. Virtue mapping.

ous leader. Similarly, understanding the operation of virtuous or corrupt aspects of behavior and performance in their home organizations and executive teams creates wide opportunities for creatively extending effective leadership. Systematic efforts to be more aware of the situations that face them and their organizations from the vantage point of the implicit or explicit opportunities to enact virtuous or corrupt behavior or to reinforce virtue or to counter corruption in their environmental exchanges supports a multifaceted and complex set of ideas and ideals through which they can select how they will guide their enterprises. Applying moral reasoning, values clarification, and ethical standards to their ideas and actions will also help executives become more confident that the decisions they make and the actions they take will produce justice for everyone with whom they are involved. Finally, leaders need to be prepared to examine themselves, their colleagues, their organizations, and their competitors from the perspective of their own virtue systems. They must have a more refined understanding of human wisdom, courage, temperance, justice, and reverence and how these aspects of a virtuous character can appear or disappear under the stresses and strains of their own and others' executive lives. Furthermore, they must be committed to continuously developing the virtuous aspects of their character with the full and certain knowledge that such characteristics cannot be consistently deployed or counted on if they are not practiced and honed just like any other aspect of human capacity.

As an example, Exhibit 4.4 provides a set of suggestions for how individual leaders or the members of a leadership team can more systematically develop their courage. Four major methods are suggested: workouts, skill building, knowing one's history, and knowing and examining what is good with respect to the development and execution of courage. Specific suggestions are made within each subsection of the exhibit, and many of these can be recognized as examples of managerial or personal competencies that the models of leadership assessment suggest are at the core of effective executive performance. However, as the exhibit and the rest of this chapter strongly suggest, practicing and possessing the competencies do not ensure that any individual leader will develop a virtuous character or, even if a leader is virtuous, that he or she will be able to act virtuously in every situation. Similarly, developing competencies that are core components of courage do not guarantee by any means that individual leaders will act courageously under all circumstances or that he or she will be wise enough to choose the correct kind of courage to exercise.

Exhibit 4.5 presents another avenue to further the development of courage in leaders. It assumes that the virtue mapping model can be further differentiated from executive wisdom and expanded to include courage as well. It provides a systematic set of questions for individuals in leadership positions to explore their thoughts, feelings, and experiences with regard to the development of courage and cowardice. It suggests that consideration be given to taking concrete action steps toward enacting more courageous behavior. The exhibit also provides a small guide that can help a person conduct a dialogue on courage with a trusted friend, colleague, mentor, coach, or other advisor. The completion of this self-reflective exercise would undoubtedly leave any individual conducting such an inquiry in a much better place to understand his or her own history, philosophy, and likely patterns of action when courage is called forth by leadership trials or life's challenges.

Peterson and Seligman (2004) defined the virtue of human courage as "emotional strengths that involve the exercise of will to accomplish goals in the face of opposition, external or internal" (p. 199). It is clear from the lessons of history and practical experience that individuals in leadership positions must possess and enact a great deal of this virtue to do their work effectively. Key questions for any leader then become the following: how do people know that they possess the virtue of courage, and how could they use such knowledge to strengthen and deepen their ability to act consistently in

EXHIBIT 4.4
Methods to Develop Executive Courage

Workouts
- Identifying events, issues, problems, challenges, situations, or people one tends to avoid or which are "frightening"
- Mental simulations and table top exercises—create scenarios and imagine "what if"?
- Practice scenarios with friends, mentors, coaches
- Graded exposures—picking lower level challenges to encounter and manage first then add more complexity, exposure, and power to them
- Reflective after action reviews—personal notes, group discussions, coaching sessions

Enhancing Basic Skills
- Communications—listening, empathic resonance, inquiry, feedback, assertion/advocacy, encouragements, self-disclosures
- Conflict management
- Problem solving
- Decision making
- Diversity awareness and management
- Self-awareness, self-management, and other reflective arts
- Negotiation
- Collaboration
- Cooperation
- Thinking skills—analytic and Intuitive
- Emotional management
- Creating personal and professional support systems

Knowing the Past and Present
- Review the following:
  - Personal history of courage and cowardice
  - Family history of courage and cowardice
  - Reference group(s) history of courage and cowardice
  - Organization and work group history of courage and cowardice
  - Historical and current role models (heroes and villains) and personal ideals and expectations
  - Family, culture, and organizational expectations of courage and cowardice

Knowing What Is Good
- Review and contemplate the following:
  - Awareness of familial, religious, cultural, social, and organizational normative expectations and values that determine what is good and bad, just and unjust
  - Ethical principles and codes of conduct
  - Religious principles, dogma, doctrine, and ideology
  - Philosophy—personal and other
  - Tests of public opinions
  - Knowing and understanding the history of humanity and its just and unjust ideologies and actions
  - Developing one's own standards for just and unjust actions and the proper emotional responses to such experiences
  - Developing one's conscience
  - Developing one's observing ego
  - Privately and publicly exposing and engaging one's instincts, needs, desires, motivations, beliefs, attitudes, and value systems

EXHIBIT 4.5
A Self-Reflective Inquiry on Courage and Cowardice

Introduction

Peterson and Seligman (2004) defined the virtue of human courage as "emotional strengths that involve the exercise of will to accomplish goals in the face of opposition, external or internal" (p. 199). It is clear from the lessons of history and practical experience that individuals in leadership positions must possess and enact a great deal of this virtue in order to do their work effectively. Key questions for any leader then become, how does a person know that he/she possesses the virtue of courage and how could they use such knowledge to strengthen and deepen their ability to consistently act in a courageous fashion? Take a few minutes to read through the following list of questions as a sort of check in regarding how you think about this virtue. If you are more intent on learning more about your experience with this virtue and how you use it in your life, take a pad of paper and write your own answers to the questions after you've taken some time to reflect on each of them.

1. What was the most frightening experience in your life? In your professional life?
2. How did you manage this experience?
3. What conflicts, issues, situations, events, people, problems, and challenges frighten you the most in your personal life? Your professional life? Your organization?
4. Are there conflicts, issues, situations, events, people, problems, and challenges that routinely produce fear in your personal life? Your professional life? Your organization? If yes, what are they?
5. What do you least like to see, say, hear, feel, think, or do?
6. What do you avoid seeing, saying, hearing, feeling, thinking, or doing?
7. How do you manage the conflicts, issues, situations, events, people, problems, and challenges that routinely produce fear in your personal life? Your professional life? Your organization?
8. Who is the most frightened/anxious/timid person you have ever known personally? Professionally?
9. How have you seen them manifest their fear or anxiety?
10. How have you seen them manage their fear or anxiety?
11. In what situation in your personal life did you most exhibit the virtue of courage? In your professional life? What happened to you and to others as a result of your courageousness?
12. From whom in your life have you learned the most about how to be courageous? How did they teach it and how did you learn it?
13. Who is the most courageous person that you know personally right now? How have they demonstrated their courage to you? What do you believe makes them so courageous?
14. Who is the most courageous person that you have ever known personally? How did they demonstrate their courage to you? What do you believe made them so courageous?
15. Can you identify three other heroes/role models of courage in your life? Why do they serve as role models for you? What did you learn to see, say, hear, feel, think, or do from them?
16. How do you know that you are being or have been courageous?
17. How do you know that you are not being or have not been courageous?
18. In what situation in your personal life did you most exhibit cowardice? In your professional life? What happened to you and to others as a result of your cowardice?
19. From whom in your life have you learned the most about how to be cowardly? How did they teach it and how did you learn it?

EXHIBIT 4.5
A Self-Reflective Inquiry on Courage and Cowardice   *(Continued)*

20. Who is the most cowardly person that you know personally right now? How have they demonstrated their cowardice to you? What do you believe makes them so cowardly?
21. Who is the most cowardly person that you have ever known personally? How did they demonstrate their cowardice to you? What do you believe made them so cowardly?
22. Can you identify three other role models of cowardice in your life? Why do they serve as role models for you? What did you learn to see, say, hear, feel, think, or do from them?
23. How do you know that you are being or have been cowardly?
24. How do you know that you are not being or have not been cowardly?
25. What knowledge, skills, or abilities do you think you might need to become more courageous as a leader? As a person?
26. What dimensions of your personal diversity (age, gender, race, national origin, religion, sexual orientation, marital status, etc.) contribute most to how you think, feel, and behave in a courageous or cowardly fashion?
27. If you wanted other people in your personal or professional life who are important to you to think of you as more courageous, what would they need to see or hear you see, say, hear, feel, think, or do?
28. What one small step could you take in the next 24 hours to address more effectively a conflict, issue, situation, event, person, problem, or challenge that frightens you in your personal life? Your professional life? Your organization? Take that step.
29. What could or will you do in the next day, week, or month to develop more knowledge, skills, or abilities that you think you might need to become more courageous as a leader? As a person? How will you do this? Take those steps.
30. What type of courage behavior gives you the most trouble when you do it—attack, retreat, resist, engage?
31. What type of courage behavior gives you the most trouble when others do it—attack, retreat, resist, and engage?
32. From whom did you learn the most about each of these forms of courage behavior?
33. What feels right or is the correct way for you to use each of these forms of courage?
34. In what situations do you typically use each of these forms of behavior?
35. What barriers might get in the way of you taking steps to develop the knowledge, skills, and abilities to become more courageous in any and all of the forms that it can take?
36. What can you do to prevent these barriers from impeding your progress in developing the knowledge, skills, or abilities to become more courageous?
37. Try to identify at least one person in your life with whom you could discuss the issue of your personal and professional courage and cowardice.
38. Make time to talk to him or her.
39. Consider starting the conversation with the following questions:
    a. Do you believe I am a courageous person?
    b. Can you give me an example of how you have seen or heard me acting courageously?
    c. Do you believe I am a cowardly person?
    d. Can you give me an example of how you have seen or heard me acting in a cowardly fashion?
    e. How did you feel about me in those situations?
    f. What did you think about me in those situations?

(continues)

EXHIBIT 4.5
A Self-Reflective Inquiry on Courage and Cowardice   *(Continued)*

g. What, if anything, do/did you wish that I would do differently?
h. What do you think I could do to improve in this area of my behavior?
i. Who are your role models for courageous behavior?
j. What standards do you hold for courageous behavior?
k. Can/will you give me an example of your own experiences with courage or cowardice?
l. Will you talk to me about the conflicts, issues, situations, events, people, problems, and challenges that frighten you the most in your personal life? Your professional life? Your organization?
m. What do you typically do when someone disappoints you regarding courageous behavior?
n. How have you worked to become a more courageous person?
40. Have the conversation.
41. Are there individuals in your life or organization whom you could ask to provide some mentoring for you in the area of courage? Who are they? How might you approach them?
42. Are there individuals in your life or organization to whom you could provide some mentoring in the area of courage? Who are they? How might you approach them?
43. What have you read recently that has taught you something about the development or engagement of human courage?
44. Does your organization/executive/management group have explicit norms or expectations for courage behavior? Cowardice? If yes, how would you describe them?
45. Does your organization or executive/management group have implicit norms or expectations for courage behavior? Cowardice? If yes, how would you describe them?
46. Does your organization or executive/management group ever explicitly discuss courage or cowardice?
47. If your organization or executive/management group does not discuss courage, why do you think that is the case?
48. What do you think would happen if you raised the issue of expectations for courage in one of your staff meetings?
49. How could you better help your boss, subordinates, peers, and family members become more consciously aware of the issues of courage and cowardice?
50. How could you better help your boss, subordinates, peers, and family members become better practitioners of courage?
51. If you were to ask your boss, a subordinate, a peer, or a family member to take one small step to become more courageous, what would that be?
52. What dimensions of diversity (age, gender, race, national origin, religion, sexual orientation, marital status, etc.) of your boss, a subordinate, a peer, or a family member contribute most to whether you believe they think, feel, and behave in a courageous or cowardly fashion?
53. What barriers do you see in the way of your boss, subordinates, peers, and family members becoming better practitioners of courage?
54. How could you help them address these barriers or how could you address these barriers directly in a personal way?

a courageous fashion? Take a few minutes to read through the list of questions in Exhibit 4.5 as a sort of check-in regarding how you think about this virtue. If you are intent on learning more about your experience with courage and how you use it in your life, take a pad of paper and write your own answers to the questions after you've taken some time to reflect on them.

SUMMARY

Contemporary models of leadership development have increasingly relied on empirically derived measures of behaviorally based competencies. The embedded assumptions of these models are that leadership should largely be judged on the basis of what individuals do in these positions and that if managers and executives can develop the appropriate kinds of competencies and levels of performance with each of them, organizations can be more assured that their leaders will be effective in their work. This school of thought and practice implicitly incorporates aspects of the historically derived emphasis on human virtue as the centerpiece of leadership development. Most competency models include some measurement surrogates for the traditional cardinal virtues of wisdom, temperance, courage, and justice. However, the historically important virtue models of leadership tried to answer a related but different core question: who are you as a person? This chapter attempted to clarify these issues, examined a coaching case study within this framework, and presented a model of virtue mapping that encourages the systematic use of the reflective awareness described in Kilburg (2006) in its application to executive wisdom to develop executive virtue. Specific suggestions were made about how to enable organizations and individuals to examine the ways in which they think, feel, and act courageously or cowardly, and methods for developing human courage were suggested as well. Most people have an intuitive feel for effective leadership. We know it when we see it and experience it directly. The central contention of this chapter is that whenever and wherever effective leadership is most often demonstrated, it will represent a combination of both specific behaviorally based competencies and virtuous aspects of executive character. Now let's go on to look at the virtues of reverence and temperance in more detail.

5

REVERENCE AND TEMPERANCE: FOUNDATIONS FOR VIRTUOUS LEADERSHIP

INTRODUCTION

As we've discussed in previous chapters, ancient Chinese and Greek models of effective leadership were based on the assumption that individuals who were motivated to assume these positions should first seek to become virtuous people. This, of course, entailed a lifelong commitment to practice virtuous behavior. Only when they were thought to have reasonably demonstrated that they understood and could consistently enact behavior that was reverent, temperate, courageous, just, and wise would such individuals be proposed for senior positions in state governance. Socrates called them philosopher kings and advocated that leaders must first be lovers of all knowledge before they were given the powers of office. Confucius' term was the Superior Man who combined refined manners and the wisdom of a sage (Confucius, trans. 1989; Kilburg, 2006; Little, 2002; Plato, 1999). In 2006, I used the term *virtuous leaders* to describe individuals who not only were able to lead their enterprises or countries successfully but also exemplified the ancient and modern ideals of people who strive to live and act rightly in this world.

Contemporary models of leadership are anchored in the precepts of 20th-century behaviorism, which in turn represented strong reactions to the trait theories that were initially advanced in the late 19th and early 20th centuries. In Chapter 4, I described how modern approaches are most often developed through psychometrically defensible methods and result in multifactored lists of behaviors defining good leaders. These competency-based systems often have descriptive terms that substitute for or specifically adopt certain of the ancient virtues. *Leads courageously, demonstrates interpersonal skill,* and *possesses integrity* are modern, descriptive terms of leadership abilities that try to incorporate some of these teachings of philosophy (Bartram, 2005).

This chapter focuses extensively on the description of the virtues of reverence and temperance in ancient and modern terms and emphasizes that future approaches to leadership development must first be grounded in the effort to help executives understand and be able to consistently enact these virtues. It will attempt to delineate ways that development programs and individual executives can pursue such experiences and create characters defined routinely by these behaviors. It provides examples of exercises and homework assignments that support such growth. Two case studies illuminate the impact of poor practice of these virtues in organizations by senior leaders.

SHOOTING THEMSELVES IN THE FOOT: TWO CASES OF LEADERS WHO UNINTENTIONALLY UNDERMINED THEIR OWN EFFORTS

"If this continues, I don't think I will be able to stay in this organization." This is an exact quote from what two highly successful, hardworking, dedicated, senior executives employed in different organizations positioned in separate sectors of the global economy said to me in the same week. Both lamentations came early in coaching sessions that led to a careful exploration of the antecedent experiences, patterns of behavior, and reactions for each of them. In each of the cases, the sessions revealed the underlying structure and process of the exchanges that were, by the explicit self-reports of these two leaders, literally traumatizing them in their relationships with their bosses. I would like to summarize what the coaching work uncovered and the general structure of the interventions that I made with both clients, then use these examples to begin a more detailed discussion of how reverence and temperance or their relative absence can significantly affect the performance of individual leaders, their colleagues, subordinates, and their organizations.

The Case of Lily and Bill

Lily and Bill had worked together in the same large functional unit for more than a decade in their previous organization. They had reported to different people in that enterprise, but over the years, they grew to know and respect each other as colleagues. Eventually, they became close personal friends because of shared interests, similar challenges in their family lives, and a deep appreciation and admiration for each other. When Bill left the organization to join a different business as a senior vice president, he knew that he had to rebuild the leadership team with whom he would work most closely. Lily was his first recruit to the new office. Bill delegated enormous areas of responsibility to her, provided a tremendous increase in salary, and allowed Lily to hire a number of people to help manage her responsibilities. The new partnership began with extremely bright hopes and high expectations.

Shortly after assuming their positions, they discovered that their predecessors had left them a tremendous financial and programmatic mess in one of their areas of responsibility. The disclosure of the problems occurred as a result of the annual financial audit of the entire enterprise, and it led to significant comments in the report of the external audit firm; major discussions between them, the board of directors and the CEO; and a very public and politically charged commitment to clean up the mess. Bill assumed the responsibility to make the necessary changes and assigned the principle clean up duties to Lily. Lily dove in conscientiously and uncovered decades worth of problems, tens of millions of dollars of misallocated and inappropriately tracked resources, tremendous weaknesses in the financial and programmatic controls of the organization, and the unwillingness and inability of her colleagues across the various affected departments to work together and take responsibility for their part in the historical problems. True to her character and competencies, she continued to dig deeply, work conscientiously, and try to hold everyone publicly accountable. In reality, that assignment alone was more than a full-time job.

However, the CEO and board had even bigger plans for Bill and his unit. During that same year, the leadership and governance of the enterprise made commitments to goals in their area that were orders of magnitude higher than anything that had ever been achieved in the past. They allocated tremendous amounts of new resources to help Bill build his organization and brought major public attention to what they were trying to achieve. Bill turned to Lily to help him build his organization, recruit and train staff, and run the operation when he was out of the office working with his leadership colleagues, organizational governance, suppliers, and regulators. Those early days were exciting and challenging.

During our discussion, Lily explained patiently that she still held tremendous affection and admiration for Bill, continued to consider him a good friend, and truly supported what he was trying to accomplish in the organization. However, she complained bitterly of being burned out by the focus on the project to repair the historical problems. Because of the governance scrutiny, financial implications, and potential for public embarrassment, those efforts had become all consuming. Lily literally worked full time trying to fix those problems even as she tried to keep her other responsibilities moving along. She was emotionally and physically tired after nearly 2 years of heroic effort. Nonetheless, she stated clearly that the project was not the major impetus to her wanting to leave the organization.

To her surprise, Lily had learned early in her new working relationship with Bill that he had some personality characteristics and elements in his leadership style that were proving to be troublesome to her. According to her description, whenever Bill was put under increased scrutiny and pressure by the CEO, board, regulators, or colleagues, his stress level would increase dramatically. When he was in that state, he would show up in the office with a very different demeanor. Usually, Bill was affable, approachable, possessed a high level of personal self-awareness, and had a good sense of humor. When he was in that mode of operation and interaction, Lily loved working with and for him. However, when under pressure, Bill could and would attend meetings, call people into his office, or simply walk into the offices of his staff and begin to authoritatively demand explanations of events, make unreasonable requests that reports be produced on very short timelines, or ask for complicated forms of data and information analysis that the organization had no infrastructure or historical capacity to produce. The demands were also accompanied by intense questioning in which he repeatedly demanded explanations for why things were not happening, going well, or proceeding as he expected. At times, the interrogations could unpredictably morph into barrages of criticism. At his worst, he would show up in someone's office, demand information, and, before the efforts to explain were completed, launch into what staff and Lily described and experienced as an angry tirade punctuated by profanity and sarcastic comments. Most often, Bill would then depart the scene of the crime, leaving the staff member(s) in emotional turmoil trying to figure out how to respond to what he wanted accomplished, yet so emotionally upset that it often took them hours to calm down. Lily reported that she routinely spent hours with staff members helping them sort out the aftereffects of these exchanges. Bill had also demonstrated willingness to engage in this pattern of behavior with Lily in meetings with multiple members of the staff or in front of others in the halls or offices of the organization.

During our conversation, Lily said that she had made efforts to bring these behaviors to Bill's attention but felt that she had not been successful because he was so sensitive to her feedback that he tended to well up with tears, complain about his stress load, and change the subject. She found it nearly impossible to have a complete conversation with him on the subject because she truly understood and had empathy for him. She also said the amazing thing was that Bill could have these kinds of intense exchanges with people and then show up in a meeting an hour or day later acting like absolutely nothing had happened. Based on how she had come to know him, Lily believed that this pattern was ingrained in his personality and that he displayed it with his family as well as at work. The one piece of clarification she did get from him during one of their fragmented conversations on the subject was that he never displayed the same kind of behavior to his boss, peers at the vice presidential level, or to anyone in governance or a powerful position who had the ability to hurt him or the company.

Deepening the conversation, Lily and I were able to discern the following pattern:

1. Conditions of increased stress and public scrutiny created the emotional background out of which these episodes of "drive-by" emotional shootings, aggressive interrogations, loss of temper, and impossible performance demands occurred.
2. These events took place two to three times per month and did not appear to have any other common stimuli creating them.
3. Lily's response to these exchanges was to want to withdraw from Bill and leave the organization. Her personal attachment to him had made it nearly impossible for her to provide the same kind of developmental feedback and firm limit setting that she was always able to provide to her staff. Despite knowing what she should do and having made a couple of incomplete and feeble efforts on her own, she simply could not bring herself to hurt him with a completely candid conversation.
4. Lily had experienced a pervasive and chronic increase in her general level of anxiety and tension because of the public scrutiny of the special project as well as to the anticipation that she could never predict or control when Bill would show up and attack her or someone else. Whenever he came after her, she was left feeling like a failure and that she had been publicly humiliated. She also described an intense, historical, and personal pattern of dealing with shame as an emotion and stated that the experience of that feeling often left her devastated for hours and, in worst cases, days. It would take her a long time to pull herself back together emotionally and to summon the motivation to continue to go to work and to engage with Bill, her colleagues, and her assignments.
5. We agreed that Bill's pattern of flashes of temper, use of criticism and sarcastic questioning, expressions of profanity, and ability to recover extremely quickly and act like nothing had happened was the core of what was driving her to want to leave the organization.

She experienced those exchanges as extremely disrespectful, intemperate, childlike, and irresponsible on Bill's part and yet felt powerless, hopeless, and helpless in the face of the pattern to do anything constructive about it.

The Case of Jim and Linda

Linda had been brought into her company as a new chief operating officer over 3 years before my discussion with Jim. She had served an intense, meaningful, and problem-filled, 18-month apprenticeship with the previous CEO, Howard Price. During that time, Linda had demonstrated her work ethic, attention to detail, analytic skills, and motivation to lead. Any job that Howard or the board gave her elicited the same kind of furious, hard-driving effort that would quickly get her to the bottom of a problem. She would then act with incredible swiftness. Often she would send lengthy e-mails to the vice presidents in the organization, providing them with detailed road maps of how to fix the problems she had uncovered. In addition, she would also send these kinds of instructions to virtually any manager or supervisor in the company, regardless of whether that person reported to her or someone else. In face-to-face meetings with individuals, she could be extremely personable, and most of the people who worked with Linda reported that they found themselves liking her. However, she could also appear extremely distracted, detached, and at times disrespectful as she checked or responded to e-mails, took cell phone calls, and allowed other people or cell phone calls to interrupt meetings.

During that apprenticeship, Linda received a great deal of coaching from Howard, the chairman of the board of directors, Dave Strickland, and me. Over the course of the 18 months, she demonstrated the capacity to consciously moderate that pattern of behavior, as she continued to master the details of both the industry and the business. The board and Howard were ready to have her assume the position of CEO, but they waited until they were sure that Linda could demonstrate the ongoing ability to relate effectively to her colleagues. Eventually, she convinced them that she could perform the duties of CEO and they promoted her.

Linda moved quickly to form her own executive team. Among other moves, she promoted Jim and gave him significantly expanded responsibilities. Jim was extremely grateful for the trust that she placed in him, and he worked exceptionally hard to master the new aspects of his job, built a more competent middle management team under him, and produced enormous cost savings for Linda in his first full year in his job. Over time, he also completed the requirements for his MBA degree, which the company had supported completely. Jim was motivated to stay in the organization and make even more significant contributions. When we had our conversation, there was no question about his commitment to the company, his gratitude to the board, and the intense satisfaction he was getting from his work.

During our discussion, Jim stated that he wanted to explore a pattern of behavior on Linda's part that had become problematic for him. It consisted of several major components. He described a series of meetings and discussions he had had with Linda about a managerial position they had agreed to add to organization. The new staff member would carry an extensive portfolio of responsibilities that would cut across two functional units in the company. Jim and his closest working partner in the enterprise, Roberta Manson, would share this person, and they were quite clear on the qualifications that they thought the potential hire should have. However, in the discussions with Linda, Jim said that he had gotten the sense that the plans Roberta and he had made did not mesh with those that Linda had apparently formulated. In those conversations, Linda conducted a relatively intense Socratic-like dialogue, asking both Jim and Roberta an extensive series of questions that seemed to Jim to be designed to move them to a particular conclusion that she had already reached. Only after three or four of these exchanges did it become clear that Linda had become concerned about the overall lack of any succession management planning in the organization and that she believed one of the most important criteria for the person filling this new position would be the individual's ability to step in for either Jim or Roberta should one of them decide to leave the company.

Jim stated that both he and Roberta would have been happy to discuss the succession issues with Linda from the outset of the deliberations and that they had experienced her behavior during the process as transparently political, demeaning to them, and, in the end, manipulative. He went on to ask me why Linda seemed to need to behave in such a fashion when everyone around her knew what she was doing. Jim said that the other members of the executive team shared his concerns.

He also added that there were two other related behaviors of Linda's that were proving to be troublesome to him and that were contributing to his declining morale and consideration of leaving the company. The executive team held a regular weekly meeting that Linda chaired. Over the course of the 18 months of her term of office, these meetings had taken on a very different structure and process than those that Howard had used. During his term of office, Howard had used a formal agenda for the weekly meetings, but he allowed a great deal of room for open dialogue and extensive exchanges on the challenges the executive team faced in leading the business. He also tried to achieve a consensus on how they were going to proceed on any specific issue. Linda had slowly but surely removed those discussions from the executive team meetings. Instead, they had become formal affairs that were driven by highly structured and succinct information updates from all of the participants. Jim reported that on many occasions, Linda would abruptly interrupt his presentations and push him either to be more succinct or simply move on to another subject. When he tried to ask questions about the updates being provided by his colleagues, Linda would cut off the questions or make sure the replies did not evolve into a full-fledged give-and-take between members of the executive team by saying things such as, "let's keep this discussion on a high level."

Finally, Jim expressed concerns that in their meetings, Linda at times appeared to be uninterested in what he was telling her. At her worst, she would diminish the importance of what he was trying to communicate or discuss. The overall experience that he said he was having with Linda seemed to focus on her need to control minutely everything going on in the company and that she was only truly interested in her own views of events, challenges, or operations. Jim said he believed every member of the executive team was having similar experiences with Linda and that the overall level of frustration with her leadership appeared to be growing among the members of the group. Despite these concerns, Jim also said that he liked Linda; he thought she was doing a good job as the CEO, felt the company was on the right track, and, quite paradoxically, for the most part, she left him alone to run his part of the business. When I asked him to estimate the percentage of the time that he experienced Linda behaving in this overcontrol pattern, after a thought-filled silence, Jim replied probably 30% of the time. When I said that I thought no leader was perfect and asked him at what level of frequency Linda's behavior would be more tolerable to him, he replied that if it occurred 10% or 15% of the time, he thought he could handle it pretty well.

As we continued the conversation, Jim and I outlined the following pattern. Linda had demonstrated a consistent need to control the activities for which she was responsible in the company. As she assumed the role of CEO, she made significant changes over the course of her first 18 months in office. The need for control now manifested most clearly in several ways:

- Linda would conduct meetings with her colleagues in which she used Socratic dialogue and other forms of communication to lead them to conclusions that it appeared she had already reached. Her use of this approach created a sense in her team members that she was being unduly manipulative and somewhat disingenuous. They strongly preferred that she would simply state what was on her mind at the outset of a conversation or set of deliberations.
- Linda had progressively changed the nature of their executive team meetings, moving away from extensive, open dialogues on

almost every feature of the company's operations and toward a highly structured set of information exchanges between them. Efforts to extend the discussion, dig into details, or express extensive views were met with significant resistance, calls for keeping exchanges brief, conversations at high conceptual levels, and changing the subject. Agenda items requiring extensive operational discussions were frequently placed in the "other items" category and were only addressed as time permitted at the end of meetings.

- In meetings, at her worst, Linda periodically appeared disinterested in what her colleagues were talking about and made frequent references to changing the job duties and responsibilities of different managers in their operations with seemingly no consideration of her colleagues' personal thoughts and feelings about such changes.

- Efforts to discuss these issues or observations of what Jim thought might be happening most often elicited intense exchanges with Linda that almost always got back to what prompted Jim's thoughts and feelings, not what Linda had done. Jim felt strongly that Linda struggled with her ability to listen to performance-based feedback from her colleagues and worked to minimize her responses to it.

My effort to intervene in both of these situations took a similar form. Both Jim and Lily knew and in fact stated that they understood I expected them to act courageously and to move in the direction of surfacing the problem behaviors. In essence, they understood that the purpose of the coaching activity was to enable them to do something different and perform more effectively in their roles with the challenges that they faced. In each case, I tried to get them to quantify the nature of the problem behaviors and to identify targets or goals that they thought their colleagues could reach. I also helped them clarify the nature of their reactions. In both cases, the behavioral–emotional sequence they were experiencing had at least the following components:

1. Behavior on the part of a superior that was experienced as disrespectful and intemperate that produced feelings of failure, being out of control or overcontrolled by the boss, followed by experiences of shame and intense loss of dignity.

2. Efforts to engage the superior in a constructive way were met with significant resistance that manifested in different ways. The inability to influence the superior created strong feelings of

helplessness, hopelessness, powerlessness, and, at its worst, the desire to leave the organization.

I suggested to both of these individuals that after they kept some records of these types of exchanges, I would help them bring the patterns to the attention of their superiors and to try to clarify behavioral expectations and perhaps changes in the operating norms of these leadership groups. I also talked with them about how to detoxify themselves from such shaming and anxiety-arousing exchanges more effectively. Finally, I emphasized to both Lily and Jim that even if they left their respective positions and organizations, they would not escape these types of problems. In virtually every organization in which I consult, there are people in senior leadership positions who behave like Bill and Linda. I strongly suggested that one of the skills they would need to improve while they were in their present positions or in any other similar leadership role in an organization was the ability to lead and coach up the chain of command. Indeed, even CEOs, who on the surface of their job descriptions seem to have all of the authority and power in their organizations, also need to be able to influence boards of directors, government and industry regulators, investment communities, and advocacy groups, any one of which can act in ways to produce these same reactions in them. Indeed, learning how to influence at senior levels in organizations is one of the most challenging aspects of executive life.

REVERENCE AND TEMPERANCE: VIRTUOUS FOUNDATIONS OF EXECUTIVE PERFORMANCE

At its essence, the core patterns described in these two case studies involve the unacknowledged, largely unconscious, and extremely destructive results of the inability of Linda and Bill to consistently enact the virtues of reverence and temperance with their colleagues. In both situations, these leaders had unknowingly created significant flight risk in key subordinates whose departures would have been devastating to their administrations. In both situations, the subordinates believed they had strong working relationships with their bosses, that their leaders were doing the right things for their organizations, and that they held largely strong positive feelings for them. However, the patterns of irreverent and intemperate behavior with which Lily and Jim had to contend had significantly undermined their commitment to their jobs and their organizations, their sense of loyalty to their bosses, and their own physical and mental well-being. Amazingly, both Lily and Jim said they did understand that their leaders would never be perfect in these areas of behavior and that they believed that they could readily tolerate what they were experiencing if it decreased in frequency by a significant amount. Both also suggested that their estimate of their current experiences were that the outbursts of irreverence and intemperance occurred several times per week or in up to 30% of the exchanges that they were having with their boss.

My coaching with these two clients had several major foci:

1. I tried to get them to be as explicit as possible about the nature of the behavior they were experiencing, the antecedents of the pattern, the consequences for them and others in their organizations, and the specific emotional responses that the exchanges were stimulating in them.

2. During the discussions, I helped them put specific labels on the behavior they were experiencing and understand that their bosses' inability to consistently display the virtues of reverence and temperance was having pernicious effects on them and their colleagues.

3. In both situations, I pushed the clients to objectify the pattern and to clarify whether they wanted and needed the behavior to disappear completely or to be reduced in scope and frequency. I also encouraged them to keep records of the behavior and their reactions to confirm the preliminary hypotheses that we had created and to serve as a foundation for a future discussion with their bosses about the changes that these clients thought needed to be made.

4. The conversations with these two clients were extremely useful to both. They reported feeling calmer, more directed, and much clearer about what had been happening to them. They also felt much better prepared to observe what was happening in future exchanges and to be able to engage those experiences more constructively for themselves.

5. Finally, both clients were encouraged to think about whether they were engaged in similar patterns with others and how holding high office in organizations created natural tensions that could increase the likelihood that they, too, or anyone for that matter, might well be pushed to act irreverently or intemperately.

If we follow the intuitive pattern and logic that are nested within these case examples, it is relatively easy to come to the conclusion that the practice of reverence and temperance on the part of leaders is crucial to success in their roles. As I suggested in the introduction to this chapter, contemporary competency models of leadership speak directly and indirectly to the issue of virtue by suggesting that they are forms or patterns of behavior to be mastered by managers. When virtues are routinely practiced by managers along with the mastery of other competencies, I would suggest that organizations are likely to see an increased likelihood of effective leadership performance. In this context, I suggest that virtuous behavior on the part of a leader in the form of the consistent enactment of reverence and temperance is vastly more complex and more important than being a skilled performer of a range of other behavioral competencies. In the pages that follow, I explore a little history in regard to these virtues, present some additional models and concepts to help us understand them, and suggest some exercises that might help leaders and those who develop them make progress in becoming more strategically reverent and temperate.

The *Oxford Dictionary of English* (1998) defines *reverence* as "deep or due respect felt or shown towards a person on account of his or her position or relationship. . . . Deep respect and veneration for some thing, place, or person regarded as having a sacred or exalted character . . . gestures of respect or veneration" (p. 1580). The same dictionary defines *temperance* as "the practice or habit of restraining oneself in provocation, desire, passion, etc. . . . rational restraint (one of the four cardinal virtues) . . . self-restraint and moderation in action of any kind . . . especially self-control, restraint, or forbearance when provoked to anger or impatience" (p. 2023). If we combine the definitions of these two virtues and focus them on how they can be enacted by leaders, we might suggest that virtuous leaders who consistently display reverence and temperance treat their colleagues, regulators, superiors, and customers with deep respect and veneration. Further, they consistently behave toward them with strategic self-restraint and moderation in self-expression even in the face of severe provocation. I would go on to suggest that leaders who practice these virtues are likely to create leadership groups and organizational cultures that foster higher levels of trust and emotional security, and, in so doing, they will establish a strong foundation for consistent and effective individual, group, and enterprise-wide performance. See Exhibit 5.1 for definitions of these leadership virtues and additional explanatory notes.

Now let's look at some historical and contemporary views of these virtues. In his analects, Confucius stated:

> The illustrious ancients, when they wished to make clear and to propagate the highest virtues in the world, put their states in proper order. Before putting their states in proper order, they regulated their families. Before regulating their families, they cultivated their own selves. Before cultivating their own selves, they perfected their souls. Before perfecting their souls, they tried to be sincere in their thoughts. Before trying to be sincere in their thoughts, they extended to the utmost their knowledge. Such investigation of knowledge lay in the investigation of things, and in seeing them as they really were. When things were investigated, knowledge became complete. When knowledge became complete, their thoughts

EXHIBIT 5.1
Definitions of Leadership Reverence and Temperance

Leadership Reverence

A disposition or pre-dispositional intention and capacity engrained in a leader's character to respond to people and the world around him/her through the ability to feel and strategically enact or express respect, shame, and awe based on the judgment of what would be most courageous, just, and wise in a given situation.

Leadership Temperance

A disposition or pre-dispositional intention and capacity engrained in a leader's character to respond to people and the world around him/her through the ability to strategically express or restrain thoughts, feelings, and behaviors based on the judgment of what would be most courageous, just, and wise in a given situation.

Reverent and temperate leaders tend to behave and to expect their colleagues and organizations to behave modestly, deal with others honestly and with integrity, tell the truth, creatively collaborate, treat everyone respectfully, and have the capacity to feel and express anxiety and regret about being ashamed or guilty about errors, mistakes, and poor performance. They work to ensure that resources and profits are distributed appropriately and when they must take adverse or injurious actions aimed at members of the organization, competitors, or the organization itself they do so with the long term intention of improving performance and not simply promoting their own self-interest; and they treat others justly and wisely.

Irreverent and intemperate leaders tend to behave and to expect their colleagues and organizations to behave arrogantly, blindly, disrespectfully, dishonestly, manipulatively, shamelessly, and act to deny feelings of shame or guilt by trying to hide errors, mistakes, and poor performance in a cowardly fashion. They work to ensure that resources and profits are distributed to protect what they experience their own narcissistic entitlement. When they take adverse or injurious actions aimed at members of the organization, competitors, or the organization, they do so to promote their own self-interest and tend to rationalize their efforts in terms of performance improvement. They tend to treat others and the organization with ignorance, contempt, and distain.

became sincere. When their thoughts were sincere, their souls became perfect. When their souls became perfect, their selves became cultivated. When their selves were cultivated, their families became regulated. When their families were regulated, their states came to be put into proper order. When their states were in proper order, then the whole world became peaceful and happy. (Little, 2002, p. 13)

These ideas were written and taught more than 2,500 years ago. Similarly, in Book Four of Plato's *Republic*, he quoted Socrates as stating,

And in truth justice, as it appears, is something of this kind. But it does not concern a man's management of his own external affairs, but his internal management of his soul, his truest self and his truest possessions. The just man does not allow the different principles within him to do other work than their own, nor the distinct classes in his soul to interfere with one another; but in the truest sense he sets his house in order, gaining the mastery over himself; and becoming on good terms with himself through discipline, he joins in harmony those different elements, like the three terms in a musical scale—lowest and highest and intermediate, and any others that may lie between those—and binding together all these elements he moulds the many within him into one, temperate and harmonious. (p. 130)

Both Confucius and Socrates are well known in philosophy and history for being students of leadership, as well as teachers and mentors to leaders. As we can see clearly in these samples of their writing and teaching, from the earliest days of recorded human history, the best teachers were carefully examining the importance of creating and living a reverent and temperate life for leaders of city-states and nations.

The historical course of the theory and practice of reverence and temperance from the time of Socrates is bound completely to the rise and fall of the Greek, Persian, Carthaginian, Roman, Moslem–Moorish, Asian, European, and other empires, and the evolution of the major religions of Christianity, Islam, Judaism, Buddhism, Hinduism, among others, nearly all of which had to come to grips with the central question of how humans could and should live good lives. All of these political and religious belief systems created practical manuals for the way in which virtues could be identified and developed. These guides were embedded in the main texts of their churches, the Torah and the Holy Bible, the Koran (Dawood, 1990), the Bhagavad-Gita (Easwaran, 1985), and the Tibetan Book of the Dead (Coleman & Jinpa, 2005). In medieval Europe, the classical Greek virtues of temperance, courage, justice, and wisdom were retained and retranslated by the Christian Church as the cardinal virtues, to which they added faith, hope, and charity (Jaspers, 1957; MacIntyre, 2008; Pieper, 1966; Schimmel, 1997). Reverence in the practice of the Church was saved for the relationship between humans and the Divine. Christian doctrine, civil law, and the aims and practices of chivalry coevolved during those centuries, leading to the adoption of the Magna Carta in England, the establishment of English common law, and the keystones for the democratic nation-states that were to follow during and after the Enlightenment (Kaeuper, 1999; Rowling, 1979).

By the mid–18th century, schools and systematized learning also became accessible to the upper middle, middle, and even some of the working classes. The invention of the printing press made reading a widely practiced skill, and increasingly average people in Europe, the Americas, and parts of Asia become became better informed via newspapers, pamphlets, books, almanacs, and other forms of information dissemination. In pre-Revolutionary America, the mechanics of leading a virtuous life become a centerpiece of public discussion and private pursuit. For example, George Washington, the first president, wrote his own book, the *Rules of Civility and Decent Behavior* (Washington, 1988). For Benjamin Franklin, the pursuit of virtue was a lifelong enterprise, and it became one of the central themes of his writing and public discourse. Franklin was especially focused on the issue of temperance and worked during his entire life to describe its practice to others and to display it personally in various ways (Rogers, 1996). The first guiding principle to which he devoted himself was "there is no happiness but in a virtuous and self-approving conduct" (Rogers, 1996; p. 14). The study and conduct of a virtuous life consumed much of Washington's and Franklin's time and energy, and many of the other leaders who participated in the establishment of the United States were serious students and practitioners of virtue as well. In summary, it seems fair to say that the elaboration, study, and practice of human virtue have been a constant part of the social evolution of humans since the dawn of written human history.

Until recently, the science and practice of psychology have had at best an ambivalent relationship with the subject of human virtue. In fact, Fowers (2005) recently stated that "psychologists persist in our efforts to eliminate virtue from theory" (p. 18). Fowers suggested in the same text that beginning with the work of Gordon Allport in 1937, the effort to deemphasize the issues of character and to elevate the scientific study of personality traits and characteristics has had a consistent and pernicious impact on the field's ability to contribute to the understanding and practice of human virtues. He also pointed out that recently a small group of psychologists have become interested in positive approaches to psychology and have begun to write about and conduct scientific studies of human virtue. As I described earlier, the work of Peterson and Seligman (2004) is of particular note in this regard.

Reverence

With regard to the study and practice of reverence, there is virtually no literature cited in the PsycINFO database on that topic. In the classification system provided by Peterson and Seligman (2004), it is not even mentioned, although the virtues of transcendence and humanity both address aspects of reverence. It would seem that as far as the field of psychology is concerned, reverence has acquired no theoretical or practical interest for more than a century. This is despite the fact that in his classic text on religious experience, William James (1902/1961), perhaps best known as the first modern American psychologist, devoted an entire chapter to the topic of saintliness and its associated practices and components. During the 20th century, reverence was largely abandoned by philosophy as well, and as a subject of study and practice, it became increasingly confined to the various religions of the world. Recently, this has been rectified to some degree by a wonderful philosophical treatise on the topic by Paul Woodruff (2001). Let's create a little space to examine some of the ideas he put forward with a particular emphasis on applications of reverence to the practice of leadership.

Woodruff (2001) defined *reverence* as "the well developed capacity to have feelings of awe, respect, and shame when these are the right feelings to have" (p. 8). He also stated that "reverence is the virtue that keeps human beings from trying to take tight control of other people's lives" Further, it "keeps human beings from trying to act like gods" (p. 4), and, "Reverence begins in a deep understanding of human limitations; from this grows the capacity to be in awe of whatever we believe lies outside of our control—God, truth, justice, nature, even death" (p. 1). Woodruff clarified as well that when the human soul is irreverent, it is arrogant and shameless. It is unable to feel awe in the face of things higher than itself. For him, irreverent souls are unable to feel respect for people they see as lower than themselves—ordinary people, prisoners, the poor, the homeless, children, subordinates.

Once he established these essential definitions and perspectives, Woodruff (2001) went on to discuss his belief that reverence "is the virtue that separates leaders from tyrants" (p. 175). Speaking specifically to the issue of how reverence informs the practice of leadership, Woodruff wrote,

> Reverence is the capacity to feel respect in the right way toward the right people, and to feel awe toward an object that transcends particular human interests. When leaders are reverent, they are reverent along with their followers, and their common reverence unites them in feelings that overcome personal interests, feelings such as mutual respect. These feelings take the sting from the tools of leadership—from persuasion, from threats of punishment, from manipulation by means of rewards. This is because there are no winners and losers where there is reverence. Success and failure are dwarfed by the magnitude of whatever it is that they hold together in awe. (pp. 175–176)

In these passages, it is easy to see that Woodruff (2001) provides a fundamental approach through which anyone can try to practice leadership. Contemporary management theory repeatedly emphasizes the need to establish a unifying vision for a given enterprise as one of the essentials for success (Collins, 2001; Collins & Porras, 1994). Put in the context of human virtue, a unifying vision is simply what Woodruff describes as that ideal that all members of any organization hold in awe. Collins (2001) differentiated this idea into what he called the three circles of the Hedgehog Concept. He maintained that great enterprises answer three questions:

1. What can you be best in the world at doing?
2. What drives your economic engine?
3. What are you deeply passionate about?

Once leaders and followers are clear about these answers, they are free to pursue their personal, professional, and organizational ends with unbridled commitment and devotion. Collins thus provides a somewhat more elaborate and elegant explanation of Woodruff's interpretation of an ancient virtue in contemporary management terms. By using Collins's (2001) ideas, we can penetrate deeper into the elegance of Woodruff's language, "whatever it is that they hold together in awe," and into the daily practices of leaders and followers trying to do what they are best at every day.

Woodruff (2001) went on to describe the difference between the good opinion and the reverence approaches to respect in organizations. In the good opinion approach, the members of an enterprise earn the respect of their colleagues through the exercise of their competencies and the success of their performances. He suggested that such an approach creates a false belief that organizational success depends on each individual being effective at his or her job. Woodruff refuted this belief with a fundamental assertion that good organizations are systems that are devised with the intent and the ability to rectify mistakes at all levels in their structure. He further asserted that no human is perfect and thus we can expect human organizations to be imperfect. Effective leaders and followers understand they are imperfect and work together against this essential nature of humanity by cocreating good organizations that can and do buffer the normal mistakes that their members make.

Finally, Woodruff (2001) provided us with astounding clarity about the central importance of respect based on reverence in organizations. He stated:

> An act of respect says that none of us is all-powerful or immortal, that no one can play god and get away with it. We will all die; we will all make mistakes. We all together seek to maintain an orderly system that is least vulnerable to hubris, to the violence of mind or action that comes from forgetting our common human limitations. An act of respect represents the thought that I cannot get away with treating you like dirt, no matter how powerful I am. No matter how low, how immature, how foolish, or how weak in mind I think you are, reverence does not allow me to overlook our common humanity and, in the case of hierarchy, our devotion to common ideals. . . . People who think they have perfect knowledge, or are guided in their decisions directly by God, are usually in for a surprise. Overconfidence is an ever-present danger in a human mind, and the best defense against it is listening to others, with reverence. (pp. 182, 185)

Woodruff's (2001) restoration of the virtue of reverence to the conceptual foundations of and the dialogue on what represents truly effective leadership was timely in that it provided additional historical and philosophical evidence for the importance of another of Collins's (2001) ideas about what makes organizations great, Level Five Leaders, whom he described as "a study in duality; modest and willful, humble and fearless" (p. 22). In the context of

Woodruff's and Collins's ideas, virtuous leaders who practice their craft with acute sensibility to reverence are better able to attract and retain gifted colleagues. The leadership group thus established and supported is then able to move organizations systematically to consistently higher levels of performance than are other types of leaders or executive groups. As Collins also described, to be sure, leaders who believe they are geniuses, who manifest characteristics such as arrogance, hubris, and narcissistic entitlement, can be successful, at least for periods of time. However, in his view, if organizations are truly in it for the long haul, there is no substitute for virtuous leaders who base their relationships and the practice of their craft on enacting the virtue of reverence.

Temperance

As opposed to reverence, the study of temperance, or the ability to appropriately express or restrain thoughts, feelings, and behavior, has continuously occupied a considerable swath of psychological territory for more than a century. One could safely say that much of the entire fields of clinical, counseling, school, and educational psychology have been preoccupied with how to identify and solve the problems of intemperate, out-of-control behavior by creating or restoring the capacity of individuals to lead reasonable and good lives. No single book or review of the literature could do true justice to the contributions of the thousands of scientists and practitioners in these fields. What follows is a simple set of highlights, an outline if you will, of just some of the ways in which the virtue of temperance has been addressed in the field under different labels.

As described earlier, temperance is one of the six core virtues in the classification system proposed by Peterson and Seligman (2004). They defined temperance as the "positive traits that protect us from excess" (p. 431). They went on to elaborate that the virtue of temperance has four subcomponents. These contributing virtues are aimed at specific forms of excess that are well established in human behavior. They describe these excesses in the following ways:

> Hatred—against which forgiveness and mercy protect us. Arrogance— against which humility and modesty protect us. Short-term pleasure with long term costs—against which prudence protects us. And destabilizing emotional extremes of all sorts—against which self-regulation protects us. It is worth emphasizing that the strengths of temperance temper our activities rather than bringing them to a complete halt. (p. 431)

Even the most cursory examination of these definitions demonstrates how closely they align with the description of Level Five Leaders provided by Collins (2001). Linking the concept of temperate leadership to the ability to transform organizations from mediocre to sustained levels of superior performance makes it clear that these ancient ideals continue to demonstrate their power in the contemporary global marketplace, an environment that Confucius and Socrates could never have envisioned.

Similarly, the importance of self-regulation has provided a consistent focus of research and practice attention in psychology for many decades. Kilburg (2006) delivered a succinct overview of the history and much of the current practice of self-reflective leadership and self-regulation as applied to management in his book on executive wisdom. He called his approach the dance of reflective engagement. It involves a balance of being able to step back from the environment in which a leader is engaged and to examine carefully what is happening and what needs to happen. As such, when reflective activity occurs, it better prepares the executive to take the action best designed to produce desired effects. Kilburg documented empirical efforts to elaborate reflective practices and their effects on leadership development, as well as the complex and well-developed theories of action that have been created during the past 50 years of psychological, sociological, and philosophical work (Carver & Scheier, 1998; Schunk & Zimmerman, 1998).

Perhaps the best and most consistent research and practice activity that pertains to the virtue of temperance arises from the study of emotional and social intelligence. Dan Goleman (1995) intensified the flurry of scientific and practice work on emotional intelligence with his thoughtful book on the subject in which he stated:

> My concern is with . . . *emotional intelligence*: abilities such as being able to motivate oneself and persist in the face of frustration; to control impulse and delay gratification; to regulate one's moods and keep distress from swamping the ability to think; to empathize and to hope. (p. 34)

Later in the same book, Goleman described a curriculum for the development of what he called *emotional literacy*. It consisted of efforts to expand competency in the areas of

- Emotional self-awareness
- Managing emotions
- Harnessing emotions productively
- Empathy: reading emotions
- Handling relationships

Goleman et al. (2002) and Weisinger (1998) further elaborated the concept of emotional intelligence as applied to the processes of leadership. Each of these books provided many case examples, useful extensions of the core concepts initially outlined by Goleman (1995), as well as suggestions for practical improvements in these skills and abilities in work settings.

In recent years, portions of the research community in psychology have vigorously pursued the subject of emotional intelligence, and a considerable debate has emerged as to whether it constitutes a separate form of intelligence or is something else (Mayer, Salovey, & Caruso, 2004a). Considerable progress has been made on the development of reliable and valid measures of the phenomenon as well (Mayer, Salovey, & Caruso 2004b). Mayer and his colleagues (2004a) defined emotional intelligence as

> the capacity to reason about emotions, and of emotions to enhance thinking. It includes the abilities to accurately perceive emotions, to access and generate emotions so as to assist thought, to understand emotions and emotional knowledge, and to reflectively regulate emotions so as to promote emotional and intellectual growth. (p. 197)

Mayer and other scientists have made systematic efforts to provide empirical support for and against the hypothetical and conceptual arguments that enhanced psychology's interest in human emotions. For example, Côté and Miners (2006) reported an elaborate study of the relationship among emotional intelligence, cognitive intelligence, and job performance. They stated that "both emotional intelligence and cognitive intelligence were positively correlated with all three measures of job performance" that they used in the study (p. 15). In their conclusions, they emphasized the following:

> It is commonly believed that organizations that attract and retain the smartest people will have a competitive advantage because cognitive intelligence helps workers to process increasingly technical and large amounts of information. . . . Our results showing that emotional intelligence compensates for low cognitive intelligence suggest that this common belief represents just one approach to building a successful organization. Organizations can also be successful if they attract and retain people who have high emotional intelligence. (p. 23)

Goleman (2006) elaborated on his original ideas in a book titled *Social Intelligence* in which among other evidence, he summarized many recent studies that used functional magnetic resonance imaging to identify centers of activity and neuronal pathways in the brain that are involved in processing emotional and social information. These areas include the premotor, prefrontal, ventromedial, orbitofrontal, and anterior cingulate cortexes; and the insula; the hippocampus; the amygdala; and the brain stem. Each of these areas of the brain may also have many substructures that are involved in processing these types of data and providing feedback, motivational information, and influencing parameters for decisions and actions that individuals take. This recent work, which incorporates psychological, social, and neurophysiological research findings, strongly suggests that the ancient observations and teachings of Confucius and Socrates on the importance and function of the human virtue of temperance were absolutely accurate despite the absence of what we would call modern research evidence.

Finally, in an interesting elaboration of the research on human emotions, Fredrickson (1998, 2009) created an innovative explanatory framework to describe the functional purposes of human emotions. In essence, she restated the well-known phenomenon that emotion and emotional information take two major forms in human experience—positive and negative. In her classification system, Fredrickson (1998) identified four positive emotions—joy, interest, contentment, and love—and went on to suggest that the purpose of these experiences is to "broaden an individual's momentary thought–action repertoire, encouraging the individual to pursue a wider range of thoughts or actions than is typical. . . . Positive emotions broaden the scope of attention, thinking and action" (p. 315). She went on to suggest that positive emotions enable *resource building*:

> whether through play, exploration, or savoring and integrating, positive emotions promote discovery of novel and creative ideas and actions which in turn expand the individual's personal resources, whether they be physical resources (e.g., the ability to outmaneuver a predator), intellectual resources (e.g., a detailed cognitive map for way finding), or social resources (e.g., someone to turn to for help or compassion. (p. 315)

Negative emotions such as anger, shame, anxiety, and sadness, on the other hand, are thought to narrow the scope of attention, restrict the momentary thought–action repertoire, and promote defensive reactions such as fight, flight, or freeze responses. Negative emotional events and sequences are thought to have had and to continue to play extremely important roles in the Darwinian evolution of mammals, including primates, and in the creation of psychopathology and stress-related illnesses. Tugade and Fredrickson (2004) and Tugade, Fredrickson, and Barrett (2004) expanded on these core ideas and presented empirical research findings that support the hypothesis that positive emotional experiences can mediate and reduce the effects of negative emotional events and thus promote human resilience.

In recent studies of positive and negative emotions most relevant to work of business teams, Losada (1999) and Losada and Heaphy (2004) presented nonlinear dynamic models of positive and negative emotions and their effects on organizational performance. Their key empirical findings illustrated that high-performing business teams have significantly higher ratios of inquiry as opposed to advocacy exchanges, almost a six to one ratio of positive to negative emotional exchanges, and nearly twice as many references to others than the self compared with mediocre or poorly performing teams. They provided a meta-learning model in which they suggested that these high-performing business teams are able to create and use psychological and social space characterized by high levels of inquiry, positive emotional exchanges, and interactions with and references to the thoughts and feelings of others as opposed to the individual selves in the group. They suggest that such business environments buffer against and help manage the stresses of the workplace and improve the ability of teams to work together. They succinctly described meta-learning as "the ability of a team to dissolve attractors that close possibilities for effective action and to evolve attractors that open possibilities for effective action" (p. 751).

This brief overview of historical information and contemporary scientific findings clearly demonstrates that the subjects of temperance and reverence introduced twenty-five hundred years ago have continuously informed and guided the day-to-day lives of many people and the thoughts and actions of leaders. Results of contemporary studies on the performance of business organizations and business teams dramatically confirm the importance of incorporating the education, training, and enactment of virtue as fundamental components of leadership development programs and processes. Although there is little confirming information about the explicit contributions of reverence to the workplace, Losada and Heaphy's (2004) study demonstrated clearly that in business teams consistently performed more poorly when they were managed by people who most frequently advocated their own views rather than elicit and listen to those of others; engaged in negatively charged and, one could safely say, disrespectful emotional exchanges; and concentrated more on themselves than on their colleagues. Indeed, there was a significant pattern reported that as these, what could be called irreverent and intemperate, behaviors increased, performance decreased. The opposite pattern was equally true—namely, as reverence and temperance increased, performance increased. So with a little history and science under our belts, let's turn our attention briefly to how we can perhaps improve the practice of these behaviors in the context of a model of virtuous leadership.

VIRTUOUS LEADERSHIP AND THE STRATEGIC PRACTICE OF REVERENCE AND TEMPERANCE

Figure 4.2 (see Chapter 4, this volume) presents a model derived from my work on executive wisdom (Kilburg, 2006). In that figure, we saw the three core processes of executive work, discernment, decision making, and taking action linked together by process loops that emphasize that constant feedback and learning occur between each of these major elements. In addition, we saw additional feedback loops attached to each of the elements that contain either virtuous or corrupted forms of behavior. If the virtuous domain dominates the deliberations and work of a leader, the three core processes are most influenced by reverence, temperance, courage, justice, and wisdom. Similarly, if corrupted forms of behavior dominate, we witness leadership guided by irreverence, intemperance, cowardice, injustice, and ignorance or stupidity. Collins's (2001) study strongly supports the fundamentals of this model because its major finding is that organizations guided by virtuous leaders make a sustained transition from good to great, whereas enterprises led by leaders who do not consistently enact these virtues appear to be unable to sustain superior performance for substantial periods of time.

Figure 5.1 presents a slight revision of my model of the six domains that lead to the emergence of virtuous leadership (Kilburg, 2006). In the figure, the individual leader interacts with the systems of his or her organization through a third element, the mediated domain. That component of the organization comprises the relationships and the subsystems of the enterprise through which the executive intervenes in, on, and with the people that comprise the institution. The enterprise itself exchanges and engages with its external environment, which can differ radically depending on the portion of the

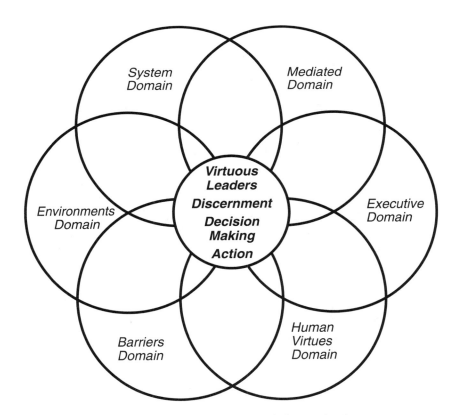

Figure 5.1. Domains influencing the emergence of virtuous leaders.

global economy in which it competes. The human virtues of the individual executive comprise the fifth domain, and in this model they refer primarily to the relative presence or absence of reverence, temperance, courage, wisdom, and justice or their corrupted opposites, the vices of irreverence, intemperance, cowardice, injustice, and ignorance. Finally, a barriers domain is denoted that comprises any element of the organization and its subsystems, the external environment, or the individual leader that might impede the emergence of virtuous leadership. It is in the subtle, endlessly complex interactions between these various domains that virtuous leadership is shaped and executed on a daily basis. It is this very complexity that accounts for the fact that any individual leader will have an extremely difficult time displaying every element of his or her virtue in every situation that she or he faces.

Figure 5.2 illustrates the model in slightly different terms. In the center of the Venn diagram, virtuous leadership, which is enacted through the core processes, arises out of the sustained action of the five core virtues of reverence, temperance, courage, justice, and wisdom. I believe that leadership without the persistent presence of all five of these virtues is doomed to systematically

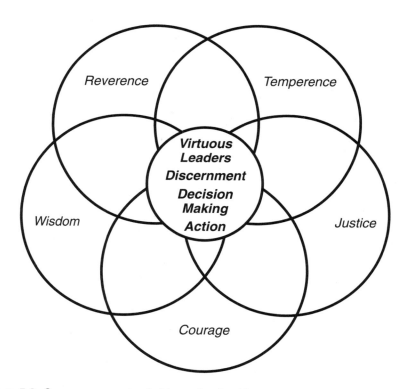

Figure 5.2. Core components of virtuous leadership.

underperform compared with leadership that concentrates on developing and using these forms of behavior on a daily basis. Losada and Heaphy's (2004) as well as Collins's (2001) studies would seem to provide strong preliminary empirical support for this proposition as well.

Figure 5.3 depicts still another view of virtuous leadership incorporating Fredrickson's (1998) model of positive and negative emotion in which the three core processes of discernment, decision making, and action taking interact with the feelings and thoughts of the executive. Those three processes, as well as the thoughts and feelings themselves, can vary around four core dimensions. They can be either intuitively or rationally derived and informed following Gary Klein's (1999, 2003) work on decision-making systems and processes in human organizations. Furthermore, the core processes can focus on positive or negative feelings within the model suggested by Fredrickson (1998, 2009) in which positive emotions are said to promote behaviors that broaden, build, and create new thought–action patterns in a person's life while negative emotions tend to focus, narrow, and elicit defensive or self-protective thought–action patterns.

Figure 5.3. Internal components of the three core processes of executive work.

At any given point in an individual leader's day, week, year, or life, these patterns of thoughts and feelings will always create or significantly influence how he or she tends to see the world, make decisions about what to do in response to it, and act as a result of the decisions that are made. I think it is also safe to say that every human being who serves in a leadership position has ingrained preferences for his or her behavior. These can be thought of as habits of mind, emotion, and behavior that create what are considered to be the most likely pathways for individuals to experience their lives. These pathways or preferences are informed by all of the elements of a person's individuality—race, gender, age, education, religion, marital status, sexual orientation, personality, and so on—and by his or her developmental history and experience. Leaders who achieve higher states of reflective awareness of these habitual pathways and thus learn to understand when, where, and how to use or move away from them in their roles as executives are more likely to be able more consistently to choose and enact effective decisions for their organizations (Kilburg, 2006).

Figures 5.4 and 5.5 present flow diagrams that attempt to specify more clearly what happens with regard to reverence and temperance in the actual practice of individual leaders. In these diagrams, patterns of positive and negative thoughts and feelings, which can be either rational or intuitive, give rise to actions that can also be positive or negative and rational or intuitive. In the center of each diagram is a depiction of the reflection and engagement model described by Kilburg (2006) in which individuals, it is hoped, give careful consideration to what they want to accomplish before they choose to say, not say, do, or not do something as a leader. Figures 5.4 and 5.5 both depict that the outcomes or consequences of such deliberations are informed internally by elements of diversity, plans, fantasies, and wishes, psychodynamics, and many other features of the inner personal landscapes of individual executives. As we saw in Figure 5.1, the external environment as well as all elements of the organization in which a leader works also can and most often do influence these processes in an individual person. In Figure 5.4, either reverent or irreverent behaviors result from the complex interaction of these internal and external processes. In Figure 5.5, either temperate or intemperate behaviors are enacted, which in turn usually represent a mixture of both restrained and expressed thoughts and feelings. In both figures, the enactment of virtuous or corrupted forms of behavior produce consequences in the environment and in the leader which further influence the internal patterns of thought, feeling, and likely behavioral responses.

The flow diagrams in Figures 5.4 and 5.5 suggest that under the best circumstances, any leader is able to sustain heightened and deepened states of self-awareness about his or her propensities to feel, think, and act in particular ways. If leaders are able to do so and to engage in the dance of reflective

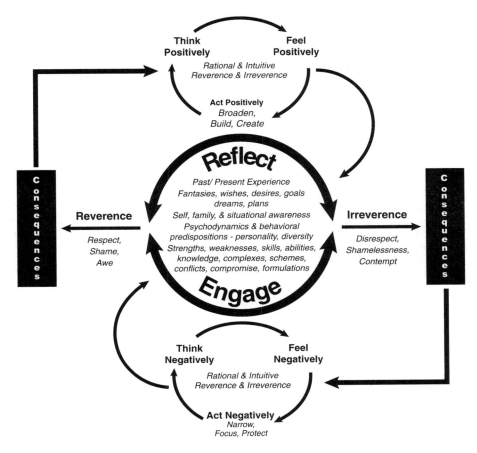

Figure 5.4. Internal components of the reverence process.

engagement in a sophisticated way, I suggest that these executives are most likely able to use reverence, irreverence, temperance, and intemperance in strategically useful ways to guide their organizations, executive teams, and leadership behavior. I believe that leaders who enact such strategic approaches to virtue are far more likely to sustain high levels of effectiveness and to continue to grow and develop their knowledge, skills, and abilities. To the extent that leaders are stuck in predispositions or deeply ingrained habits that are not virtuous, I believe we are likely to witness consistent problems with their performance, and their organizations are also likely to struggle as well.

The advantage of using flow charts to break down these components of behavior is that they allow us to see the various elements and how they might relate to each other to produce something like what we experience in our lives

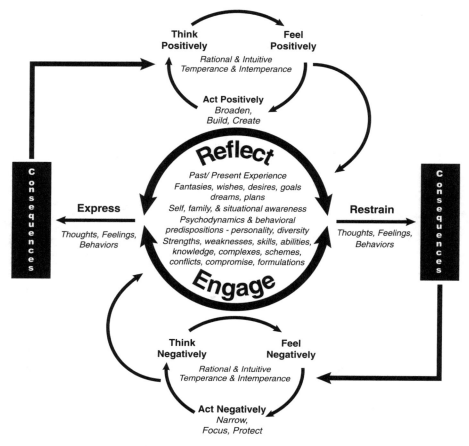

Figure 5.5. Internal components of the temperance process.

as leaders, followers, or consultants. In reality, as Goleman (2006) reported in his book on social intelligence, human beings are hardwired neurologically to perform some of these internal sequences in mere tenths of a millisecond. In other words, these patterns of thought, feeling, and action can take place faster than a person can blink an eye. So although the flow charts would seem to indicate that executives exert considerable, moment-to-moment influence on everything that they think, feel, and do, the reality is that, like most people, they simply act and react their way through most of their days. To be sure, the figures presented here also allow us to analyze these complex sequences into some of their component parts to examine them and to provide diagnostic and intervention suggestions for leaders and those who work to develop them. However, I want to be clear that I do not believe any individual executive has these processes and structures consistently under his or her conscious control.

I hope that these definitions of reverence and temperance and the figures presented here provide clearer pictures of how they fit into a larger model of virtuous leadership and perhaps how they work inside individual executives. We can now reasonably ask the following questions: Can we help executives to become both more aware of how they experience and enact these virtues? How might they become better practitioners of both of them? Exhibits 5.2 and 5.3 present structured inquiries on personal and leadership reverence and temperance. These questions are designed to lead anyone who spends time reflecting on them to gain an increased personal, interpersonal, and executive–organizational awareness of how they learned about reverence and temperance, how they practice them in their daily lives, and what effects their current patterns of behavior have on them, their organizations, and the people close to them. They also suggest structured ways in which a leader or leadership team could undertake an initiative to change how they behave in these dimensions. Anyone conducting these inquiries and attempting to implement a change based on the improved awareness the processes create is likely to improve their sensitivity to how these virtues or their corrupted alternatives influence their lives. If changes are attempted, the process is also likely to demonstrate that while individual acts of virtue are relatively easy to conceive and put into practice, enacting reverence and temperance routinely as part of leading a virtuous life as a leader is likely to be a somewhat more difficult and time-consuming endeavor.

It is always extremely useful to understand the personal history behind a given component of character or behavior. Through such explorations, you can discover unseen or unrecognized patterns, create roadmaps to better performance, and help others to better work with you in a wide variety of ways. Given the working definitions of leadership reverence and temperance provided in Exhibit 5.1, make some time to work through the list of questions in Exhibit 5.2 that focus on the evolution and practice of the virtue of reverence in your life and work. When you have done so, consider finding someone you know and trust with whom to share your findings and to discuss your observations.

The virtue of temperance has been defined as the practice of restraining oneself under conditions of desire or provocation. It can also be described as the ability to express oneself in a wise, measured, and effective way despite conditions of desire or provocation. In other words, when enacted well, the virtue of temperance enables any leader to find the right thoughts, feelings, words and deeds to respond to situations that confront him or her on a daily basis. At its core, temperance requires leaders to have the capacity to assess the world and then to create and enact a measured and effective response to it that serves both the individual and the organization he or she serves—see the definition provided in Exhibit 5.1. Take a few minutes to work through the list of questions in Exhibit 5.3 to get a better idea of your current patterns of personal

EXHIBIT 5.2
An Inquiry on Personal and Leadership Reverence

Introduction

It is always extremely useful to understand the personal history behind a given component of character or behavior. Through such explorations, you can discover unseen or unrecognized patterns, create roadmaps to better performance, and help others to better work with you in a wide variety of ways. Given the working definitions of leadership reverence and temperance provided in Exhibit 5.1, make some time to work through the following list of questions that focus on the evolution and practice of the virtue of reverence in your life and work. When you have done so, consider finding someone you know and trust with whom to share your findings and to discuss your observations.

Patterns of Reverence in Your Life

During the course of your personal and professional life to this point:
1. Who treated you with the most reverence?
2. Who treated you with the most irreverence?
3. What lessons did you learn from him/her, them?
4. In what situations were you treated the most reverently?
5. What happened; why do you think it happened; what were the effects on you; on others?
6. In what situations were you treated the most irreverently?
7. What happened; why do you think it happened; what were the effects on you; on others?
8. How did being treated in these ways—reverently or irreverently—make you feel; others feel?
9. How did being treated in these ways—reverently or irreverently—make you think and believe; others think and believe?
10. How did being treated in these ways—reverently or irreverently—make you behave; others behave?
11. Do you believe these experiences changed you permanently? How? Why? How do you know? Made you a different person? How? Why? How do you know?
12. Do any of those situations continue today?
13. What are your reactions when you find yourself in them?
14. Whom do you treat with the most reverence in your life?
15. Whom do you treat with the most irreverence in your life?
16. Whom and what do you most respect in your life? How? Why?
17. Whom and what do you most disrespect in your life? How? Why?
18. From whom did you learn the most about reverence in your life?
19. From whom did you learn the most about irreverence in your life?
20. How do you feel, think, and behave toward those individuals (questions 18 & 19) now?
21. What leaders in the past or present do you most revere? Why?
22. What leaders in the past or present do you least revere? Why?
23. Do you believe that you should make changes in whom and what you revere or treat irreverently? How could you do that? Why do you believe you should make those changes?
24. How do you think you might resist making such changes?
25. How could you manage such resistances and prevent them from inhibiting the changes you might try to make?
26. How will you know that you have made the changes to which you committed?
27. How can you ensure that these changes will be maintained?
28. From which leader(s) did you learn the most about reverence?

EXHIBIT 5.2
An Inquiry on Personal and Leadership Reverence   *(Continued)*

29. Do you believe that your family should make changes in whom and what it reveres or treats irreverently? How could it do that? Why do you believe it should make those changes?
30. How do you think your family might resist making such changes?
31. How could your family manage such resistances and prevent them from inhibiting the changes it might try to make?
32. How will you know that your family has made the changes to which it committed?
33. How can your family ensure that these changes will be maintained?
34. From which leader(s) did you learn the most about irreverence?
35. What does your organization most revere?
36. In your organization, whom do you treat with the most reverence? The most irreverence? How? Why?
37. In your organization, who treats you with the most reverence? The most irreverence? How? Why?
38. What does your organization/senior leadership team most revere? How? Why?
39. How does what is revered affect you and others in the organization positively? Negatively?
40. How does what is revered affect the organization's performance positively? Negatively?
41. Are there disconnects between what your organization/senior leadership team says it most reveres and what it actually does? How? Why? How do those disconnects affect the other members of the organization or its performance?
42. Does the organization/senior leadership team need to change what it reveres? How should that be done? Why?
43. How could you participate or lead the effort to make such changes?
44. What resistance do you expect to encounter if such changes are attempted?
45. How do you think you can most effectively manage such resistance?
46. How will you know that your organization/senior leadership team has made such changes?
47. How can your organization/senior leadership team ensure that these changes will be maintained?
48. What/whom does your organization/senior leadership team treat most irreverently? How? Why? (Ask yourself questions 39–47 with regard to what the organization/senior leadership team treats most irreverently.)

and leadership restraint and expression, how those patterns evolved historically, and what aspects of the patterns are working well or may need to be modified.

Similarly, Exercises 5.1 through 5.4 present a series of activities that can also improve your sensitivity to these virtues or their opposites and to develop further your capacity to practice reverence and temperance in strategic ways in your life. Exercise 5.1 provides a series of questions and thought experiments that, if followed, may well improve your individual capacity to experience and enact these virtues. In particular, the exercise encourages anyone who tries its various components to use his or her empathic skills and abilities to imagine how friends, family members, and colleagues both live their lives and use the virtues of reverence and temperance to help them live.

EXHIBIT 5.3
An Inquiry on Personal and Leadership Temperance

Introduction
The virtue of temperance has been defined as the practice of restraining oneself under conditions of desire or provocation. It can also be described as the ability to express oneself in a wise, measured, and effective way despite conditions of desire or provocation. In other words, when enacted well, the virtue of temperance enables any leader to find the right thoughts, feelings, words and deeds to respond to situations that confront him or her on a daily basis. At its core, temperance requires leaders to have the capacity to assess the world and then to create and enact a measured and effective response to it that serves both the individual and the organization s/he serves—see the definition provided in Exhibit 5.1. Take a few minutes to work through the following list of questions to get a better idea of your current patterns of personal and leadership restraint and expression, how those patterns evolved historically, and what aspects of the patterns are working well or may need to be modified.

Questions on Temperance
1. Are you able to identify easily the following emotional states in yourself?
   - Joyful
   - Loving
   - Contented
   - Sexually aroused
   - Curious
   - Angry
   - Sad
   - Ashamed or guilty
   - Anxious
   - Disgusted
2. Are you able to identify easily those emotional states in others?
3. How do you experience those emotional states psychologically?
4. How do you experience those emotional states physically?
5. How do you most typically express those emotions?
   - When you are by yourself?
   - When you are with family members?
   - When you are with friends that you trust?
   - When you are with acquaintances you know but may not trust?
   - When you are with colleagues at work whom you trust?
   - When you are with colleagues at work whom you know but may not trust?
   - When you are with strangers in social settings?
   - When you are with strangers in work settings?
6. How do you most typically restrain the expression of those emotions?
   - When you are by yourself?
   - When you are with family members?
   - When you are with friends that you trust?
   - When you are with acquaintances you know but may not trust?
   - When you are with colleagues at work whom you trust?
   - When you are with colleagues at work whom you know but may not trust?
   - When you are with strangers in social settings?
   - When you are with strangers in work settings?

EXHIBIT 5.3
An Inquiry on Personal and Leadership Temperance *(Continued)*

7. Are the members of your family able to identify easily the following emotional states in themselves?
   - Joyful
   - Loving
   - Contented
   - Sexually aroused
   - Curious
   - Angry
   - Sad
   - Ashamed or guilty
   - Anxious
   - Disgusted

8. Are the members of your family able to identify those emotional states in others?

9. How do your family members experience those emotional states psychologically?

10. How does your family experience those emotional states physically?

11. How do the members of your family typically express these emotional states when they are with each other? With others outside the family?

12. How do the members of your family typically restrain the expression of these emotional states when they are with each other? With others outside the family?

13. What would the behaviors involved in your expression or restraint look like to those who know you well?

14. What would the behaviors involved in your expression or restraint look like to those who do not know you well?

15. What would the behaviors involved in your expression or restraint look like to those with whom you work—peers and colleagues, subordinates, supervisors?

16. Do these expressions or restraints change when the person or group you are interacting with is of a different race, gender, age, religious background, ethnic origin, marital status, or sexual orientation?

17. With whom is it easiest to express yourself?

18. With whom do you restrain yourself the most?

19. Why do you think these patterns exist?

20. From whom did you learn the most about emotional expression or restraint?

21. What were the major lessons that you learned from these mentors?

22. Do those lessons still influence your behavior today?

23. Are those lessons functional, constructive, and helpful or are they dysfunctional, destructive, and hurtful to you?

24. What were the major patterns of emotional expression and restraint in your family of origin?

25. Have you ever tried to consciously change the way you express or restrain your emotions? Did you succeed or fail? How and why do you think you succeeded or failed?

26. From whom do you most often solicit feedback or other sources of evaluation about how you express or restrain yourself?

27. Does that feedback assist you when you need it?

(continues)

EXHIBIT 5.3
An Inquiry on Personal and Leadership Temperance   *(Continued)*

28. Does that feedback hinder your development?
29. Do you consciously practice the way in which you express or restrain yourself emotionally?
30. Has your work group or leadership team ever discussed their past or current patterns of emotional expression or restraint?
31. Has your work group or leadership team ever identified constructive or destructive patterns of emotional expression or restrain in which they engage?
32. Has your work group or leadership team ever tried to establish norms or behavioral expectations for the expression or restraint of emotions or thoughts?
33. Does your work group periodically or routinely evaluate how it performs in the arena of expression of thoughts and emotions?
34. Has your work group or leadership team ever been able to change the way in which it expresses thoughts or emotions? How and why did it succeed?
35. Has your work group or leadership team ever tried and failed to change the way in which it expresses thoughts or emotions? How and why did it fail?
36. If you had the authority to change any one thing in how your work group or leadership team expresses or restrains the expression of emotion and thought, what would that be? What do you believe others would want to change in the group or team?
37. Who was/is the most effective person at practicing strategic temperance you ever met?
38. Who was/is the most effective leader at practicing strategic intemperance you ever met?

You can take several additional steps to further your personal and professional understanding and capacity to express or restrain yourself. Consider the following:

- Sit down with someone who knows you well and whom you know well and work through the above list of questions together. Solicit their honest and tactful opinions about yourself and try to provide yours to him/her.
- Pick one of the emotions or a pattern of expression or restraint that you would like to improve upon and create a homework assignment for yourself such as:
  a. Count the number of times in a day, week, or month that you observe yourself engaging in the pattern.
  b. Create a new or different way of expressing or restraining the emotion or the pattern.
  c. Practice the old pattern or way of expression or restraint in an exaggerated fashion with a friend or trusted colleague.
  d. Practice the new pattern or way of expression or restraint with a trusted friend or colleague.
  e. Once you feel confident with the new pattern, take it to work with you and try it out.
  f. Ask for feedback on your efforts from colleagues, superiors, or subordinates.

EXERCISE 5.1
Improving Your Capacity for Reverence and Temperance

Introduction

To strategically enact the virtues of reverence and temperance, one must be clear that each requires an acute sensitivity to emotion in oneself and others. If a person wants or needs to become more effectively reverent or temperate in life, perhaps the single best step to take to begin such improvements is to work to increase sensitivity to emotions in the self through the practice of self-awareness and sensitivity to emotions in others through the practice of empathy. Consider undertaking one or more of the following activities to broaden the foundation for your use of reverence and temperance in your life.

Activities to Consider

1. Take some time and reflect on when you feel awe, respect, or shame in your life.

2. Why should you feel awe, respect, and shame in those situations or with or about those individuals, groups, or organizations?

3. Who should feel awe, respect, and shame in those situations or with or about those individuals, groups, or organizations?

4. Where should you feel awe, respect, and shame in those situations or with or about those individuals, groups, or organizations?

5. When should you feel awe, respect, and shame in those situations or with or about those individuals, groups, or organizations?

6. How do you experience awe, respect, and shame in those situations or with or about those individuals, groups, or organizations? How do you know you are having such emotional experiences?

7. Do you struggle with treating others with respect and find yourself routinely comparing yourself to others or to idealized standards or role models, critical of yourself or others more than is warranted, condemning yourself or others, or treating yourself or others contemptuously? Are you routinely suspicious, distrustful, skeptical, or cynical of other individuals, groups, organizations? How does such behavior manifest in your life? What effects does it have on you and your capacity to relate to other people, groups, or organizations?

8. Is there someone, a group, or an organization that inspires awe or disgust in you? Who or what does so? How do you know that this is the case?

9. Is there a person, a group, or an organization that you treat with the utmost respect or contempt? Who or what generates such responses from you? How do you know that this is the case?

(continues)

10. Is there a thought, feeling, behavior, person, situation, activity, group, or organization that generates high levels of shame or shamelessness in you? Who or what generates such responses from you? How do you know that this is the case?

11. If you find the foregoing steps useful, take some additional time and reflect on when and with whom you feel the following emotional states:
    - Curiosity or interest
    - Joy
    - Surprise
    - Sexual arousal
    - Anxiety
    - Contentment
    - Guilt
    - Sadness
    - Anger
    - Dissmell
    - Disgust
    - Contempt
    - Envy
    - Jealousy
    - Pride
    - Love
    - Affection
    - Relief
    - Hope
    - Compassion (empathy/sympathy)
    - Aesthetic emotions (beauty, wonder)

12. Why do you think you have those feelings in those situations or with or about those individuals, groups, or organizations?

13. Who should have those feelings in those situations or with or about those individuals, groups, or organizations?

14. Where should you have those feelings in those situations or with or about those individuals, groups, or organizations?

15. When should you have those feelings in those situations or with or about those individuals, groups, or organizations?

16. How do you experience those feelings in those situations or with or about those individuals, groups, or organizations? How do you know you are having such emotional experiences?

17. With whom, about what, or in what situations are you most likely to fight in your life?

EXERCISE 5.1
Improving Your Capacity for Reverence and Temperance   *(Continued)*

18. From whom, what, or in what situations are you most likely to flee in your life?

19. With whom, about what, or in what situations are you most likely to freeze in your life?

20. Think about a person whom you know well and like a lot. Make some time and try to imagine what that person's life is like on a daily basis. What is important to him or her? What does this person like, hate, spend time doing, avoid?

21. Think about the way in which that person expresses reverence and temperance. What or whom does this person revere, treat with respect, hold in awe, disrespect, hold in contempt?

22. Think about how that person might experience those other emotions identified in step 11. Are there situations, events, people, groups, or organizations that you know for certain generate those feeling states in that person? Are there other situations, events, people, groups, or organizations that you can imagine might generate those feeling states in that person?

23. Why do you think he or she has those feelings in those situations or with or about those individuals, groups, or organizations?

24. Where should he or she have those feelings in those situations or with or about those individuals, groups, or organizations?

25. When should he or she have those feelings in those situations or with or about those individuals, groups, or organizations?

26. With whom, about what, or in what situations is that person most likely to fight in his or her life?

27. From whom, what, or in what situations is that person most likely to flee in his or her life?

28. With whom, about what, or in which situations is that person most likely to freeze in his or her life?

29. How do you imagine he or she experiences those feelings in those situations or with or about those individuals, groups, or organizations? How would you know he or she is having such emotional experiences?

30. Try a similar exercise for a group that is different from you in some major aspect of diversity—race, ethnicity, age, gender, sexual orientation, religion, education, and so on.

Exercise 5.2 encourages you to conduct the inquiries provided in Exhibits 5.2 and 5.3 as a starting point. It then provides a set of suggestions for activities you can undertake to try to practice, change, or experience how you use these virtues in your life. The suggestions also include the possibility of involving others whom you trust in the processes of learning about and trying to improve your ability to be reverent and temperate.

Exercise 5.3 focuses on how a leadership or business team could discuss and begin to practice these virtues more consciously and conscientiously in team members' daily interactions. It suggests that teams set aside time to explore the topic either in regular or specially designed meetings. Teams can use the inquiries in Exhibits 5.2 and 5.3 and Exercises 5.1 and 5.2 to start the discussions by encouraging individual explorations of these virtues. The exercise also provides a set of systematic suggestions for how a group might try to change how they enact reverence and temperance together.

Finally, Exercise 5.4 provides an opportunity to deepen your understanding of events, people, or situations that are most likely to lead you to behave irreverently or intemperately in your life. It begins with a request that you try to remember such occurrences in some detail and then to examine how such history and experiences may well have contributed to patterns of behavior in your life. It culminates in a framework that asks what changes you might want to try to make in these patterns and then takes you back to the systematic steps to guide change efforts provided in Exercise 5.2.

A SHORT RECONSIDERATION OF THE OPENING CASE STUDIES

Now that we have explored some history, research, and important concepts regarding the practice of reverence and temperance by leaders, let's return briefly to our opening case studies in which Bill and Linda were experienced by key subordinates as behaving in ways that, if not modified, were likely to lead to the departure of people on whom they depended extensively. The fact that reverence and temperance have been studied, advocated, and practiced by leaders for thousands of years speaks clearly to the timeless importance of the contribution they make to the effectiveness of any executive's performance. As we saw in these case studies, despite the ready availability of considerable information regarding reverence and temperance, neither Linda nor Bill were nearly as competent as they needed to be in those domains. Even worse, they were both struggling severely with a fundamental lack of awareness of the impact of their irreverence and intemperance on their colleagues and their organizations.

In my coaching of Lily and Jim, I focused on first helping them be concretely aware of the type of behavior that was causing problems for them

EXERCISE 5.2
Improving Your Practice of Reverence and Temperance

Introduction
Thousands of years of human history demonstrate that individuals can be taught how to behave virtuously and can learn how to improve their performance in these areas when they are motivated to do so. If you are interested in conducting some experiments to improve aspects of your virtue, consider undertaking one or more of the activities outlined here.

Activities to Consider and Implement

1. Complete the inquiries on reverence and temperance provided in Exhibits 5.2 and 5.3 in this chapter.

2. Were there any specific patterns, events, situations, people, issues, problems, or stories that drew your attention more than others? Why do you think that these items have such power and intensity for you?

3. As a result of your considerations, are there emotions, thoughts, or behaviors that you believe you might like to express or restrain more strategically? Which ones? Why those? How do you believe such expression or restraint would better help you, others, your work group or executive team, your family, your organization, your community? With whom do you want to express or restrain those thoughts, emotions, or behaviors? When or in what situations do you want to express or restrain those thoughts, emotions, or behaviors? Where do you want to express or restrain those thoughts, emotions, or behaviors? Why do you want to express or restrain those thoughts, emotions, or behaviors?

4. Identify someone who knows you well and discuss what you learned as a result of completing the inquiries.

5. To improve your capacity to enact the virtue of temperance, pick one of the emotions, thoughts, or behaviors that you would like to strategically express or restrain more effectively. Which one did you pick? Why? How do you believe such expression or restraint would better help you, others, your workgroup or executive team, your family, your organization, your community? With whom do you want to express or restrain those thoughts, emotions, or behaviors? When or in what situations do you want to express or restrain those thoughts, emotions, or behaviors? Where do you want to express or restrain those thoughts, emotions, or behaviors? Why do you want to express or restrain those thoughts, emotions, or behaviors?

6. Before you undertake any effort to initiate the changes, take some time and ask yourself, trusted other(s), or a coach if one is available to you what barriers might be in the way of successful implementation. If you have trouble imagining any barriers, then take some time and imagine that you have failed to do what you set out to do. Ask yourself what might have gone wrong. Make a list of the ideas you produce from this discussion.

(continues)

7. Take some time to rank order the ideas from most to least likely to interfere with implementing your improvements.

8. Consider what steps you could take to minimize the likelihood that the top three barriers will interfere with your implementation plan(s).

9. Establish one or two goals for you on the change(s) you want to undertake. Make the goals specific, measurable, achievable, reinforceable, timely, and capable of engaging the support of others.

10. Identify how you will measure or otherwise obtain feedback that will tell you if you are making progress.

11. Implement your plan(s).

12. Solicit regular feedback on what you are trying to accomplish and discuss what you learn and experience with trusted others or a coach if you have one available to you.

13. After a reasonable period of time, conduct a formal discussion with trusted others or a coach if you have one available to you to determine how you have done and the impact that the change(s) have made on you, a group, your family, a leadership team, or the organization as a whole. If any, what additional steps or refinements do you want to make, and what specific activities individual members of any leadership group should undertake to continue to improve?

14. If you are so motivated, pick another change that you want to make and repeat the process.

15. To improve your capacity to enact the virtue of reverence, pick a person, group, organization, or situation to respond to in your world with whom or which you want to enhance your ability to feel and strategically enact or express respect, shame, or awe or restrain disrespect, shamelessness, or contempt based on your judgment of what would be most courageous, just, and wise.

16. Which one did you pick? Why? How do you believe such expression or restraint would better help you, others, your work group or executive team, your family, your organization, your community? With whom do you want to express reverence or restrain irreverence? When or in what situations do you want to express reverence or restrain irreverence? Where do you want to express reverence or restrain irreverence? Why do you want to express reverence or restrain irreverence?

17. Before you undertake any effort to initiate the changes, take some time and ask yourself and trusted other(s) or a coach if one is available to you what barriers might be in the way of successful implementation. If you have trouble imagining any barriers, then take some time and imagine that you have failed to do what you set out to do. Ask yourself what might have gone wrong. Make a list of the ideas you produce from this discussion.

18. Take some time to rank order the ideas from most to least likely to interfere with implementing your improvements.

19. Consider what steps you could take to minimize the likelihood that the top three barriers will interfere with your implementation plan(s).

21. Establish one or two goals for you on the change(s) you want to undertake. Make the goals specific, measurable, achievable, reinforceable, timely and capable of engaging the support of others.

22. Identify how you will measure or otherwise obtain feedback that will tell you if you are making progress.

23. Implement your plan(s).

24. Solicit regular feedback on what you are trying to accomplish and discuss what you learn and experience with trusted others or a coach if you have one available to you.

25. After a reasonable period of time, conduct a formal discussion with trusted others or a coach if you have one available to you to determine how you have done, the impact that the change(s) have made on you, a group, your family, a leadership team, or the organization as a whole. What additional steps or refinements, if any, do you want to make, and what specific activities should individual members of any leadership group undertake to continue to improve?

26. If you are so motivated, pick another change that you want to make and repeat the process.

and then proceeded to push them to extend their understanding of the consequences. In other words, I used the models outlined in Figures 5.1 through 5.5 to guide my own explorations of their situations and to help illuminate what was happening in and to them as they described their experiences of being treated irreverently and intemperately. In addition, I tried to make them create specific estimates of the frequency with which they encountered the corrupted behaviors and encouraged them to collect data on just how often those patterns were being experienced.

I also suggested that they needed to be clear with themselves about what their preferences were with regard to the amount of irreverence and intemperance they could endure in their relationships with their bosses. Such estimates and requests specifically confronted them with the reality that no leader is perfectly virtuous in their lives as well as the fact that Bill and Linda at times might well have justifiable reasons to behave in intemperate

EXERCISE 5.3
Improving the Practice of Reverence and Temperance
in Your Leadership Team

Introduction

Currently, the research literature is extremely explicit on the subject of performance improvement in virtually every domain of human ability that has been studied. The three major steps that anyone or any group can take to improve performance are to establish a set of goals or aspirations, intensively practice the skill or ability that is the target of improvement over time, and obtain expert feedback on actual performance. The following exercise is designed to help your leadership team improve its awareness of how it is practicing the virtues of reverence and temperance and to identify and initiate such changes that the members of the group believe need to be made.

Activities

1. Start with a discussion of the virtues of reverence and temperance at one of your regular executive team meetings. Ask yourselves whether you are satisfied with how your team and the other members of the organization are practicing those virtues and whether improvements could be made that would help the group and the enterprise. If the consensus is that improvements could help, try the following steps.

2. Have each member of the group complete the inquiries on reverence and temperance provided in Exhibits 5.2 and 5.3 in this chapter.

3. Take some formal time at a regular executive team meeting to discuss what the members of the group learned as a result of completing the inquiries.

4. Ask each other whether there are any lessons that could be generalized from the discussion. Write down those lessons and disseminate them to the group after the meeting.

5. Ask whether there is collective impression or sense that there is a need to make improvements in how the individuals, group, or organization practices reverence and temperance.

6. Ask the group to return to a follow-up meeting during which they will be expected to make suggestions for what these improvements should be and how they should be made. When the group meets to have the discussion, have each member take a turn and make one suggestion that he or she has devised. Keep a list of the suggestions made. Continue to go around the group until each member's list is exhausted. If someone else has made the same suggestion, go on to express the next original idea on your list. Send the full list to the members of the group and have each of them try to organize the list into categories that make sense.

7. At the next group meeting, review the categories that have been created and try to make one coherent classification of the suggestions. Discuss your findings.

8. Make a determination about which of the suggestions you would like to implement first, and then plan how you will try to do so.

9. Before you undertake any effort to initiate the changes, take some time and ask each other what barriers might be in the way of successful implementation. If you have trouble imagining any barriers, then take some time and imagine that you have failed to do what you set out to do. Ask yourselves what might have gone wrong. Make a list of the ideas you produce from this discussion.

10. Take some time to rank order the ideas from most to least likely to interfere with implementing your improvements.

11. Discuss what steps you could take to minimize the likelihood that the top three barriers will interfere with your implementation plan(s).

12. Establish one or two goals for your group on the change(s) you want to undertake. Make the goals specific, measurable, achievable, reinforceable, timely, and capable of engaging the support of others.

13. Identify how you will measure or otherwise obtain feedback that will tell your team whether you are making progress.

14. Implement your plan(s).

15. Solicit regular feedback from each other and those outside of the group on what you are trying to accomplish and discuss what you learn and experience together.

16. After a reasonable period of time, conduct a formal discussion at one of your regular meetings to determine how you have done, the impact that the change(s) have made on the individuals in the group, the team itself, and the organization as a whole, if any, what additional steps or refinements you want to make, and what specific activities individual members of the group might undertake to continue to improve.

17. If you are so motivated, pick another change that you want to make and repeat the process.

18. If you do not want to take the time during regular meetings to conduct this process, consider organizing a retreat for a day or two that will focus the attention and energy of the entire group on these activities.

19. If you do not have confidence that your team will be able to conduct the exercise without assistance, consider hiring a professional facilitator or consultant to help manage the processes and ensure that you will all follow through on the processes.

20. Do not be afraid to improvise, add steps, or change anything identified in this exercise that will help your team improve its capacity to express and experience reverence and temperance.

EXERCISE 5.4
Exploring Your Hot Buttons and Triggers

Introduction

All people have experiences in their lives that predispose them to react strongly to situations, people, events, and behaviors in others. When these patterns are deeply ingrained, they can serve as hot buttons that almost automatically trigger feelings, thoughts, and behaviors in response to them. At their worst, these patterns can result in extreme reactions that cause significant damage to relationships, reputations, careers, families, executive and work teams, and organizations. To improve our ability to manage our responses to such hot buttons, it is vital to have a better sense of what they are and how they might work. If you are interested in pursuing such knowledge, consider undertaking the following activities.

Suggested Activities

1. Find a quiet place and time when you will not be disturbed for a while, say 30 to 60 minutes. Take a few deep breaths and put yourself in mood to consider some people, scenes, and events in your life. Taking each in turn, try to remember a time, place, or situation when you
    - lost your temper and yelled at or hit someone
    - had someone lose their temper at you and yelled at or hit you
    - cried over a loss or injury
    - caused someone to cry because of a loss or injury
    - felt humiliated or ashamed
    - caused someone to feel humiliated or ashamed
    - felt guilty
    - caused someone to feel guilty
    - became extremely frightened
    - caused someone to become extremely frightened
    - found yourself insanely envious of someone
    - found yourself insanely jealous of someone
    - caused someone to be envious of you
    - caused someone to be jealous of you
    - experienced extreme happiness or joy
    - caused someone else to be extremely happy or joyous
    - became disgusted to the point of nausea
    - caused someone to be disgusted to the point of nausea
    - felt overwhelmingly sexual
    - caused someone to feel overwhelmingly sexual
    - really wanted to compete with someone or for something
    - felt severely wounded by the words or actions of someone
    - severely wounded someone else by your words or actions
    - experienced something that really surprised you
    - really surprised someone else

2. In these situations, who was involved? What happened? When did it occur? Where did it happen? What led up to the situation or event? What were the consequences? How did it change you or others? What predisposition, pattern, or trigger did it create for you?

EXERCISE 5.4
Exploring Your Hot Buttons and Triggers   *(Continued)*

3. Do these memories and events still inform your relationships, interests, behaviors, feelings, thoughts, or patterns of what you like or what you tend to avoid?

4. In your present personal or work life, what situations, types of events, patterns of relating, individual people, groups, organizational or environmental issues stimulate the same kinds of patterns or reactions in you?

5. Are there any changes you might like to make in your thoughts, feelings, or behaviors as a result of this reflection? If yes, consider undertaking Exercise 5.2 with this change as the target or goal of your work.

or irreverent ways. In particular, when the effectiveness of their organization's performance is threatened by poor work on the part of their teams or key colleagues, each of them is naturally going to feel anxious, angry, and perhaps publicly embarrassed. Even the anticipation of such negative emotional states may lead to requests for improved performance, threats of consequences if goals are not met, or in some cases demonstrations of disappointment or clear anger over the potential of overt failure of subordinates. Indeed, both Lily and Jim needed to become better practitioners of these virtues with their own subordinates, which subsequent coaching sessions addressed.

In the end, Lily and Jim understood that they both had an obligation to talk frankly with their colleagues about the impact that their outbursts and lack of control had on them and others in these organizations. Creating such dialogues requires both courage and wisdom, two additional and exceedingly complex virtues themselves. However, if they could or would not provide the feedback to Bill and Linda, make clear what their needs and preferences were for change, and express a willingness to work constructively with their bosses on these developments, the likelihood that their lives would improve was next to zero. Without such dialogues and in the absence of any other disconfirming information, it is nearly impossible for anyone to change their behavior.

Indeed, in feedback-free environments, every person most often merely continues to do what comes naturally until or unless we encounter opposition, pressure, adverse feedback, or demands for change. Encountering such resistance to our natural patterns of behavior can be challenging at best and extremely painful at worst. However, creating such tensions for leaders can ultimately improve their ability to perform. Imagine world-class athletes trying to improve their performance without the objective measures provided by stopwatches and officials with tapes and video cameras. It simply cannot be done. The problem for senior executives inside their organizations is that their power and prestige often enable them to create self-deluding, self-fueling, defensive operations that cover up and deny problems with their performance (Argyris, 1990, 1993). It takes time, energy, and extraordinary commitment on the part of everyone on a leadership team to improve. As Collins's (2001) study demonstrated, such changes can take considerable time to accomplish.

In my experience, it is not all that unusual to encounter people in leadership positions who do not receive developmentally oriented feedback on a regular basis. In fact, many organizations appear to have created entire cultures that can be described as "no news or bad news" environments. In such organizations, as long as a person produces in accordance with expectations that may or may not be made explicit, he or she is more or less free to continue to think, feel, and behave in any way that seems natural to them. However, when numbers are not produced or when the grapevine begins to express reservations about a leader's behavior, pressure may build informally for someone to speak out to the affected person. In the worst of these types of enterprises, such feedback arrives only when a leader who has been struggling is asked to leave the organization. However, it is also the case that in many instances in today's business world, many executives simply do not wait for development to happen to or for them. In the best of circumstances, leaders take the responsibility for their own growth extremely seriously and become the primary source of motivation for constructive change in their lives. I have had the privilege of working with many executives who take the examples set by historical figures such as Confucius, Socrates, Franklin, Washington, Lincoln, and Gandhi extremely seriously and establish their own strategic agendas for lifelong change. In my experience, those types of leaders also are increasingly understanding that such development requires a commitment to the study and practice of virtues such as reverence and temperance.

In summary, I believe that if we stood back from our active engagement as leaders, or as coaches and developers of leaders, and asked ourselves what we think constitutes world-class executive performance, we would inevitably find ourselves considering that the same time-tested qualities of character that were intimately described by our illustrious ancients, Confucius and Socrates, were intimately entwined in the daily lives of leaders achieving in such a fashion. Furthermore, careful reading of virtually any era of history would demonstrate that the times when virtuous leadership was absent in a country, empire, or organization were often dark and dangerous for their members or citizens. The opposite is equally true. The periods of human history in which *Homo sapiens* progressed smoothly and accomplished a great deal were most often those in which leaders tried and succeeded to behave virtuously on a daily basis. If leaders consistently demonstrate these character traits, then people who follow them are better able to do the same themselves, and they expect more from each other.

6

THE EVOLUTION OF EXECUTIVE
CONSCIENCE AND THE PRACTICE
OF JUSTICE

INTRODUCTION

On June 19, 2008, evening news shows on major media outlets in the United States featured a story in which two corporate hedge-fund managers, Matthew Tannin and Ralph Cioffi, at the soon-to-be-defunct financial firm of Bear Stearns were arrested by agents of the Federal Bureau of Investigation and charged with nine counts of securities fraud, wire fraud, and conspiracy (Goldstein & Henry, 2008). At their arraignment, federal prosecutors alleged that in early 2007, they knew that their funds, which were based on mortgage-backed derivative securities, were all but worthless. Internal e-mail communications between the individuals clearly stated that they understood the precarious position of their operations and yet despite their legal, professional, and moral obligations to inform their investors, they continued to make extensive public statements that the funds were sound, performing well, and provided significant additional growth potential. As they attempted to entice existing and potential customers to put more money into their fund, at least one of the individuals was alleged to have withdrawn several million dollars of his own money from the same investment pool.

Although Tannin and Cioffi were subsequently acquitted in federal court, this story completed yet another tawdry chapter in the ethical and moral history of Wall Street financial firms. Given the lessons of the past 25 years, one would think that leaders in these organizations would be extensively trained and personally prepared to address such fundamental moral problems when they arise in contemporary enterprises. Headlines and scientific studies suggest that despite the creation of extensive additional federal regulatory burdens through requirements of the Sarbanes–Oxley Act, any number of business leaders continue to make decisions and take actions that demonstrate astounding lapses in moral reasoning and judgment. The 2010 federal reforms aimed at tightening financial regulation represent further attempts to bring more ethical discipline to the U.S. financial community.

As I finish writing this book, the entire global economy anxiously vibrates each day as the intermediate and longer term implications of the extraordinary misjudgments and misdeeds of the subprime mortgage industry in the United States and Europe continue to emerge and undermine the collective security of many nations and billions of people. Anyone with a normally reflective mind who examines such events asks such logical questions as: How did the internal controls of so many successful financial institutions fail simultaneously? Why did the regulatory structures of so many governments fail to detect and take constructive action to minimize the negative impacts of such poor corporate strategies and decisions? In all of the board rooms, executive suites, governmental offices and hearing rooms, why were the people with active consciences and the capacity for advanced moral reasoning not asking extremely hard questions about what these organizations were doing? Once again, most of us who were not directly involved with these organizations or their decision-making processes end up simply shaking our heads in a form of dysphoric wonderment and asking how this latest example of extensive, collective leadership folly will be resolved. However, as discussed in detail in Chapter 3, we know implicitly and explicitly that this latest chapter will not represent the end of such incompetent and negligent leadership. Indeed, deep down, I believe most of us intuitively understand that leaders and the processes through which they direct their organizations possess inherent flaws and challenges that often create the opportunity for faulty moral reasoning, individual and organizational corruption, and illegal action.

The purposes of this chapter are to provide two brief historical vignettes illustrating both moral and immoral leadership, succinctly explore the concepts that moral philosophers and other scholars have given us to examine various aspects of these challenges, and finally to review a set of tools and methods that may help leaders and those who develop them address how they can more reliably emerge as moral agents in their organizations as they struggle to live and direct their enterprises in and through the virtue of justice.

EXAMPLES OF MORAL AND AMORAL LEADERSHIP

What follows are two radically different historical case studies. The first summarizes what occurred between two high school students who found themselves in the middle of the busing implementation process during the desegregation of South Boston High School. The second is a hypothetical examination of the conversations that may have occurred between the top leaders of Enron Corporation as they attempted to manage the financial and media crisis that led to the destruction of that company. They are presented as illustrations of range of processes of moral reasoning in which human beings sometimes engage and as a method to introduce how leaders need to become better practitioners of the complex virtue of justice.

South Boston High School

Robert Coles (2000) told a story about a young White woman named Alice who attended South Boston High School during the period in which court-ordered busing was being used to solve long-standing segregation problems in the city school system. The tale was reported by an African American student named Mary Ann whom Coles had gotten to know as part of his research efforts aimed at trying to understand what was happening with and to the children who were at the epicenter of society's efforts to correct centuries of abusive, segregationist education policies.

Coles (2000) described Mary Ann as "a remarkably stoic and farsighted person who kept telling me she could 'understand' the evident anger of some of the white people of the city. 'It's new and they're scared,' she said tersely" (p. 220). Approximately 4 months into her 1st year at the high school, Mary Ann's grandmother, a central figure in her emotional and family life, died suddenly. Mary Ann began a protracted grieving process, and as part of that experience, she started to wear black clothing to school every day. Mary Ann described her exchanges with Alice this way:

> A girl came up to me in the hall; they never talk to me, and a lot of times they whisper swearwords, so I was surprised. She asked if I "was alright." I said yes, sure. She said she noticed I was wearing black all of the time. I said yes, my grandma died. She said she was sorry. Then she told me her father died a year ago, and she knew what I was going through. It was nice of her. (p. 221)

Alice continued to talk to Mary Ann in school despite the considerable social pressures not to do so. She sent Mary Ann a sympathy card and in their discussions told her that she was sorry for the problems that had been occurring at the school. Alice told her that she regretted her initial outspoken disapproval of the integration project. Mary Ann told Coles,

She told me she owes us [the African American students] an "act of contrition," and I didn't know what she was talking about. So I asked her, and she said the priest told her, if you do something, and you figure out it's wrong, then you should recognize that you've made your error, and try to make up for it in some way. You face up to what you've done and pray you won't do it again. I think that's why she sent the card to us, "an act of contrition." (Coles, 2000, pp. 221–222)

Coles went on to suggest that the White, predominantly Catholic students were familiar with contrition as enacting regret; it is

something priests say when they want you to apologize and admit you've made a mistake. For the black child "contrition" conveyed a certain elusive mystery. "I think it means you've done something that can get you in trouble, but whether you meant to do the wrong thing, that's up to God to decide, so you can't be sure, and He's the one who is watching and He knows." (Coles, 2000, p. 222)

In his later attempts to comprehend his experiences with these young people more completely, Coles frequently discussed them with the legendary psychoanalyst Erik Erikson. His reply to Coles was as follows:

Maybe we should take a step back. Maybe we should stop (only for a few minutes!) being child psychiatrists or psychoanalysts—or even social observers, versed in the knowledge of "group dynamics and social stress." There is no question that those children are going through a lot of personal turmoil . . . with people keeping their distance from one another, the whites versus the blacks. . . . But why not look at what this school crisis has done—at the emergence of leaders, young people who go beyond the "society" around them, and become moral leaders! (Coles, 2000, p. 225)

In their further exchanges, Erikson and Coles went on to discuss how moral leadership emerges in the interaction between individuals, their inner psychological worlds, and their social circumstances. Erikson himself was intensely interested in this phenomenon, which he explored through his psychohistorical biographies of Luther (Erikson, 1962) and Gandhi (Erikson, 1969). Summarizing Erikson's additional comments about the situation at South Boston High School, Coles quoted him as follows:

I wouldn't try to formulate this with too much emphasis on either the mind or religion and the Bible! I'd think of what these young people are doing for the rest of us as well as for themselves: they are showing us— showing that priest!—what happens when moral values are really put to the test, when someone has to "take the lead" in life, live up to what is said in church or at home or in a classroom by a history teacher or a literature teacher or a Sunday school teacher. If you live up to values, you're doing that, taking the lead with regard to them: that's moral leadership—

what Gandhi tried to find "doable" for himself. It's important for us to remember this—that moral leadership as we study it in history and politics (from the distance of time and events we never get to see or learn about in any detail) is also moral leadership that can happen right in front of us or not far away. (Coles, 2000, p. 226)

This simple case history and the additional analysis of it provided by Coles and Erikson cut to the center of the issue of how we define the virtue of justice as it is experienced in life and work. Nearly every day, each and every human being on the planet faces a series of decisions, each of which when carefully deconstructed possesses moral attributes. We either face or avoid questions such as, Should I drive faster than the legal limit to save a little time? Did I really put in a full day's work for my pay? Am I teaching my children to do what I say and not what I do? Am I trying to do something that may be within legal bounds in my business but I fundamentally know it's the wrong thing to do? As Erikson said, moral leadership happens right in front of us. It comes out of our mouths and is evident in our actions and those with whom we work and live. We don't need to look at historical figures such as Gandhi or Hitler to learn the fundamental principles. We all have values. Virtually every human has a sense of what it is to live justly or unjustly. The major problem is that many, many people and many individuals in positions of extraordinary authority do not take the lead with regard to living through and enacting moral principles. Let's look at a more well-known case to examine hypothetically what sometimes can happen to leaders when they face extremely difficult situations.

A Fateful Meeting at the Enron Corporation

As of this writing, it has been 10 years since Enron declared the largest bankruptcy in the history of the country. In the time since, we have been made privy to much of what happened inside what was repeatedly hailed as the prototypical modern corporation, one that many on Wall Street and in the business media promoted to others as a model to emulate. A number of books and articles have chronicled the core pieces of the story (Byrne, 2002; McLean & Elkind, 2003; Smith & Emshwiller, 2003; Swartz & Watkins, 2003), but with the plea bargain between Andrew Fastow and the U.S. Department of Justice, the public trials of Ken Lay and Jeffrey Skilling, and the Supreme Court decision to overturn the initial court verdict on the actions of Arthur Andersen, we have all been public witnesses to the crash of this organization and its tragic aftermath.

Having worked with a fair number of leadership teams as both a member and a consultant, I have repeatedly tried to imagine what might have been happening at the very top of the Enron organization as this terrible problem came to a head. Because the case led to changes in corporate accountability legislation in the form of the Sarbanes–Oxley Act and restatements of corporate earnings at hundreds of large companies around the world, historically, the debacle may well represent the 21st-century equivalent of the Rockefeller oil trust scandal of the last century that gave rise to the original Sherman antitrust legislation. Disclosures of leadership wrongdoing at a number of other large companies that followed the Enron debacle have resulted in the indictment of other corporate executives as well.

Although we witnessed the public disclaimers of the former CEO of Enron, Jeffrey Skilling, and the now-deceased chairman of the board, Ken Lay, both of whom vehemently denied that they knew what was really happening with the financial management of the corporation, in my opinion, it strains any and all human attempts at understanding to believe their statements. Anyone who has worked with senior leadership teams in publicly held corporations knows that CEOs and Chairpersons demand to know precisely this kind of information at the earliest moment possible and ritually and systematically punish subordinates who fail to inform them. The fact that Lay and Skilling were present along with the other members of the full board of directors to approve the major steps recommended by Fastow to move the losses off of Enron's formal accounting ledgers and into the special purpose organizations is proof positive that they fully comprehended what they were trying to accomplish. I want to explore further the issue of moral agency in leadership and the enactment of the virtue of justice with a succinct analysis of what I believe might have occurred. I want to emphasize that what follows is merely a work of my imagination; I have no evidence that the hypothesized events and activities actually took place. Nevertheless, the scenario I paint is based on significant experience in organizations and with many leaders facing similar kinds of problems.

My hypothesis begins with a meeting held in Ken Lay's office. It was after 5 p.m. when Jeff Skilling and Andy Fastow arrived. Jeff had only recently been appointed as the CEO after 10 years of near-constant effort to gain the position. Given his experience in the company and relationships with almost everyone, Skilling had settled into his position quickly and was already making a significant impact on the enterprise and its people. Ken had asked them to come in to discuss the problem that Andy had briefly outlined to him earlier in the week. In short, the company had placed some major bets in various derivative markets and energy futures that had gone completely sour. As a leadership group, they were feeling pretty good that their personal friend George Bush had been elected president in November 2000 and that their kind of high-flying, laissez-faire, corporate leadership was being extolled by the business media as required for the future of the global economy. However, they were also worried about the opening phases of the deflationary sell-off in the stock market. Above all else, they had worked to raise the price of Enron's stock. It had made them wealthy and famous. They would fight to defend that price with all they had, and after all, losses, even very large losses, were to be expected in their kind of business model.

As they sat down together, Ken asked Andy to describe the problem as he saw it. Andy quickly sketched the outline. Their organizational design and strategy, lovingly and aggressively developed with the assistance of Jeff and his colleagues at McKinsey & Company was based on the principles of arbitrage and derivative trading that first emerged on Wall Street in the 1980s. Starting with natural gas, they had led the way in creating new investment and trading vehicles in the energy industry. Because of their work and that of other companies, it was now possible to trade almost any form of energy as futures, commodities, and various forms of derivative securities. What agricultural and other forms of commodities trading did for the Chicago Board of Trade, Enron was trying to do with energy and for Houston. The core of the strategy involved hedging one form of energy trading against another to try to ensure substantially more gains over losses. The progressive nature of the gains they made and reported to the investment communities supported the high stock price. To me, Enron was a sort of publicly traded hedge fund in energy. Anyone could buy into the action for about $90 per share in 2000 dollars. Up to that point, their strategy had been a huge success, but because of a string of unanticipated and largely unpredictable reverses in a number of their deals, caused at least in part because of the rapidly burgeoning collapse of the stock market, the company now faced the need to declare a couple of billion dollars in losses. They did not know how badly their stock would be hurt, but they did know that senior executives in many other companies routinely lost their jobs over much smaller financial problems. In a sense, their organization and the execution of their strategy had run away from them because of external situations that were beyond their control and despite their best leadership efforts.

After Andy outlined the problem, Ken raised several questions about the potential impact on the stock, the likelihood of being able to offset the losses with other gains, and how to manage the media spin for Wall Street. Jeff, an exceptionally sharp business analyst, was probably and appropriately skeptical about the possibility of a quick, multibillion dollar turn around in a global economy that seemed to be rapidly heading into a recession. As the newly appointed CEO, the dream job he had campaigned rigorously for, and public maven of these kinds of aggressive, high-risk corporate strategies, he was hard-pressed to come up with a creative answer in the time frame that they had. With a PhD in economics, Ken also understood the fundamentals well. Jeff and Ken turned to Andy, who as the CFO knew the accounting rules like the back of his hand and who had been creative in the extreme in finding ways of positively and inscrutably portraying the status of the company in its quarterly financial reports to Wall Street. Largely because of Andy's capacity for opaque and indecipherable communication, Enron had the reputation on Wall Street of being virtually impenetrable from a financial and corporate strategy perspective. Aspects of their financial filings were worded in such a fashion that they were impossible to understand without the company dictionary, and they were not sharing that with anyone. Andy had no immediate answers either. Ken pointed out that they had real time clocks ticking in the sense that their next earnings summary was due soon, and they had the full board of directors to inform about the challenge. All three leaders admitted there was a major problem, knew that they had to find a solution quickly, and palpably feared what would happen to each of them if this was handled in the wrong way. After some additional discussion, they all agreed to put on their thinking caps to try to come up with some potential solutions.

Even looking back now, we do not know that such a meeting took place. In fact, both Lay and Skilling denied knowing what was really going on in any substantive detail. As reported by a variety of sources (Byrne 2002), there is stunningly little concrete evidence to show that the two of them had much of anything to do with what eventually unfolded in the first half of 2001. Neither sent nor responded to e-mails. Neither signed major documents. There is virtually no paper trail connecting them to events outside of the skimpily recorded deliberations of the board of directors. However, it strains everything I know about organizations and leaders to believe for a moment that they did not have at least a broad understanding of what the company was trying to do. Mentally, I have put myself in the position of being a coach to one or more of them as they walked through this crisis. My first piece of advice would have been that they talk to lawyers familiar with such situations to get a good idea about the legal risks for them as individuals. The absence of paper trails suggests strongly to me that all of them had access to and took the advice of their counsel in response to their evaluation of the problems they faced. As a result, they created "plausible deniability" for themselves. It is now clear that using Fastow's testimony, prosecutors made a criminal case against Lay and Skilling.

From my vantage point as an experienced executive coach, here are the principle aspects of my assessment of their leadership dilemma. First, they did not really foresee this happening. They had been successful in building Enron as a new type of energy trading company for more than a decade. They had all made a lot of money and become personally famous in the process. They fully believed that their strategies and methodologies would insulate them from the emergence of the worst cases. Second, as a result, they had not created the fiscal infrastructure, policy foundation, decision support systems, organizational culture, group processes, media strategy, or level of executive and emotional maturity to manage such an enormous problem. Third, their approaches to leadership had been conditioned by hard-driving, individual initiative; a seemingly endless series of personal and corporate successes; and a high media profile that positioned them as the executive dream team of the 21st century. As human beings, they were completely unprepared for a public failure of this scale and the inevitable consequences of extreme humiliation, extraordinary anxiety, sense of powerlessness, depression, and the probability of job loss that they faced. In addition, any true sense of personal conscience or moral agency as applied to their professional lives probably was hopelessly submerged in the ocean of their executive entitlement, belief in themselves, publicly evangelical commitment to unfettered global capitalism, and the nearly endless chorus of public adulation. Finally, their lack of awareness of group dynamics and behavior, organizational culture, and their own personality patterns had created a decision-making process that was fatally flawed.

Using Argyris's (1993) terminology, their espoused theory of executive leadership may be hypothetically characterized by explicitly stated beliefs that they were

1. penetrating point business strategists.
2. unflinchingly courageous and self-confident in facing the problems of leading a huge, 21st-century business organization in highly turbulent, global energy markets.
3. individually and collectively capable of creatively thinking their way through any problem that they faced.
4. really incapable of failing.
5. appropriately putting company profitability and earnings as the central value through which everything that they or anyone else did or said must be harshly judged.

In reality and as viewed from the advantageous position of being historically privileged outsiders, we can see that their leadership approach was characterized by unstated and probably largely unconscious patterns of behavior in which they

1. had a history of being less than truthful with each other and with those around them.
2. tended not to talk to each other in an open and honest fashion in which they could discuss their true feelings and thoughts.
3. believed and felt as though they were entitled to the power, prestige, perks, position, and money that they had because of their hard work and the public recognition of same.
4. were relatively impervious to feedback from those around them and actively engaged in behavior that discouraged or punished those subordinates who would contradict or challenge them.

5. at an unconscious level were chronically anxious about how they could keep their extraordinarily successful business going in the face of mounting losses, a deepening global economic storm, rapidly changing markets and emerging competition, their public commitments to an aggressive, all-out growth strategy, and the impossibly high expectations of Wall Street.
6. often acted out these tensions with subordinates, vendors, and business partners in humiliating, aggressive, and controlling interactions that had created an understandable climate in which virtually everyone avoided telling the truth to those in power.
7. systematically avoided any discussions in which questions of morality and business ethics were raised and examined with any degree of sincerity.

In such an environment and with such a hypothetical set of leadership characteristics, they decided that they had to rapidly search for and find a creative fix for their problem. They set off to develop a solution that would

1. allow them to save face and ultimately prevent any major public disclosure that would adversely affect the reputation of the company, the stock price, or their job security.
2. be an example of the type of cutting-edge business strategies that they had been accustomed to inventing.
3. get them through what they firmly believed was a short-term crisis.
4. avoid any questions or discussions of morality or ethical impropriety.

In my imaginary scenario, they went back to their offices and began to think and work individually. They also had a series of quiet, intense, and very private, off-the-record consultations with a small number of "trusted advisors," including attorneys.

As the subsequent disclosures of Enron business practices revealed, Fastow and his financial team had become adept at creating a series of unique financing and organizational structures through which they plowed the revenues and expenses that ultimately appeared on the company's balance sheet. Their operative principles seemed to be to maximize income statements, minimize reported losses, and, above all else, support the stock price. The options-based compensation policies of the company gave the executive team ample incentives to do anything they could to drive the stock price higher. With some exceptions, those policies had worked nearly to perfection until 2000.

In his own considerations of the problems facing the company, Fastow had the advantage of being able to talk to his wife, who was also a senior financial executive at Enron. At some point in his private deliberations, he came to the conclusion that it might be possible to extend their previously creative and successful approach of using "special organizational arrangements" to carry the financial burdens of the debt. In essence, they would invent new organizations, transfer the debt to them, report the transfers in their financial statements in ways that no one but a few trusted insiders could understand, and hope that no one would really notice what had happened. Their own experience and, in all probability, their lawyers told them this was extremely risky and that they would need to have the approval of both their board of directors and the auditors. Again, I am creating a complete hypothesis here.

They may have been told by counsel that if such governance and accounting approvals were forthcoming, they would create a paper trail that could possibly protect them if the details ever became public. The declarations of the Fastow's and their attorneys through the processes of indictment and plea bargaining demonstrated that this was the core of their defense. In essence, he claimed he had done nothing wrong because the board voted to support the recommendations and the auditors had approved of the actions. The only person in the whole process who appeared to stand firm and raise questions about the propriety of what they proposed to do was Carl E. Bass, the lead auditor from the Arthur Andersen Corporation. For his acts of moral courage, he was removed from the account by his company (Byrne, 2002).

To resume our imagined scenario, a relatively short time after their initial meeting, Jeff and Ken were presented with the high-risk plan by Andy that would allow them to "fix" their immediate problem in a creative fashion. Again meeting at the end of the day in Ken's office, Andy sketched the broad outline of an organizational design that would incorporate separate enterprises to which they would transfer the debt. The liability would be formally removed from Enron's balance sheet, but they would need to report the relationship with the new organization as part of their normal financial filings. As with many of their past transactions, the description of the new arrangement would be rather vague and difficult for anyone to decipher, even those with true financial expertise. The financial aspects of the venture would be present in their reports but delivered in such a fashion that it would take a real economic detective to unravel the full scope of what had been done. To accomplish this, the three of them knew from their conversations with various attorneys that they would need to stay formally in the bounds of standard accounting practices and the Enron board of directors would need to approve of the transaction. A key part of the plan required that their external auditors at Andersen more or less would know and approve of what they were trying to do. Without their agreement, the full extent of the losses would probably be made public with the consequent negative outcomes. Andy may or may not have disclosed at this point that if approved, his plan would personally net him approximately $25 million. Another key part of the plan involved obtaining financial support for the new organizational entities. Andy had designed them in such a fashion that the banks and investment houses who bought in would make incredible, short-term returns on their money and thus be reluctant to blow the whistle on the design.

After discussing the pros and cons in fairly theoretical terms, they may have briefly entered into an exchange about legal risks. Sitting where I am right now, I sincerely doubt that any of them truly understood the magnitude of what could happen if their plan came to be publicly understood. Why should they? In essence, they had been operating in similar ways for years with largely positive consequences. The world around them had systematically rewarded them in the past; why would it not in the future?

However, at some level, they also did understand that the magnitude of the risks involved was larger than in the past. It may have been in such a consideration that the issue of the ultimate downside risk was raised. In essence, anyone can see a distinct line of logic for the three of them that goes as follows:

1. We need to take some major risks to bring the company through a rather difficult passage.
2. If the worst happens, it may be some time before any of us would be able to work as a senior executive in a large firm again. Indeed, it might be impossible.
3. If the risks are that large, what would it take financially to merit taking them, and which one of us would be willing to do so?

The meeting ended with a commitment to explore the proposal further and to reconvene quickly once they had some time to reflect. In reality, it not only created some time for individual reflection, it also provided an opportunity for additional legal consultation. What we can infer is that at some point, Fastow decided that the risk for him came with a price tag of $25 million. Skilling and Lay came to different conclusions, choosing not to participate personally and directly in the implementation of the decisions but at least agreeing to take it to the board and do what they could. They must also have approved the structure of the deal because it came to the board and was approved. We now know that the whole plan was a type of scam that, once uncovered, led to the company's declaration of bankruptcy in less than 6 months, to the imprisonment of both Fastow and his wife Lea; to the conviction and imprisonment of Skilling; and to the conviction of Lay, who died of a heart attack several months after the jury returned its verdict.

If we briefly compare these two case examples, the differences are stark and startling. In the first, a young White woman courageously risked her reputation and network of social connections to reach out and establish a relationship with an African American student in one of the most racially torn high schools in the country. She did this because of a discussion with her priest and the convictions of her own personal conscience. In their exchanges about the situation, both women were able to articulate and explore moral principles and moral action. They actively demonstrated their commitment at the time to be moral agents in their lives and to live and work actively through the virtue of justice.

At the Enron Corporation, senior executives and all of their directors, consultants, and business partners in the middle of an enormous organizational crisis appear to have completely avoided the subject of what was the morally correct action to take. They collectively concocted and executed a business plan that, when publicly disclosed, led to the demise of their business, careers, and executive lives. In the ensuing discussions, public presentations, and court cases, most of them continued to deny any true wrongdoing. The boldness, brashness, and extent of their lies and misdeeds were breathtaking and stand in stark relief when compared with the lives and acts of two normal high school students. In the Enron case, the executives committed every one of the seven deadly errors described in Chapter 3: failures of execution; failures of integrity; failure, unwillingness, or inability to take timely and needed action; emotional incontinence; domination dynamics; inflated expectations; and unbridled secrecy and dishonesty. At the South Boston High School, not one of these errors was committed.

So the question can be raised logically: How can we increase the likelihood that human beings who accept positions of leadership in our organizations will behave more like Mary Ann and Alice and less like Ken, Jeff, and Andy? What principles and methods are more likely to produce executives who can both reason and act as moral agents in their enterprises? Let's first turn to a brief review of moral philosophy and psychology and some of the principle findings of contemporary research efforts to define and explore the issue of justice as applied to work settings.

MORAL REASONING AND THE VIRTUE OF JUSTICE IN HISTORICAL CONTEXT

The subjects of ethics, morals, and moral reasoning have spawned an absolutely enormous literature over the five millennia of recorded human history. Nearly all of the greatest products of ancient philosophy focused extensively on these issues. Our beloved texts of religious teaching, the Jewish and Christian Bibles, Muslim Koran (Dawood, 1990), Hindu *Bhagavad-Gita* (trans. 1985), and Buddhist Tibetan Book of the Dead (Coleman & Jinpa, 2005) extensively address the subject of how to live a moral life. Many other sources of information and ideas about moral development are widely available (e.g., Kohlberg, 1981; Newman, 1996; Radhakrishman & Moore, 1967). As of this writing, PsycINFO lists 1,915 citations on moral reasoning and an even more impressive 5,426 citations on moral development. Interestingly, there are only 62 citations that simultaneously explore the subjects of moral development and leadership. Google lists 92,600,000 Internet citations on the subject of ethics. Amazon's online book store has 246,560 titles available for purchase on the subject of ethics. In short, ethics, moral reasoning, and moral philosophy are among the most important and extensively researched and discussed subjects that humanity has ever explored. However, despite what we know and know how to teach, leaders continue to get it wrong, to reason in a faulty and sometimes morally delusional fashion, and to behave in corrupt and illegal ways. One question that arises immediately is how can anyone expect to summarize or develop even a modest comprehension of this vast body of knowledge?

Table 6.1 makes a modest effort at organizing an overview. It presents a succinct list of major contributors to our store of human concepts and knowledge about the virtue of justice and offers a few of the central concepts that continually inform academic and philosophical research and leadership practice. Although the list of scholars and their ideas is all too limited, in nearly every course on ethics and moral development, these core concepts are explored because they represent the essential outline of what students study. Beginning with the aphorisms that characterize the work of the Chinese masters Confucius and Lao Tzu and traveling down the 2,500 years since their writing led to the establishment of the approach to leadership development and human life that still influences contemporary China, these ideas represent many of the essentials of moral reasoning and ethical practice. The content of Table 6.1 more or less speaks for itself, but if we look closely at the summaries, several generalizations suggest themselves. They are as follows:

- *Virtue*—Moral living and ethical leadership practice primarily depend on a foundation of virtuous behavior. Although the virtues identified by different authors vary, they nearly all include versions of reverence, courage, temperance, wisdom, and justice. In addition, all of these authors agree that virtue can only be attained through practice during a life dedicated to achieving higher levels of expertise and experience with them. They all also agree that the leaders of human organizations should be chosen only from the ranks of the most experienced and virtuous people.

TABLE 6.1
Major Contributions to Justice Theory and Leadership in Human Affairs

Individual	Significant contribution
Confucius	*The Analects* (trans. 1989) ■ Humans improve through learning and self-development and the extension of one's good mind and development to others. ■ Humans create their own destiny. ■ Morality depends upon the performance of one's duties. ■ Wisdom, humanity, courage, and righteousness/propriety as the "Four Beginnings" of an ethical system. ■ Do not do to others what you do not want them to do to you. ■ To be human practice earnestness, liberality, truthfulness, diligence, and generosity. ■ Lead through reverent, virtuous service.
Lao Tzu	*Tao Te Ching* (trans. 1989) ■ Taoism—the natural order of the Universe is to return to where it starts. ■ The complementarity of opposites—yin and yang. ■ Lead without action. ■ The best man is like water . . . it benefits all things and does not compete with them. ■ The sage disregards the extremes. ■ Cultivating virtue in oneself is the path to living a virtuous life. ■ Benefit others do not injure. ■ Act but do not compete.
Socrates/Plato	*The Republic* (trans. 1999) ■ Leaders as "Philosopher Kings"—well trained and virtuous lovers of knowledge who live and lead through courage, temperance, wisdom, and justice. ■ Leaders practice their craft for the benefit of others as their duty to their fellow citizens. ■ Justice is the virtue of the soul and vice is its vice. ■ Political life should be regulated by those who are not attracted to it. ■ Justice described through the metaphors of the sun, the line, and the cave, which all promote the lifelong study of goodness, the development of the ability to see both the tangible and the intangible, and the love of knowledge rather than belief as the pathway to freedom.
Aristotle	*Nicomachean Ethics* (trans. 1908) ■ The study of ethics and politics go hand in hand. ■ Humans seek happiness, defined as *eudemonia* or living reasonably and virtuously in the pursuit of rational and effective ends. ■ Virtue is pursued through thought and character. Virtuous thought is obtained through teaching and

(continues)

Individual	Significant contribution
	learning and virtuous character is developed through practice and the development of good habits.
	■ Virtue as the golden (reasonable) mean between two vices—bravery between fear and hubris, generosity between lavishness and miserly, temperance between rage and meekness.
Buddha	The First Sermon (Jaspers, 1957)
	■ The cause of human pain is craving for pleasure, lust, passion, existence, nonexistence.
	■ Pain ceases when craving is replaced with abandonment, release, forsaking, and nonattachment.
	■ Teaching the "Four Noble Truths" - the truth of suffering, the origin of suffering, the cessation of suffering, and the eightfold path.
	■ The path to release from craving is the "Eightfold Path"—right views, right intention, right speech, right action, right livelihood, right effort, right mindfulness, and right concentration.
	■ Leaders as truth finders and teachers of the noble truths.
Augustine	The Confessions (trans. 2003)
	■ Wisdom is acquired through faith in God, its word, and moral laws.
	■ Eternal salvation is obtained through devotion to God, its word, and moral laws.
	■ Conventional wisdom, studies of philosophy, and pursuits of the flesh blind humans to the truth of God.
	■ Religious conversion to Christianity is the pathway to seeing and practicing truth.
Moses Maimonides	*The Guide for the Perplexed* (trans. 1956)
	■ The 613 precepts of the Pentateuch—a complete code and potential solutions to the questions of moral, religious, and social duties of Jews.
	■ Grand efforts to compare and reconcile the work of Aristotle with Torah.
	■ Pursuit of wisdom in the knowledge of God, workmanship, moral principles, and cunning - planning and strategy in practical, political, and social matters.
	■ Pursuit of other virtues such as loving kindness, judgment, piety, humility, and righteousness.
	■ Human awakening through the awareness of God and the practice of its laws.
Nicoló Machiavelli	*The Prince* (1582/1964)
	■ Desperate times call forth different aspects of leadership virtue and behavior.
	■ Obtaining and exercising political power at times requires ruthless actions to manage difficult situations.

Individual	Significant contribution
	■ Order and justice depend first and foremost on establishing executive authority. ■ Traditional normative expectations for moral and ethical behavior are subordinate to the requirements of political success and the exercise of executive authority. ■ How to use goodness and evil in the service of the state/organization. ■ The appearance of vice and virtue can be quite paradoxical and must not be confused with what is required for success.
Immanuel Kant	*Grounding for the Metaphysics of Morals* (1785/1993) ■ Morality must be based on reason not religious revelation. ■ Respect for the dignity of every human. ■ The categorical imperative—act only in ways that you will it as a universal law that everyone would follow—behave only in ways in which you would have everyone behave. ■ The purpose of human reason is to help individuals develop a good "will" to pursue the highest ends with the best means. ■ Human action and reason must be guided at all times by duty and the aim of duty must be to enact universal law. ■ Humanity and morality alone possess dignity which is above all other prices that we pay for our place in the world.
Thomas Hobbes	*Leviathan* (1651/1962) ■ Humans are motivated simultaneously by their fear of death and need for security. ■ Humans are naturally self-interested, assertive, and seek power. ■ War/competition is a state of nature. ■ Humans fight because of competition for resources/gain, to protect themselves and others from those who would enslave them, and to protect their reputations/sense of self-respect. ■ People trade liberty to the state in return for security, the social contract. ■ Societies are formed for gain, glory, or love of ourselves. ■ People should know how to treat others because they know how they want to be treated themselves. ■ All humans are more or less equal in their faculties. ■ Humans have natural rights to self-protection and liberty; to seek peace; and, if peace is not forthcoming, to make war and defend themselves.

(continues)

Individual	Significant contribution
John Stuart Mill	"What Utilitarianism Is" (original work published 1863; see Mill & Bentham, 1987) ■ Utility or the greatest happiness principle—actions are right to the extent that they promote happiness is the fundamental rule of human behavior. ■ Leaders should multiply happiness for the greatest number of people. ■ Utility helps leaders to settle conflicts between different duties. ■ Moral leaders take the interests of others into account. ■ The intention of an act describes the morality of the person while the consequences describe the morality of the act. ■ Systems of ethics are designed to inform humans about their correct duties. ■ Humanity has learned a lot about morality, ethics, and leadership and there are many different paths to each. Utility is a reasonable first principle to begin the journey to increased understanding and better practice.
Friedrich Nietzsche	*Thus Spake Zarathustra* (1883–1885/1993) ■ Utility and egalitarianism create societies of mediocrity—nations of slaves to the majority. ■ All human progress really depends on the efforts of superior people; those who can and do rise above average and make unusual contributions that advantage everyone else. ■ Societies should encourage the development of "supermen"—people who are courageous, visionary, and capable of independent thought and action. ■ The creative force in humans is the will to power best expressed in art, philosophy, and self-control; the desire to improve oneself and one's world not just to accept what is given; and in an exuberant approach to life that cultivates virtues such as honesty, sympathy, and generosity. ■ The average person longs for happiness and is willing to accept mediocrity as the price for it. ■ There is no after life, only our ability to make the best of the one we are given by nature.
Max Weber	*The Theory of Social and Economic Organization* (c. 1915/1975) ■ Charismatic leaders elicit strong personal reactions from followers in the form of commitment to a mission and devotion to duty. ■ Religion and religious beliefs inform the foundations of capitalism.

Individual	Significant contribution
	■ The authority and power of charismatic leaders derives from their ability to inspire others not from formal position power or organizational rules or routines. ■ Charismatic leaders are imbued with special powers and characteristics by the worship/admiration of their followers. ■ Charismatic leaders have a duty to followers to exercise their gifts on their behalf. ■ Rational bureaucratic rules will seem irrational to the charismatic leader and vice versa. ■ Napoleon's rule of genius lasts only as long as followers believe leaders possess that quality.
Ruth Benedict	*Patterns of Culture* (1934) ■ Culture is the ultimate determiner of normality, morality, and ethics. ■ Morality represents the habitual and ritual behaviors of groups of humans. ■ Culture has taken an extraordinarily wide range of forms in human history. ■ In some cultures, people who would be defined as extremely abnormal in contemporary western societies would function easily. ■ For the Kwakiutl Indians of Northern Pacific America, the highest good was to give away what was most valuable. ■ The morals, ethics, and normative expectations for behavior in any society are selected over time from a larger universe of possibilities and then ritually taught to its members. ■ Any individual who arrives in a new culture or society is at risk for being defined as abnormal, immoral, or unethical if s/he does not learn and at least publicly subscribe to what is the commonly accepted right ways of behaving.
Jean Piaget	*The Moral Judgment of the Child* (trans. 1965) ■ Humans develop their moral reasoning ability through childhood and adolescence. It is a subset of their general cognitive abilities. ■ The stages of cognitive and moral development move from the simple to more complex and each subsequent stage depends upon the skills and abilities that have emerged in the previous one. ■ In early stages, children learn and learn how to apply "rules." ■ In middle stages, children learn about responsibility, lying, respect, and moral realism as it is practiced in their worlds.

(continues)

Individual	Significant contribution
	■ In the later stages of development, children learn about retributive, distributive, and other forms of justice. They also learn about duty and living a disciplined life. ■ Societies and families play distinctive roles in helping children learn the appropriate content and codes of moral reasoning while they simultaneously develop biologically and psychologically.

Lawrence Kohlberg	*Moral Stages and Moralization: The Cognitive–Developmental Approach* (1981)
	Moral reasoning and behavior develops through a series of three levels and six stages.
	■ Level One—Preconventional
	  a. Punishment and Obedience Orientation
	  b. Instrument and Relativity Orientation
	■ Level Two—Conventional
	  a. Interpersonal Concordance Orientation
	  b. Law and Order Orientation
	■ Level Three—Postconventional, Autonomous, or Principled
	  a. Social Contract Orientation
	  b. Universal Ethical Principles Orientation

John Rawls	*A Theory of Justice* (1971) ■ Justice as fairness. ■ Social contracts provide a procedural methodology and interpretation of Kant's rational choice as the foundation for ethics. ■ Every citizen has an equal right to a social system with the most extensive liberties that allows the same liberties for everyone. ■ Social and economic inequalities are just only if they result in benefits for everyone, especially the least advantaged in society. ■ Positions and offices are open to all under fair equality of opportunity.
James MacGregor Burns	*Leadership* (1978) ■ The relationship between leaders and followers must be based on shared values. ■ Leaders and followers assist each other in developing morally and in operating daily on more advanced ethical principles and practices. ■ Burns explicitly embraced Kohlberg's taxonomy of moral development. ■ Transforming leaders constantly engage followers and other stakeholders in discussions of values. ■ Leaders use conflict creatively to improve the understanding of values and identify and achieve common goals when possible.

Individual	Significant contribution
John Thibaut and Laurens Walker	■ Two forms of values—modal values related to the means of accomplishing activities such as due process and end values such as justice and equality. *Procedural Justice: A Psychological Analysis* (1975) ■ Differentiation of the psychological reactions to the issues involved in distributive justice—how individuals fair in how goods, power, services, recognition are divided among the members of a group—and procedural justice—the processes that are used to both make the decisions about such divisions and to actually enact those choices. ■ Set the stage for thirty years of scientific work exploring how justice works in organizations and between leaders and followers. ■ Leads to extended theory and empirical support for the importance of preserving procedural justice in leader–follower exchanges. ■ Subsequent scientific findings demonstrate consistent positive relationships between leader–follower exchanges characterized by the experience of positive procedural justice and a variety of organizational outcomes.

■ *Golden Rule*—Human justice begins with the enactment of the "golden rule"—do unto others as you would have them do unto you. Embedded in this approach is both an understanding of and commitment to the practice of this methodology for every member of a human community. Three of the five essential leadership virtues focus on the challenge of how humans should treat each other. The golden rule provides a cornerstone for these deliberations.

■ *Complementary Conflicts*—Certain moral principles are complementary to each other, thus creating a perpetual type of conflict. The primary form that this dialectic tension takes is in the pull between the utility—egalitarian perspective, which emphasizes the greatest good for the greatest number of people and everyone should be treated equally versus the subjectivist–narcissistic–charismatic position, which argues for decisions based on what is good for the individual and the view that human progress depends on the creativity and inventiveness of unique and talented people.

- *Contractual Relationships*—Moral conflicts are perpetual and inevitable because they involve fundamental questions about the distribution of goods, status of individuals, processes through which decisions are made, multiple loyalties that people possess, and their attachments to each other, institutions, belief systems, and tribes. The best way to address the issues of justice inherent in such conflicts and determining fair solutions is for humans to develop relationships based on contractual understandings and commitments. In this fashion, the obligations that people have toward each other can be identified and addressed when they are not met.
- *Duty*—Moral and ethical leadership is based on clarifying the nature of duties that the members of an organization or society have toward each other and discharging those duties with the highest forms of devotion and competency.
- *Developmental Process*—The capacity for moral reasoning and ethical behavior changes through time. The moral competencies of children are different from those of adults, and they are and should be held to standards and expectations that are appropriate for their levels of development. Moral development can be facilitated through time by education, role modeling, mentoring, experience, and other actions.
- *Cultural Foundations*—Cultural differences can and do make enormous contributions to how moral and ethical behavior is determined. What is normal and moral for one group of people might well be seen as crazy or evil by another. One must try to comprehend the cultural foundations underlying the behavior being displayed to determine the motivations and methods of individuals involved and, in doing so, avoid the rush to immediate judgment about what is right and wrong.
- *Values Clarification*—Leaders and their followers do their best work when they clarify the values that they share and use conflict creatively to deepen their mutual understanding and make choices that most clearly reflect their shared commitment to what is important to them. Leaders and followers should be willing to engage constantly in a dialogue about their values as a core methodology for setting direction for their mutual action.
- *Extreme Environments*—When faced with extraordinary or extreme external circumstances, leaders and followers may need to reconsider their values and moral principles. Decisions and actions that might need to be taken under such conditions would often be considered immoral or unethical in different

times. Warfare, dangerous changes in external environments, or times of ecological, economic, and social crisis might necessitate such considerations.

- *God's Laws*—Morality is the essential province of divine judgment. Humans exist to discover, obey, and teach the laws of God. People who are blind to these universal truths should be converted, educated, saved, or shunned. Heresy, heretics, and unbelievers represent deviations from the true path of moral life and are often dealt with harshly.

A careful examination of these principles yields a variety of questions and conclusions. For example, if these lessons of history, philosophy, psychology, and politics are so well known and easy to articulate, why does humanity still so often struggle with leaders who act immorally and unethically? What can and should be done to better prepare leaders to address moral conflicts when they arise in their organizations? Are humans so different from each other that the issues of choosing values, deciding on the nature and enactment of duty toward each other and themselves, and determining how social and psychological contracts should be formulated are fundamentally impossible to address? Across the millennia of recorded human history, such questions have haunted societies, and the answers that they have each formulated and enacted have varied widely with different types of results. What is clear is that every human society and organization cannot escape the necessity of confronting moral and ethical questions and of dealing with the consequences of the solutions that they formulate. These lessons of history and hard-won fruits of intellectual endeavor and human experience are clearly available to any leader to help him or her address these challenges.

THE PRACTICE OF JUSTICE IN ORGANIZATIONS—LESSONS FROM CONTEMPORARY PSYCHOLOGICAL SCIENCE

In the vast landscape of the psychological literature that addresses the issues of moral development and moral reasoning, a substantial body of research has emerged that specifically focuses on the issue of how justice is practiced and experienced in human organizations. Most studies of justice trace their origins to a monograph authored by Thibaut and Walker (1975) that attempted "to define and clarify the nature of procedural justice through the application of social-psychological methods to some classical and controversial issues posed by divergent views about ideal legal processes" (p. vii). In essence, these authors tried to apply psychological science to legal decision making. Their assumptions were that humanity faced a future that would involve increasing levels and types of conflict with more and more dangerous consequences if they remained unresolved. They suggested strongly that the procedures used to address such complex issues were crucial to humanity's success and that procedures providing more control to the people involved in conflicts were more likely to lead to satisfactory solutions. Their basic finding was that research subjects were willing to give up control of the decision phase of legal conflicts as long as the kept control of the process and could present their own arguments in their own way. Subsequently, this has become identified as the *fair process effect* or *voice effect* (Lind & Tyler, 1988). Thibaut and Walker also addressed questions of bias, contracts, and different control processes, and their studies led to a general finding that their experimental subjects strongly preferred procedures in which more information was disclosed in conflicts and the biases of the involved parties were exposed. Research participants' perceptions of fairness and sense of satisfaction increased significantly when such disclosure was made.

This set of studies spawned an extensive exploration of many facets of justice. Colquitt, Conlon, Wesson, Porter, and Ng (2001) published a meta-analytic review of 25 years of this literature. They stated that

> justice in organizational settings can be described as focusing on the antecedents and consequences of two types of subjective perceptions: (a) the fairness of outcome distributions or allocations and (b) the fairness of the procedures used to determine outcome distributions, otherwise known as forms of distributive justice. (p. 425)

In addition, Colquitt et al. examined forms of procedural justice that appear in the literature as studies on process control, consistency, and interpersonal treatment. They reported that although Thibaut and Walker and others initially focused on perceptions of justice in legal settings and exchanges, Leventhal (1980) and Leventhal, Karuza, and Fry (1980) began to extend the research to other organizational settings.

Leventhal's (1980; Leventhal et al., 1980) work added six additional criteria to determine whether a procedure was fair. These specified that procedures should

- be applied consistently across people and time,
- be free of bias,
- ensure that accurate information is collected and disclosed,
- have processes to address flawed decisions,
- respect personal or prevailing ethical standards, and
- guarantee that the opinions of the various people involved are addressed.

Greenberg (1990, 1993) broadened the understanding of procedural justice to include types of interpersonal treatment such as efforts to preserve the dignity and sense of self-respect of those involved in a conflict or process and what he referred to as informational justice. The latter involves efforts to help participants understand why certain procedures were used in a situation or explanations concerning why the outcomes were distributed in a given fashion.

Table 6.2 presents a summary of Colquitt et al.'s (2001) findings with regard to whether these types of procedural justice affect different forms of organizational outcomes. As can readily be seen, the existing literature strongly suggests that it has significant effects on various forms of organizational behavior such as job satisfaction, organizational citizenship behavior, job performance, withdrawal from the organization, and negative emotional experiences related to work. Interestingly, although all of these types of results demonstrated that procedural justice influences various aspects of organizational effectiveness, none of the studies examined by these authors addressed the most visible and frequently used financial measures of performance, such

TABLE 6.2
Measures of Effectiveness and Outcomes Associated
With Organizational Justice

Measure of effectiveness	Organizational Justice	
	Yes	No/Don't Know
Profitability		■
Return on Investment		■
Return on Net Investment		■
Market Share		■
Market Capitalization		■
Annual Total Revenue		■
Organizational Growth Rate		■
Outcome Satisfaction		
Pay	■	
Promotions		
Work Conditions		
Job Satisfaction	■	
Organizational Commitment	■	
Trust	■	
Evaluation of Authority—		
Agent Referenced	■	
Evaluation of Authority—		
System Referenced	■	
Organizational Citizenship		
Behaviors—Individual Referenced	■	
Organizational Citizenship		
Behaviors—System Referenced	■	
Withdrawal	■	
Negative Reactions	■	
Performance	■	

as return on investment, market capitalization, or total net financial return. It is as though the psychosocial examination of the practice of procedural justice clearly indicates that it also has economic impacts on organizations but stops well short of specifying what those effects might be. Colquitt and his colleagues examined 300 articles published from 1975 to 1999 for their review, a truly significant volume of research on a single topic over a 25-year time frame.

However, it is important to realize that these studies represent only part of the evolution of the research on the practice of justice, ethics, and moral reasoning in organizations (Cropanzano, Byrne, Bobocel, & Rupp, 2001; Lebacqz, 1986). Other authors have examined such subjects as how leaders justify their misdeeds (Folkes & Whang, 2003), the practice of justice ethics by leaders in Eastern and Western cultures (Meara, 2001), and how procedural and interactional justice mediate the perceptions of leaders and followers of their mutual contributions to the organization and their citizenship behaviors (Bhal, 2006). Avery (2003) demonstrated in laboratory studies that the personality dimensions of extraversion and self-efficacy significantly predicted the value of voice or allowing the expression of views in relationships. Turner, Barling, Epitropaki, Butcher, and Milner (2002) demonstrated that leaders who practiced a more transformational approach to their work were found to score the highest in moral reasoning compared with those who were more transactional in their preferred styles. Similarly, De Cremer (2006) presented results indicating that when leaders were perceived as using a transformational approach and practicing procedural justice, they produced strong, positive emotional responses in research subjects. De Cremer (2007) extended the findings of his earlier studies by demonstrating that leaders who practiced an autocratic form of leadership were more likely to produce negative emotional effects in experimental subjects. Finally, Phillips, Doiuthitt, and Hyland (2001) demonstrated that team-member satisfaction improved as leaders efforts to involve them in decisions increased. Finkel and Moghaddam (2005), Lapsley (1996), and A. G. Miller (2004) provided extensive reviews on the literature on rights and duties, moral psychology, and good and evil. W. B. Pearce and Littlejohn (1997) discussed the issues involved in the evolution and management of moral conflict.

Other authors, such as W. J. Booth (1994) and Lachapelle (2005), have begun the difficult work of examining the relationships among moral philosophy, moral reasoning, and the rapid evolution of the global economy. In addition to these resources, conventional studies of business ethics have yielded a wide variety of books on the subject (Ciulla, 2003; Velasquez, 1992). In my earlier work (Kilburg, 2006) I extensively explored the issue of executive wisdom as part of a more comprehensive model of virtuous leadership that also incorporated the virtue of justice. Despite the extensive nature of the science, philosophy, and religious literature available to guide humans who find themselves in leadership positions, as we explored in the Enron case, many of them continue to fail even the most fundamental tests of ethical behavior.

The study of leadership failure has been deeply rooted in history. In fact, one could say that history itself represents the examination of leaders, how they succeed or fail, and the consequences of those actions and events. Psychology and other academic disciplines have been interested in what creates the conditions for leadership success and failure. Hogan, Curphy, and Hogan (1994) summarized the literature on leadership effectiveness and failure and pointed out that executives fail in their positions as much as 50% of the time. Finkelstein (2003) examined the failures of more than fifty corporations to determine how and why their leaders were not able to meet the challenges they faced. He found patterns of environmental stresses and leadership behavior that systematically contributed to the disasters that he documented. Similarly, Dotlich and Cairo (2003), Hammett (2007), Hartley (2003), Lipman-Blumen (2005), and Picken and Dess (1997) all produced extensive reviews and analyses on the issue of executive performance and failure and reached similar conclusions to those identified by Finkelstein. Kellerman (2004) examined the problem as well and stated that the foundation for bad leadership rested on a complex combination of traits, character, psychological needs, and group dynamics. In a recent book, Price (2006) explored the literature and arguments concerning the ethical failures of leaders. The main school of thinking on executive ethical disasters emphasizes volition—that leaders know what is right, ethical, and moral and yet choose to do otherwise. In contrast, Price argued for a cognitive explanation of the phenomena in which leaders come to believe that the collective ends that they desire to achieve give rise to a complex set of rationales through which they ultimately decide that they are exempt from normal moral constraints and that others also may be excluded from ethical protection.

Sorting through these resources and others, it becomes extremely clear that scholars and practitioners have collectively produced an excellent set of descriptions of what poor and unethical executive performance looks like and a wonderfully rich and detailed group of explanations for why individuals fall prey to these problems. In general, these explanations can be clustered into a few major items.

- *Comprehension*—Leaders fail to truly understand the nature of the environmental challenges that they and their organizations face, leading to the creation of faulty discernment, decisions, and actions.
- *Sacrifice and Trauma*—Human beings who rise to leadership positions sacrifice a great deal of themselves and their families' well-being along the way (Boyatzis & McKee, 2005). The conditions of personal sacrifice combine with the rewards that

organizations provide to them for their performance to sow the seeds for cognitive distortions, emotional problems, and need states that drive disordered thinking, feeling, and behavior.

- *Personality*—Some individuals possess personality traits and components of character that can express themselves in and through leadership positions in extraordinarily destructive ways for them and those who work in their organizations.
- *Dynamics*—Leaders and their followers can cocreate group, organizational, and societal dynamics of such enduring and intense destructiveness that the shape and direction of history is forever changed.

These patterns have been visible across organizations, political systems, and societies for thousands of years. Within empires, nations, and organizations, history describes the rise and fall of leaders who are beloved and extraordinarily productive and those whose legacies are still poisoning the broad human community today. A number of questions naturally arise. What can be done about these human tendencies, if we understand what can and does happen to produce unethical and immoral leadership? Why don't we act to counter those processes? How do we move systematically to improve the likelihood that our executives will perform in ways that uplift their enterprises and societies from a moral perspective? The next section of this chapter suggests several exercises that are likely to improve any individual leader's moral behavior if they are implemented systematically.

SUGGESTED PATHWAYS TO DEVELOPING JUST LEADERS

I believe we can start to consider how to improve the likelihood that leaders will practice their arts in increasingly just ways with several simple assumptions. First, the vast majority of people attracted to and promoted into positions of leadership will not have spent a substantial amount of time studying the vast history and literature of ethics and moral development. They will be oriented primarily to solving the problems they face with practical and workable solutions and for the most part will assume that as individuals, they are decent people. Second, most organizations possess only primitive means to address moral and ethical questions, although many may well have extensive legal resources available to them. Third, the globally competitive environments in which most organizations currently operate allow little time for executives to practice careful deliberation on ethical or moral challenges. Finally, leaders and those who help to develop them could benefit from a few essential tools that would increase the likelihood that they would practice improved moral reasoning in their daily work.

Exercise 6.1 suggests that leaders begin moving toward improving their ethical practices by clarifying their personal, moral point of view (Kilburg, 2006). The questions presented take an individual through a meditation on how they have evolved as moral human beings. Each of the inquiries can take a few minutes, hours, or days depending on the amount of time someone wants to invest. At the end of the reflection, the exercise suggests that the individual formulate a 50- to 100-word summary that represents his or her moral point of view. The succinct summaries presented in Table 6.1 as well as most of the references in this chapter can provide additional assistance for anyone who wants to dig deeper into the moral and ethical literature. I believe that people who take the time to construct such a short guide and then refer to it regularly are likely at least to pause and ask themselves whether a situation they are facing must be addressed within such a moral perspective.

EXERCISE 6.1
Articulating a Moral Point of View

Imagine you're going to be interviewed for a 2- to 3-minute spot on the evening news concerning your personal and professional morals. You will be asked to give a succinct statement in front of a television audience to summarize your thoughts. In preparation for this event, please take 15 to 20 minutes and answer the following questions as best as you can. Then summarize your own individual moral point of view in the space provided.

1. In what religious, ethical, or moral traditions were you raised? What do you believe those experiences contribute to your own moral perspective?

2. Who is the person in your own life who provided you with the best moral guidance? Why was he or she so effective?

3. In your personal experience, who best represents someone who both has and abides by a moral position in life? Briefly describe why you believe this is so.

4. Who is the most immoral person that you personally know or have known? How did you discover the lack of morality? What did you learn from him or her?

5. What three books, plays, movies, or other sources of learning have most instructed you in moral reasoning or moral conflict? How and why did they influence you?

6. In your training as a leader what enables you best to identify and manage ethical and moral issues?

7. Identify three of the most important issues or moral principles a leader should keep in mind.

8. Please provide a brief (50–100 words) synopsis of what you believe best describes your current moral point of view.

Exercise 6.2 provides another resource to extend moral and ethical sensitivity via a list of 21 questions that focus on a range of issues related to the subject. The inquiries begin with an examination of many of the issues raised in Exercise 6.1 but then branch into such challenges as what resources are available to address ethical challenges within an organization and the kinds of socially constructed biases or episodes of personal history that may he affecting a leader's ability to discern, decide, or act morally. The final questions ask executives to examine whether they are actively engaged in trying to improve the moral capacities of the people who work in the organizations they lead. Again, the questions presented can result in a quick examination of perspectives, problems, and practices or lead to much longer deliberations on these concerns.

Exercise 6.3 extends the work of the first two exercises by focusing on creating what Thompson (2006) called a *moral compass*. She emphasized that leaders who take the time to create such a tool for themselves are far more likely to consult it when they perceive that they are maneuvering in troubled ethical times. The compass possesses four components—moral vision, code, fitness, and performance. Thompson suggested that it is insufficient simply to develop ideas about morality and ethics. In reality, the practice of effective moral leadership demands that executives actively practice their ethics to keep themselves and their organizations in shape for the challenges that the world inevitably presents. The compass becomes a vehicle that can enable improved performance in these domains, and as history and the leadership derailment literature suggest, moral and ethical lapses often produce lasting negative effects for individual executives and their organizations.

On the basis of the findings suggested in the literature on organizational justice and leadership effectiveness presented earlier, there are at least two other forms of practice or areas of skill development that leaders could pursue to help them become better able to enact the virtue of justice. The phenomenon of voice or enabling participation by the members of an organization in decisions that are relevant to their lives and work suggests that executives could and should become expert practitioners of communication skills. This arena has been also extensively studied, and a wide variety of excellent resources are available to assist anyone who wants to learn to be better at the arts of empathic listening, inquiry, self-disclosure, dialogue, interviewing, advocacy, and feedback (Annis Hammond, 1996; Daniels & Ivey, 2007; M. H. Davis, 1996; Flick, 1998; Folkman, 1996; Gordon, 1975; Hargie, 2006; Ickes, 1997; Kegan & Lahey, 2001; Patterson, Grenny, Maxfield, McMillan, & Switzler, 2008; Patterson, Grenny, McMillan, & Switzler, 2002; Skolnick, Dulberg, & Maestre, 1999; Whetten & Cameron, 1993). The consistency and strength of the empirical findings on the positive effects on organizations of leaders who can enable the participation of their followers

EXERCISE 6.2
Moral and Ethical Questions Leaders Can Ask Themselves

1. What, if any, moral or ethical characteristics, problems, or conflicts does the decision or action I am about to make raise for me, for others, for my organization?

2. What moral or ethical principles typically guide me when I must make decisions or take actions on behalf of myself, others, or my organization?

3. In what religious, spiritual, moral, or ethical practices do I routinely engage that help me develop as a leader?

4. Do I have a consistent moral and ethical framework to guide my decisions and actions?

5. Do I consider myself as a moral agent in my organization?

6. How would I articulate my moral and ethical framework to someone else?

7. What resources do I possess or have access to that can help me examine the moral and ethical aspects of the decisions and actions that I routinely take?

8. Is there someone close to me on whom I can rely to tell me the absolute truth from his or her perspective about the decisions and actions that I take and about how she or he comprehends who I am as a person and as a leader? Do I routinely or periodically solicit that person's ideas, reactions, or guidance?

9. Can I always argue the pros and cons of a decision or action I am considering from the viewpoint of those individuals who might oppose the choice or act?

10. Do I take the time to try to understand who benefits most from a decision or action I am about to take and who might be harmed or oppressed by it?

11. Do I consciously try to balance the political, economic, social, psychological, and moral components of the decisions that I face and actions that I take? If not, why not and what do you believe it may cost you and your organization?

12. How often do I pause and consider the long-term implications, costs, and benefits of the decisions I make or actions that I take for those other than the key stakeholders in my organization? Did those considerations change the nature of the decision or action? Provide an example. What did you learn by the process? If it changed you as a leader or as a person, how and why?

13. Do I understand and try to keep in conscious contact with beliefs, attitudes, values, and characteristics of my personality and dimensions of diversity that may induce specific or systematic bias into the decisions I make and actions that I take?

(continues)

14. Have I ever used my knowledge of such beliefs, values, and other factors to change the direction of one of my decisions or actions because I came to see that I was biased in a particular and unhelpful or destructive direction? Give an example of such a process. What did you learn about yourself as a result of what you did? What was the result of the decision or action? Did the outcome of the decision or action change you in any way? If yes, how and why? If no, why not?

15. Do you conduct an ethical audit of your organizations and its practices, policies, and procedures? If yes, with what results? If no, why not?

16. Have you put in place any institutional systems that act as moral or ethical check-points or brakes on yourself, your leadership and management team, or the other employees in the organization, for example, ethical codes, institutional review processes or boards that examine decisions and actions before they are taken, after-action review processes that are routinely engaged as efforts to learn and raise ethical or moral questions, external review committees, board subcommittees on ethics? Do you have case examples of how such systems have helped to avoid ethical problems or resolve them when they are discovered?

17. As a leader or a person, have you ever faced private or public accusations that you were behaving immorally or unethically? What were the charges? Who made them and why? What was the effect on you, your organization, your family, your relationships, and your career? How did you handle that situation? What was the outcome of that process? What did you learn from what happened? If it changed you as a person or as a leader, how did it do so?

18. Have you ever been treated unjustly, immorally, or unethically by another person, leader, or organization? What was the effect on you, your organization, your family, your relationships, and your career? How did you handle that situation? What was the outcome of that process? What did you learn from what happened? If it changed you as a person or as a leader, how did it do so?

19. Have you ever been treated justly, morally, or ethically by another person, leader, or organization? What was the effect on you, your organization, your family, your relationships, and your career? How did you handle that situation? What was the outcome of that process? What did you learn from what happened? If it changed you as a person or as a leader, how did it do so?

20. Do you provide mentoring or coaching support to your key subordinates on moral and ethical matters? If yes, what do you do and what effects does it have? If no, why not?

21. Have you asked the members of your leadership team to consider how to improve the moral and ethical strength of your organization and its people? If yes, with what result? If no, why not?

EXERCISE 6.3
Evolving Your Moral Compass: A Crucial Tool for Executive Success

Thompson (2006) suggested that all leaders must develop a "moral compass" that will serve them during the inevitable trials and storms that assail humans who pursue the higher purposes and challenges of these positions. Such a tool incorporates and expands on the knowledge of one's moral point of view and, according to Thompson, helps provide guidance when leaders confront significant challenges and need to work with people whose beliefs, values, and behaviors may be radically different from theirs. Thompson's moral compass contains the four major interacting elements described here. Take some time to examine the descriptions below and the questions associated with them to continue the evolution of your own moral compass as a leader.

Moral Vision
The spiritual and emotional component of your compass, moral vision is often expressed through the ideals and values you hold, the myths that inform your life, and the images that constantly provide power to your experience.

- Who are the heroes and villains in your life and why?
- What is your vision for an ideal world?
- What noble causes ignite your imagination?
- What would you consider as the highest achievement possible for you in your life?
- For what do you want others to look to you or up to you?
- What moral, professional, or personal situation would you most want to avoid in your life?

Moral Code
Your moral code is the set of rules, norms, and behaviors that guide your behavior as a leader on a daily basis (see Exercise 6.1).

- Have you read a good book on moral philosophy? If no, why not?
- Are you familiar with a variety of approaches to moral reasoning such as utilitarianism, virtue ethics, religious beliefs and dogmas, justice theory, human rights theory, cultural relativism, or social contracts?
- To which moral theories or points of view do you subscribe?
- How would you describe your basic values?
- How do you communicate your basic values to others and enact them in your life?
- What do you do when you are asked or someone tries to force you to act against your basic values or fundamental, moral point of view?

Moral Fitness
Activities and practices in which you deliberately engage to develop virtues, avoid vices, clarify values, increase moral and ethical awareness, and to try to bring your beliefs into full, free, and conscious action in and through living.

- Do you accept the responsibility for being a moral leader in your organization and life and take constructive action to raise moral and value issues at work and home?
- Are you committed to being a moral agent in life?
- What concrete steps do you take to remain morally aware in your life and at work?
- Do you have routine moral and ethical practices in which you engage—going to church, reading, meditation, participation in various organizations or groups with moral aims, deliberately practicing virtues?

(continues)

EXECUTIVE CONSCIENCE AND PRACTICE OF JUSTICE   *181*

- Do you have a model of what your character should be and routinely question whether you are living up to that ideal?
- Are there others in your life to whom you turn for moral advice, explorations, or support? Do you meet and talk with them regularly?
- Do you give yourself, ask others to give you, or accept challenges that develop your moral character and virtue?
- Is there anything in you, your life, or relationships that undermine(s) your ability to stay morally fit? If yes, briefly describe it.

Moral Performance

Moral performance is what leaders actually do as they practice moral and ethical behavior in their lives and positions. Performance is realized as the stresses and strains of responsibility that constantly test the moral and ethical fiber of executives.

- What moral or ethical challenges are you currently facing in your life or work?
- What moral or ethical challenges have you faced in the past that strengthened you and your moral compass?
- What moral or ethical challenges have you faced in the past that weakened you and your moral compass?
- Are your colleagues and organization prepared to address moral and ethical challenges when they arise? If not, what could you do to improve their capacity to do so?
- Do you routinely try to discern and address moral and ethical conflicts or challenges such as:
  —Personal versus organizational goals and interests?
  —Employee and other stakeholder interests versus society as a whole?
  —Honesty versus protecting someone or something else that you value?
  —Loyalty between two people, organizations, interests, or ideals?
  —Doing what you believe is right versus being merciful in a given situation?

is one of the most striking results of the scientific study of management. It should not be surprising that improving a leader's capacity to communicate and to facilitate exchanges with the people with whom she or he works would also increase their ability to practice the virtue of justice.

The literature also suggests that another way to decrease the likelihood that leaders will behave badly and unjustly is to improve how they manage the tremendous and inescapable stresses of their positions. The negative effects of stress on individuals have been widely documented (Henry & Stephens, 1977; Puryear Keita & Sauter, 1992; Quick, Quick, Nelson, & Hurrell, 1997). A wide variety of constructive and effective interventions have also been developed to assist individuals and organizations manage these challenging problems by improving their coping skills and resilience (Murphy, Hurrell, Sauter, & Puryear Keita, 1995; Reivich & Shatté, 2002; Roskies, 1987). Boyatzis and McKee (2005) suggested strongly that if executives want to sustain their capacity to lead and avoid many of the traps that lead to malfunction and derailment, then they must systematically engage in practices that will improve their overall health and well-being. Again, this is a consistent, empirically supported finding in the clinical psychology and organizational health literatures that should be used by leaders to help them increase the likelihood that they will be able to act justly in the chaotic conditions that they routinely face.

Finally, Exercise 6.4 presents four brief case studies that are examples of common dilemmas leaders face in organizations. In keeping with the performance dimension of Thompson's (2006) moral compass, leaders and those who help develop them can and should make it a common practice to present and work through approaches to moral and ethical problems. Constant attention

---

EXERCISE 6.4
Examples of Organizational Cases Requiring Considerations of Justice

---

Case 1

You are the CEO of a major organization and receive information that one of your key products—a significant contributor to the financial performance of your organization—has adverse health risks and consequences for children. If you pull the product from the market, your profits and reputation will suffer immediate damage. Your board of directors and the investment community have been consistently pushing you and your management team to make even bigger improvements in your organization's profitability. How would you handle this challenge?

Case 2

You are a senior executive in your organization reporting to the CEO, and a junior member of your staff comes to you with objective evidence that your best friend and colleague in the company may well be acting unethically and in significant violation of well-known policies. You know that your friend has been under significant personal stress at home and that his or her part of the business has been under a lot of pressure to improve performance. The CEO of the enterprise is relatively new and has demonstrated that she has high standards for executive performance. How would you proceed in this situation using your moral compass?

Case 3

You are the CEO of your organization, and your board of directors has encouraged and pressured you to expand the market for your products into Asia. Neither you nor the members of your executive team had experience in that region, but you have persevered and are on the verge of negotiating a distribution agreement with a potential organizational partner. As the deliberations near conclusion, the representatives of your potential partner tactfully but forcefully suggest that to begin distributing the products, creative ways of compensating the governmental officials in several countries will need to be included in the understanding. You have no personal experience in addressing these issues. How would you proceed?

Case 4

You are the CEO of a corporation that decided it had to merge with a major competitor to continue to grow and perform financially for stockholders. You know that you will retire when the deal is finally made and you will receive an enormous personal compensation package if it is successful. Integrating the operations of the two companies will require massive layoffs in both organizations if the financial goals of the merger are to be met. Your organization has a history and culture that has avoided such layoffs whenever possible in the past. What challenges do you see here, and what would you do in this situation?

---

to these challenges and the development of a wider set of concepts and practical experiences can only help executives sort through the problems of justice that they regularly face. I believe that leaders must assume they will consistently be confronted by such issues and prepare themselves for the complex and sometimes career-threatening processes that they will need to master.

In the introduction to this chapter, we saw that moral problems and issues can arise in the lives of any human being, from high school students to executives of globally recognized corporations. The case examples also demonstrated that age, level of education, and socioeconomic status do not predict whether someone will be able to face a challenge and act justly and with moral integrity. The short summary of the extraordinarily extensive literature on these topics presented in this chapter only begins to suggest how important it is to the welfare of individuals, families, organizations, societies, and the future of humanity.

7

THE ARTS OF STRATEGIC INFLUENCE: MAKING EFFECTIVE PERFORMANCE POSSIBLE

THE CASE OF THE BRASS RING

"I'm not sure I can stand any more of this crap," Linda Thornton said with an unmistakable emotional urgency. At the time, Linda was the executive vice president and basically the chief operations officer of the largest subsidiary of a multidivision corporation. She had spent the previous 15 years of her career climbing the executive ranks of the company. Widely admired and systematically recognized for her significant and sustained contributions to the growth of the enterprise, she had been promised the position of CEO of the subsidiary when the incumbent, Walter Johanson, retired. That promise had been made by Walter himself as well as the CEO of the entire business, Stephen Robinson. The problems she was encountering stemmed from the fact that Mr. Robinson had decided to leave the company for a similar position in an even larger organization. His replacement, Max Sternberg, had been Stephen's number two. The board of directors had given him the position as an interim appointment, and he had survived the energetic search process of a board subcommittee, which had taken approximately 6 months. Max knew about the agreement that had been reached regarding Linda's corporate future and had been a steadfast ally of hers for years. Linda had staunchly supported Max throughout his trial, and he had continuously reassured her of his intention to follow through on the commitment that Stephen had made.

Unfortunately, Walter had no intention of following through. After a period of time in which he was overtly supportive to her, he subsequently appointed several other vice presidents whom he had carefully cultivated. They in turn had formed a kind of defensive perimeter around him. Linda increasingly struggled to do her job because her colleagues often worked actively and covertly to undermine her leadership. When she turned to Walter for support and direction, he often sided with the other vice presidents. All of this continued across a backdrop of effective organizational performance in the subsidiary, much of which Linda and her teams orchestrated. When Linda asked Max directly when a formal succession process would begin, he told her that it would be in the foreseeable future but that he needed to be mindful of the politics of the board of directors where Walter also enjoyed considerable public support. She felt trapped because even though Max neither liked nor trusted Walter, he was reluctant to move politically. Her own relationships with board members were extremely positive, and many of them also knew about the agreement and were supportive of her aspirations and ambitions.

"What's happened now?" I asked.

"Walter and his minions have made some financial commitments for the company that are really risky. I think they've hidden some of the transactions from the corporate finance people with some slick accounting. There's going to be real trouble because I just told Max."

"What did he say?"

"Well, he was his usual self. He's outraged by the possibility that Walter has been doing this, but he's unwilling to confront him or to take it to the board. He doesn't believe he has the votes necessary to remove Walter at present, and he's just fuming and stalling me. The idiots [Linda's term for the vice presidents who supported Walter] keep doing stupid things that just get in our way and cost us money. They think they are business geniuses and have proposed a whole bunch of risky nonsense that will just burn capital. In the meantime, I can't get what I need to take care of the essentials of the business, and our future performance may be compromised because of it."

"Besides trying to persuade Max, what else have you done recently to try to change the situation?"

"Outside of doing my job as well as I can and trying to keep my family sane, not a lot."

"Who else have you discussed the situation with?"

"Only a couple of my closest allies. Walter wouldn't take well to anything he perceived as a threat on my part."

"What about the other business units' CEOs?"

"Only one of them knows. The other five have problems of their own, and they're trying to learn how to work with Max. It's a very queasy time for everyone."

"Is there anything else you've thought of to try?"

"Quite frankly, I've been in touch with several headhunters. There are a couple of interesting job possibilities that I might like to pursue."

"Does anyone else know you've been approached?"

"No, I haven't told anyone. Loyalty is a huge issue for Max, and if he knew that I was actively looking, I can't predict how he'd respond."

At this point in the conversation, it was pretty clear to me that Linda was stalemated. Her current position in the organization was threatened, and her performance was being undermined by the passive–aggressive efforts of her competitive colleagues. The idiots had become sycophants of Walter and fawned on his every word in public. Walter still publicly professed his commitment to Linda while privately doing and saying things that got back to her indicating just the opposite. Unless she found some new way to unlock the situation, she faced an uncertain future in this organization.

"Are you truly prepared to move?" I asked carefully.

"Well, I've talked to my husband, and he's just about had it. The kids are well situated in high school, so we wouldn't move them. If I took something, I'd need to commute for a couple of years."

"That would be pretty tough."

"Tell me about it."

"Do any of the jobs make career sense to you?"

Linda went on to describe three possibilities, one of which involved becoming the COO of a larger business reporting to the CEO–chairman of the company. The scope of operating responsibilities would be extensive, but she wouldn't control the financials or business strategy. In essence, all three positions were senior executive positions with line responsibilities but not true executive authority.

"None of these positions offers what becoming CEO here would. Before I could be the CEO of a larger unit, I'd need to have line authority over finance and strategy. The COO position is the best of the lot, but I'm unclear about what is truly involved."

"What would happen if you looked at the position?"

"If they found out, Walter would be elated and Max really mad."

"Could you do the opening phases in confidence?"

"It's always risky, but yes, I think I could do the airport interview thing and perhaps even a first set of on-site meetings without too much trouble."

"You could go, collect more information to determine whether it is a viable opportunity, and then decide on next steps."

"Yes."

"Is there any way of decreasing the risk of injuring your relationship with Max if you did so?"

"What do you mean?"

"Well, it may be impossible for you to talk to him directly about this potential position, but he surely knows that you are a viable candidate for other companies."

"Oh yes, he's even encouraged me to go look in the past before he became the CEO."

"And you've always decided to stay."

"Yes."

"What would happen if others who knew both of you expressed some concerns to him that the situation is leading to you becoming a flight risk for the organization?"

"What do you mean?"

"What do you think Max's response would be if one of the people on the board who knows you pretty well talked to him about the reality that you could leave if the situation is not resolved in due time?"

"He'd take it better than if I told him because it wouldn't be a direct threat and wouldn't violate his sense of propriety and loyalty."

"And if he heard similar concerns expressed by others in the company without any specific reference to a particular job?"

"It would make him even more nervous, but I don't think he'd hammer me."

I reflected on the conversation for several moments, then tried to summarize what I thought. "The issue here seems pretty clear to me. You are at an impasse in your position, career, and organization. Unless something significant changes soon, you are likely to leave the company anyway because the levels of frustration and emotional turmoil you experience are rising steadily. The influencing strategies you have used successfully in the past in this organization—including rational persuasion, hard work, relationship development, coalition building, and so on—are no longer getting the job done. You need to take some reasonable risks to change your approach, yet have no guarantee of success."

"That sums it up nicely."

"Well, could you change your strategy and add some additional components?"

"You mean go and look at some jobs."

"Precisely! You're actually in a powerful market position right now. If headhunters are actively soliciting you for specific executive positions, it's clear that you have a good reputation and public professional capital. That could disappear quickly if Walter moved against you or succeeded in getting one of the idiots promoted. If you actually had a good job to go to, how would it make you feel?"

"Better. Miserable that I needed to leave and commute, but in the longer term, I know it's a smarter thing to do."

Linda and I then spent some time discussing how she could open a search while simultaneously reducing the risk of retaliation from either Max or Walter. The new tactics that she would add to her long-term strategy of succeeding Walter as the CEO of the company included the following:

- Following up with two of the headhunters to begin the next and more formal job search process
- Discussing the situation with three of the people with whom she had the most supportive relationships and soliciting their help in raising Max's awareness about the growing risk that she might leave the organization
- After the initial rounds of interviews and testing possibilities, asking Walter for some guidance in general terms about how to proceed with the development of her career (This would be done with the understanding that he would not so secretly relish the possibility that she would leave and that he would immediately tell Max that it might be possible. It was hoped that this step would confirm the possibility of her departure in Max's mind without any direct threat being made or concrete action step taken by Linda in public view.)
- Prepare to talk explicitly to both Walter and Max in the event that the search process moved forward
- Prepare her family for the possibility that she might need to commute to work in another town for a while
- Manage her own emotional reactions to the situation by simultaneously allowing herself to become truly interested in new career possibilities and preparing to leave her company, which now presented a very different leadership culture than the one which had become her historic professional home

We also spent a fair amount of time trying to clarify just what she would say to her colleagues about the possible searches and alternative possible reactions from Max and Walter should her activities become more public.

Over the next 4 months, Linda put the additional components of this influencing strategy into practice. She remained scrupulous about her own professional performance during this time period to forestall any potential criticism from Walter or the idiots that she was weak or a lame duck. She picked up the tempo of her meetings with the CEOs of the other business units in the company and with the members of the board to whom she had direct access. She conducted two airport interviews, and the potential COO position proved much more interesting to her than she had imagined. With the support of her husband, she moved forward with that search. I continued to talk with her regularly during these events. Simultaneously, she was tracking Max's increasing mistrust and dismay about Walter and his performance.

Several months later, when Max formally requested the audit committee of the board of directors to pay closer attention to the financial reporting being provided by Walter and his colleagues, the external auditing firm and the board members uncovered some serious reporting improprieties. As these came to light, the governance support that Walter had enjoyed evaporated. Max announced his intention to replace Walter to a narrow group of board members and other executives in his company, including Linda. As these events took place, Max brought Linda progressively closer to him. She proved to be an able partner for him during a trying and challenging set of investigations and negotiations. Max formally offered Linda the job approximately 8 months after the conversation that started this chapter. By then, Linda had withdrawn from the other search. She never had to reveal that process directly to Max because he chose not to ask her about it. However, Linda knew that he had been kept informed by several of her allies in the organization.

THE ESSENTIALS OF INFLUENCE

This abbreviated case study demonstrates some of the complexity and difficulty that leaders at the top of organizations encounter as they try both to promote their own careers and to perform effectively as executives. In my experience, many managers tend to believe that the nearer to the top of an enterprise you are, the easier it is for you to get things done. In reality, that is seldom the case. As the span of control and areas of responsibility rise for leaders, they experience tremendous increases in public scrutiny and criticism of their actions and the performance of their units. In addition, it is rare that they have the ability to direct others in their actions unilaterally. It is most common for a senior executive to face a set of colleagues who are equally ambitious, have their own power bases in the organization, pursue their own personal and unit interests, and may well aggressively defend their positions.

Despite their tremendous authority and range of decision-making powers, leaders who rise to the level of CEO/chairperson of major companies most often find themselves facing a complex environment comprising board members, investment or funding communities, government agencies and regulatory officials, various branches of the global media, public advocacy groups, labor unions, and other critics who have explicit expectations about what they should be doing with the organization. In short, the higher anyone goes in any administrative hierarchy, the greater the need for a deeply sophisticated understanding of politics, power, and influence and the skills necessary to implement complex strategies and tactics through and in human relationships across this broad array of targets.

By the time Linda encountered this career and leadership challenge, she had been working on her political and influencing abilities for decades. She had built constructive and supportive relationships through which she managed her own responsibilities, collected intelligence about what was happening inside and outside of the company, and provided herself with personal support. The series of highly charged, extremely risky, and convoluted conversations we had over the course of these events never required that I educate her on the centrality and importance of these relationships—the nuances of communication, rational argument, subtle emotional appeals, coalition politics, and specific negotiations or trading exchanges that were necessary for her to win this position. Rather, they focused on the intimate and intricate details of the strategies, maneuvers, conversations, and action steps that she undertook. It required me to see the environments in which she was working with as much objectivity as possible while simultaneously appreciating the subjective reactions that she and the other people with whom she was engaged would have to any particular action, including not taking any action. At every turn in this maze of exchanges, paradoxically, I needed both to trust and challenge her perceptions, intuitions, thoughts, and feelings. This type of work makes your head hurt, your heart ache, rubs your nerves absolutely raw, and causes massive loss of sleep. It is the essence of life as a senior executive and as a coach/consultant to these professionals. Sustaining success at the top requires a commanding comprehension of power, politics, influence, negotiations and other skills especially conflict management, persuasion, understanding organizational, group, and individual dynamics, organizational strategy and tactics, and a host of other leadership disciplines. Developing such a nuanced and differentiated set of knowledge, skills, abilities, and experiences takes a long time and a lot of effort. There are no short cuts.

The centrality and importance of these issues is reflected in the psychological literature. As I write this chapter, the PsycINFO database lists 219,858 references to the term *influence*, 63,454 references to *power*, and 4,080 to *persuasion*. The topics of politics, negotiations, group dynamics, organizational strategy, and the other related fields of study have produced their own extraordinary research and practice literatures. These disciplines and their histories are now so large and both integrated and differentiated that there is no way for one human being to comprehend fully everything that has been written, advocated, or experienced. In addition, the disciplines of political science, diplomacy and international affairs, history, sociology, anthropology, and others offer tremendously useful and insightful understanding of these topics, making the task of staying on top of the conceptual and practice literatures even more difficult. Fortunately, there is no real need for senior executives or their coaches and consultants to have such knowledge in complete depth. Over the past 50 years, many excellent books have been produced summarizing much of what has been learned and a huge number of superb and useful journal articles have also appeared. The treatment of these subjects for this book does not require anything like a comprehensive review, but I think it may be helpful to provide at least a minimal set of readings through which readers can conduct their own explorations and understand more fully the other concepts, skills, and methods that will be introduced in this chapter.

Texts on power, politics, influence, persuasion, and leadership have appeared regularly. Alvesson (1996); Bazerman and Lewicki (1983); Berridge (2002); Blau (1964); Broom (2002); Burns (1978); Cialdini (1993); Conger (1998); Etzioni (1975); Freeman (1997); Goleman, Boyatzis, and McKee (2002); Hagberg (2003); Kipnis (1976); Korda (1975); Mintzberg (1983); Mumby (1988); Nicolson (1996); Patterson, Grenny, Maxfield, McMillan, and Switzler (2008); Pfeffer (1981, 1992); Siu (1979); Yates (1985); and Yukl (2010) offer a sampling of such books across a 45-year time span. Each of them provides both general conceptual material and many of them add special emphasis. For example, Kipnis (1976) was one of the most prolific early researchers on the subject of social and managerial influence. Bazerman and Lewicki (1983) emphasized the importance of negotiations in power exchanges. Berridge (2002) and Freeman (1997) focused on the practice of diplomacy in international relations and power exchanges. Cialdini (1993) examined key aspects of human persuasion. Goleman et al. (2002) looked deeply into the uses of emotional intelligence by leaders. Kotter (1985), Mintzberg (1983), Pfeffer (1992), and Yukl (2010) provided interesting overviews of power and influence and their uses by managers. Nicolson (1996) examined the issues with a view of the overriding influence of gender dynamics on power and influence in organizations. Finally, Yates (1985) explored the relationship between political processes and the exercise of leadership and management in organizations.

As I stated earlier, articles appearing in a wide variety of journals on these subjects now number in the hundreds of thousands across the behavioral and social sciences and the humanities. General subject headings for these research studies and conceptual pieces include power and politics, the strategies and tactics involved in human influence, the importance and subtle dimensionality of relationships, the processes involved including defensive reactions, and the varied dimensions of diversity that can come into play in these circumstances among others. These research efforts also stretch across the past 50 years and continue with some degree of vigor as we move deeper into this century. The literatures on power, politics, diplomacy, and the histories of their applications stretch back to the beginning of human history.

Excellent examples of these papers can be discovered as follows. The work of French and Raven (1959) and Raven (1992, 1993, 1999), who fundamentally altered humanity's comprehension of the dimensions of social and interpersonal power, has been extended in a huge number of directions by other theorists and scientists. Abdalla (1987) looked at supervisory social power; Aguinis, Nesler, Quigley, and Tedeschi (1994) examined cognitive perceptions of power; and Allen, Madison, Porter, Renwick, and Mayes (1979) did an early review of organizational politics and the tactics used by leaders. Astley and Sachdeva (1984) studied power from an interorganizational perspective, and Atwater (1988, 1995) explored the interactions between supervisors' sources of power and some characteristics of the organizations in which they worked. Gaski (1986) extended the examination of power and influence to market channels. Kanter (1979) discussed how leaders fail in the exercise of power and influence. Kramer and Baron (1999) provided a comprehensive overview of organizational politics and called for revisions in the research agenda for science in this area. Early in the study of these issues, March (1962) discussed businesses in terms of how they operate as part of political coalitions. McClelland and Burnham (1976) reviewed power from the perspective of how it influences human motivation, and Mechanic (1962) provided an early understanding of how individuals on the lower rungs of organizational hierarchies also exercised significant power and influence. Tushman (1977) encouraged researchers and practitioners to use the lenses of power to study and engage the operations of organizations. Boyle and Dwyer (1995); Boyle, Dwyer, Robicheaux, and Simpson (1992); and Wilkinson and Kipnis (1978) demonstrated that businesses can use aspects of power to influence and change each other. Yukl and Falbe (1991) studied how power can be used and expressed down and across organizational hierarchies. These articles provide a gateway to the extensive literature on power and politics in organizations.

Another extremely interesting and pervasively studied aspect of this topic focuses on the strategies and tactics used by people to influence each other in organizational settings. Ansari and Kapoor (1987) and Deluga (1991) discussed the use of various tactics used by subordinates to influence their bosses. Ansari, Tandon, and Lakhtakia (1989) reversed this dimension and looked at how leaders influenced subordinates in their chains of command. A significant number of other studies and conceptual papers emphasized the similarities and differences involved in influence approaches depending on whether the efforts were directed up, down, or across chains of command and structures in organizations (Bohra & Pandey, 1984; Case, Dosier, Murkison, & Keys, 1988; Cohen & Bradford, 1989, 1991; Crosby,

Evans, & Cowles, 1990; Dosier, Case, & Keys, 1988; Franklin, 1975; Kipnis & Schmidt, 1985; Kipnis, Schmidt, Swaffin-Smith, & Wilkinson, 1984; Kipnis, Schmidt, & Wilkinson, 1980; Lewicki & Litterer, 1985; Newton & Burgoon, 1990; Schilit & Locke, 1982; Tandon, Ansari, & Kapoor, 1991; Tjosvold, Andrews, & Struthers, 1992; Tjosvold, Johnson, & Johnson, 1984; Yukl & Falbe, 1990, 1991; Yukl, Falbe, & Youn, 1993; Yukl, Guinan, & Sottolano, 1995; Yukl, Kim, & Falbe, 1996; Yukl & Tracey, 1992). Barry and Bateman (1992) and Barry and Watson, (1996) studied communications and other influencing methods in the context of managerial dyads, emphasizing the distinctions between what happens when just two people are involved in such exchanges as opposed to larger numbers of individuals. These studies simply illustrate the extensiveness of the available literature.

A third major topic in the study of influence and power concerns the nuances and complexities of human relationships and how those dimensionalities can also affect how leaders make change happen in their organizations. Atwater (1988); Gurtman (1992); Keys, Case, Curran, Miller, and Jones (1987); and Rotter (1980) demonstrated that the degree of trust subordinates have in their supervisors makes a major difference in how they respond to power exchanges. Bono and Anderson (2005) examined the types of assistance transformational leaders derived from networks of advisors. Boss (1978) emphasized that trust influenced problem solving in group scenarios. Dillard, Kinney, and Cruz (1996) demonstrated that influence was related to the emotional reactions of humans in close relationships. Falbo and Peplau (1980) described how power strategies worked in intimate relationships. Imai (1993) studied how power motivation and behaviors affected perceptions of social power in interpersonal relationships. Rosenbluth and Steil (1995) described a set of predictors of intimacy for women of different sexual orientations in intimate relationships. These studies are illustrative of the many dimensions of relationships that come into play when humans try to influence each other in work or personal situations.

Other dimensions of diversity have been examined to determine their effect on influence and power in human relationships. Examples of these studies include the work of Ashforth and Lee (1990); Bennett (1988); R. Z. Booth, Vinograd-Bausell, and Harper (1984); Caldwell and Burger (1997); Grams and Rogers (1990); and Kipnis, Silverman, and Copeland (1973), which looked at various types of personality characteristics, defensive behaviors, and race in influencing and power exchanges. These types of articles demonstrate the need to look closely at the wide variety of dimensions of diversity that are automatically in play for all of the parties involved in relationships in which deliberate efforts to change attitudes, beliefs, values, emotions, thoughts, or behaviors are enacted.

Finally, well-known and widely cited studies have accentuated the importance of understanding the various processes involved in influencing.

Benson and Hornsby (1988) examined the relationship between politics and compensation in organizations. Emerson (1962) demonstrated the significance of dependency components of power relationships. Kotter (1977, 1985) extended the examination of power dependency analysis. Salancik and Pfeffer (1977) examined a variety of contingencies that had impacts on influencing and power exchanges. Tepper, Eisenbach, Kirby, and Potter (1998) found that participants in influencing exchanges resisted power strategies under different circumstances, particularly when they perceived them to be unfair or unjust. Erez, Rim, and Keider (1986) explored the relationships between agents and targets in influencing processes. Cocivera (1998, 2002) did two graduate-level studies that provided one of the most comprehensive research-based views of the key components of influencing processes presented in the literature to date. These studies illustrate that the processes involved in influencing efforts are themselves important pieces of this complex puzzle that leaders constantly must address and solve.

A Conceptual Model of Influence

In studying the literature on influence over the past couple of decades, I have been slowly but surely trying to build a conceptual model that would help guide my practice in this arena both as a leader and as a coach or consultant to other executives. It is clear that there are a plethora of approaches and findings to choose from and what has motivated me is the desire to discern key elements that have reliably appeared in various articles and texts. What follows in this next section is an attempt to provide an overview of what I have developed. Keep in mind as we walk through the various elements in this approach that it is what I used in the work that I did with Linda that introduced this chapter. I will refer back to that case study to illustrate various components of the model and methods.

Figure 7.1 presents the first core element of the model. It depicts a Venn diagram with two components, the influencing agent on the left-hand side and the influencing target on the right-hand side. Between them is a space that I have labeled the zone of behavioral influencing and interaction processes. Within each of the lobes of the Venn diagram, we see the same fundamental pieces in play for both the agent and target. These include the various dimensions of the individuals' diversity, such as personality, psychodynamics, knowledge, skills, abilities, experience, roles, and, following both this book and Kilburg (2006), their wisdom and virtue systems. We can also see their sources of personal and position power, their experiences with power and influence, their histories with each other and the organizational and environmental contexts in which any influencing, power, or political process would take place.

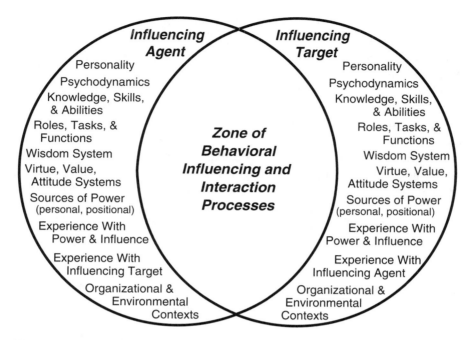

Figure 7.1. Influencing model I.

The zone of influencing processes emerges out of this enormously complex set of dimensions, and both the agent and the target organize, engage, react to, and play through these initiatives with each other. The figure presumes that the influencing processes occur in and through the relationship that the target and agent share. Even in cases in which the agent and target are strangers to each other, some effort must be undertaken at least to understand how such a relationship could or would unfold in a more personal way. In other cases in which the agent is trying to influence others with whom she or he has no direct contact through the relationships she or he has, the agent will need to imagine and perhaps simulate what will happen between those with whom there is direct versus indirect contact. Having such a model available as a baseline provides a first level of diagnostic capacity in the sense that it helps to direct your attention to the fundamental issues of who is involved in the influencing engagement. As anyone can easily imagine, the complexity of any episode of influencing rises rapidly with any increase in the number of agents and targets.

In Linda's case, she was involved in a multilevel and multidimensional effort to influence a variety of people. Her primary targets were Max and Walter. Ultimately, she needed Max to fulfill the promise that the organization had made to promote her. She also needed Walter to step down. She had used her relationships with both of them over the course of several years to achieve her goals. However, she also needed to use her relationships with a number of others within their mutual acquaintance to create impacts on both of them. Ultimately, she also needed to go outside of the existing network of relationships to create new ones and the realistic possibility that she would depart to help her break the impasse that she experienced. In these processes, she had to refine further and use an extraordinarily nuanced understanding of both Max and Walter as people and leaders for her strategy to work.

Figure 7.2 provides a somewhat simplified view of Figure 7.1 to demonstrate the core geographic elements involved in any particular influencing scenario. To put it in its clearest terms, any influencing agent must have an overarching understanding of whom she or he is trying to move as well as intimate knowledge of the organizational culture, history, structures, processes, goals, and other factors in which they are working. Finally, the agent must look outside of the both the target and the organization to the external environment for other issues, resources, and information that may be helpful in either designing or conducting any influencing effort. In Linda's case, she

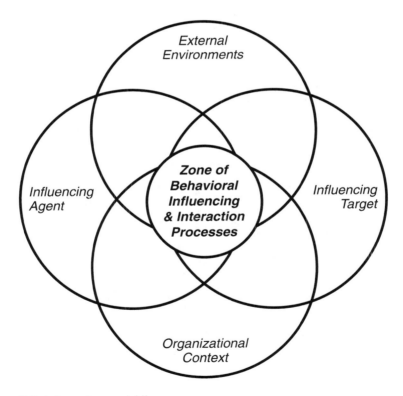

Figure 7.2. Influencing model II.

knew herself and the other executives and the organizational environment extremely well, as if it were her family. In the opening phases of our coaching and strategy work on these issues, it was clear to both of us that she needed to go to the external environment to develop a broader understanding of the possibilities that might exist for her and to create the potential for another significant source of power through and with which she could influence Max and others in her home organization. In the majority of significant influencing efforts in which executives engage, there is a continuous need to stay oriented to what is happening in all four of these domains to determine whether their strategies and tactics are working or need to change. In Linda's case, as she acquired significant sources of new information regarding each of these areas, she would often reach out to me to help her recalibrate her initiatives.

Figures 7.3, 7.4, and 7.5 provide a series of flow charts that illustrate the mutual process that an influencing agent and his or her target go through during one of these types of engagements. Keep in mind that I have created these diagrams based on my reading of the historical and current literature on power and influence. The elements contained have been documented in many of the references cited earlier in this chapter.

In Figure 7.3, we see the process begin with the influencing agent. The diagram identifies many of the internal components and dimensions of diver-

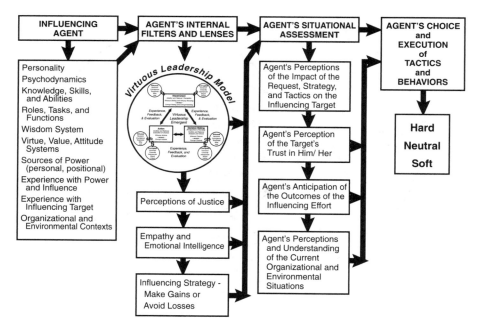

Figure 7.3. Influencing process map I.

sity that may influence an individual as he or she contends with the need to influence someone in his or her environment, in essence, repeating part of the contents of Figure 7.1. After accessing and using some or all of these facets of themselves, the leader or influencing agent then enters into the formal process of developing a strategy through and with which to affect a target. The agent overtly and covertly makes rational and intuitive connections with the various lenses and filters through which they conduct themselves and their lives. These include their virtue systems that we have explored in depth in previous chapters. Of special interest in this process are the perceptions of justice the agents use to manage their lives, their emotional intelligence that, for this book, has focused largely on the implementation of the virtue of temperance, and their empathic abilities though which they can anticipate the potential reactions of their target(s). In addition, individuals must choose a general, coherent strategy that involves whether they are trying to make gains in the situation or simply attempting to avoid losses. I have more to say about this latter topic in just a bit.

The influencing agent also conducts a situational assessment, which Figure 7.3 describes as including his or her perceptions of the effect of any potential strategy on the target, the degree of trust that may exist between them, and the potential outcomes of the initiative. Finally, the agent takes account of the external environment and the organizational context in which the effort will occur. On the basis of this comprehensive assessment, the influencing agent selects the tactics and the behaviors she or he believes will create the best outcomes and then executes them. In the literature on power and influence, such methods are often labeled as *hard, neutral,* or *soft.* Again, we discuss tactics and methods in a subsequent section of this chapter. It must also be noted that although Figure 7.3 displays this process as involving a logical and somewhat linear progression, in many, if not most, situations, a leader involved in deciding and executing an influencing effort will also be using his or her intuition to a great extent. Thus, the elements involved in any such analysis like what is portrayed in this figure may be included or excluded in rational and overt ways or in irrational and covert processes. Multilevel feedback loops may well exist between the agent's internal dimensions of diversity, her or his lenses and filters, the way in which she or he conducts and uses an environmental assessment, and the tactics and behaviors that result. In my experience, it is often the case that the approaches to influence that are favored by a leader are strongly influenced by his or her history; experience; type of education; and other personal characteristics such as personality, gender, and race. All of these sources of variance in any situation are compounded by their habits, preferences, and skills. The more an influencing agent understands about himself or herself, the situation, and the potential target the more likely that the strategies, tactics, and behaviors selected will be more effective.

Of special interest here for influencing agents and their coaches and consultants is the need to assess and take into account the defensive structures and processes that are routinely used by any target, by the groups in which the agent and target are members, and by the organization as a whole. In an earlier work (Kilburg, 2000), I provided a detailed exposition of this subject as well as some suggestions for how coaches can best access and work with and in defensive scenarios. Argyris (1990) also provided a detailed analysis and suggestions of how to approach defensive operations as they manifest in organizations. In Linda's case, she needed to pay particular attention to Max's propensity to engage in denial and repression of his thoughts and feelings about Walter and the potential consequences of leaving him in his position for a substantial period of time. Similarly, Max tended not to pay particular attention to the costs that Linda was paying in the situation. His rationalization of the political situation cemented his unwillingness to move, particularly because it was tied directly to his consciously experienced anxiety about his own personal and professional job security. In organizational terms, there was ample history to support Linda's concerns that the leadership of the company was capable of scapegoating and acting out against any leader perceived to be too deviant for the dominant coalition. In addition, like many other large organizations, there were many political alliances and subgroups that operated with varying degrees of effectiveness, including the team around Walter, whom she referred to as "the idiots." That group routinely acted out the wishes both of Walter and of the other members as they individually and jointly pursued their ambitions and goals. These assessments of the defensive perimeters and operations of the individuals and organizational structures and processes need to be made explicit when any leader faces the kind of complex and threatening challenge that confronted Linda.

Figure 7.4 presents the same processes from the vantage point of the target of influence. To respond effectively, the agent must understand his or her own dimensions of diversity, lenses and filters, and strategies. As the figure depicts, the agent will conduct a similar environmental and organizational assessment. The targets choose their own responses to the efforts to influence them, and those tactics and behaviors can be organized into four major categories. In general terms, targets tend to refuse to respond in any constructive way to the influencing strategies and tactics; create overt, active, and covert and passive means of resisting the initiatives; or comply in some formal or informal way with what the agent wants. In the best scenario, the target decides consciously or unconsciously to make a full commitment to what the agent wants by way of a response. As you examine the various components identified in these figures, it is easy to begin to understand how complex and difficult many influencing initiatives quickly become.

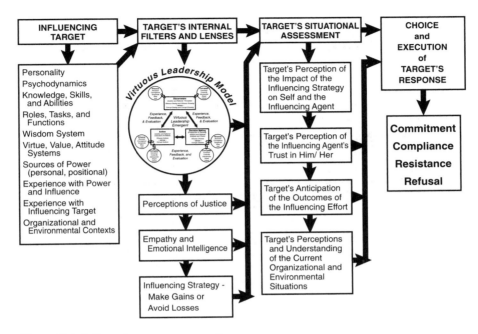

Figure 7.4. Influencing process map II.

Figure 7.5 combines the previous two figures and demonstrates that the responses of the target are absorbed by the influencing agent. In other words, in the context of a relationship between them, an influencing target almost automatically becomes an influencing agent as a result of how she or he reacts to the efforts to move him or her. Refusal responses thus will have different effects on an agent than an open and welcoming commitment to do what was suggested or demanded. The mutually interactive aspects of these exchanges describes a specific kind of dyadic relationship—namely, one in which the parties are actively trying to change the other member of the dyad. As the number of people involved in any influencing process increases, the potential number and variety of interactions and exchanges rises almost exponentially because of the size and shape of the subgroups involved. A leader targeting one member of his or her staff will face very different types of problems than one who is trying to change the attitudes, values, beliefs, assumptions, or performance of hundreds or even thousands of colleagues. The sophistication and complexity of larger scale influencing efforts thus require more in-depth consideration of the array of targets and how to reach them.

In the case of Linda, she needed to know her organization with a great deal of depth and sophistication. She also had to understand the specific individuals whom she was targeting in highly nuanced ways. In particular, we spent a great

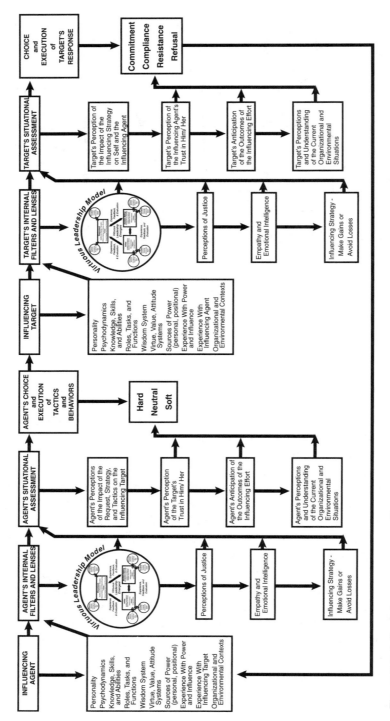

Figure 7.5. Influencing process map III.

deal of time discussing the potential responses of Max, Walter, and the board members whom she wanted to use to influence both of them. The individuals whom she used as strategic allies among her colleagues also warranted considerable discussion because of the potential for disclosure or betrayal of her efforts and the potential need for the exchange of promises and favors to move them in the desired direction. As opposed to many other actions that leaders undertake, these influencing engagements often provide them with pretty effective feedback on whether their approaches are working. In Linda's case, the stakes for her career both inside the company and in the industry made this whole sequence of activity extraordinarily risky and anxiety arousing. For if at any point in the processes Max were to be significantly offended by what she was doing or Walter threatened to the point of wanting to take direct punitive action against her, she could have lost her job and perhaps any significant opportunities for senior executive positions in similar organizations. Thus, leaders and their coaches and consultants must be extraordinarily attuned to these risks and to the likely responses of all of the people involved if they are to succeed.

In keeping with what I described earlier as the large-scale strategies that agents engage in their influencing efforts, Figure 7.6 presents a framework within which to understand these components of the influencing process. In the first column of the figure, I have displayed the typical array of potential targets for influence from the individual; to another person or group; to whole organizations; and, in larger engagements, to markets, communities, nations,

Target/ Focus of Influencing Effort	Make Gains			Avoid Losses		
	Compel	Deter	Engage	Compel	Deter	Engage
Self						
Other(s)						
Organization(s)						
Social Systems						
Markets						
Environments, Communities, Ecologies						

Figure 7.6. General goals and methods of influencing initiatives.

and whole ecologies of nations. In general terms, leaders enact two generic influencing and power strategies. They either seek to make gains in conjunction with or at the expense of their targets, or they seek to limit the losses that others try to inflict on them. Lasswell (1958) and Mearsheimer (2001) provided particularly acute analyses of these processes in the context of domestic and international politics. Under those two major headings, I have inserted three additional columns labeled *compel, deter,* and *engage.* Compelling approaches to influence usually involve the use of hard tactics and behaviors such as threats, force, or pressure of various kinds to ensure that the target will either comply or commit. Deterrence approaches can also engage similar tactics in response, usually with the intent of either refusing or resisting the influencing effort. Engagement strategies more often involve the use of neutral or soft tactics such as negotiations, rational argument, and simple requests in the effort both to build relationship(s) and to accomplish the baseline goals of the initiative usually seen in compliance and commitment responses. These approaches can be broadly compared with those used to describe the various forms of courage behavior in Chapter 4.

Again, these influencing processes can quickly become complex with the number of people involved and the types of ends being pursued. In the worst historical cases, empires and nation-states are compelled to submit to the wishes of competitors through the means of warfare, leading at times to the death of entire populations and the end of history for the losers. In contemporary free markets, this also happens with great frequency as hostile takeovers virtually end the existence of business enterprises and thousands and sometimes tens of thousands of people lose their jobs.

In Linda's situation, she was engaged simultaneously in making gains and avoiding losses. For a variety of reasons, she believed that it was best for the organization and for her to succeed Walter sooner rather than later. Indeed, Max himself had said as much to her on numerous occasions. However, Max's reading of the political landscape inhibited him from taking direct and forceful action. Linda faced the need to either wait for the situation to unfold on Max's terms or to intervene. She obviously chose to intervene. Although her primary strategy was to make gains in the sense of being promoted, she simultaneously was trying to avoid the potential loss of her job and the destruction of her reputational capital in the industry. She needed to have a clear-eyed understanding of both of these major components of her approach and to select and enact the appropriate tactics and behaviors that would support both over time. She was clearly able to do so in an extremely adroit fashion, but the processes involved were stressful throughout the time it took for her to be appointed.

Figure 7.7 directs our attention to yet another significant dimension of influencing situations. It depicts the various locations for organizational influence in a simple but descriptive fashion. In essence, leaders must understand

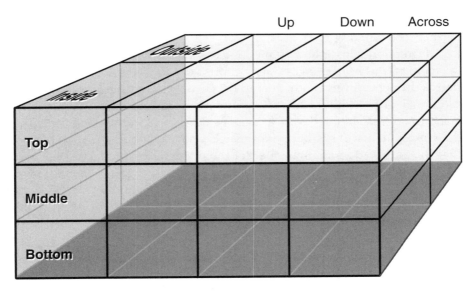

Figure 7.7. Organizational location for influence.

explicitly where they sit in the structure of their enterprise—at the top, middle, or bottom. In large and highly differentiated organizations, there can be many levels and folds within each of these major subsections. In complex, multiple-division companies like the one in which Linda worked, these hierarchical structures are repeated in all of the components of the business. Thus, Walter's position, which she sought, was but one of several CEO–presidential positions in the subsidiary companies of the larger organization. Max led a senior team of people who managed the entire institution, and Walter was just one of nearly a dozen direct reports to him.

If leaders understand clearly where they sit in the organization, it is easier to conceptualize any influencing initiative as needing to be directed up, down, or across the chain of command, and whether it must include efforts to reach outside of the whole organization to the environments in which it relates and the other organizations that reside there. In general terms, the range and types of influencing tactics and behaviors available to a leader shifts dramatically depending on these directional choices. For example, within prescribed limits, leaders are specifically empowered to use authority-centered directions, threats, other forms of coercion, and intimidation when trying to influence subordinates who report to them. Such hard tactics are not usually available when trying to influence bosses, so those efforts most often engage soft or neutral tactics, such as negotiations, rational persuasion, exchanges of favors, and ingratiation. Influencing efforts across an organization can incorporate soft, neutral, and hard tactics, but special precautions must be taken whenever the harsher roads are taken.

Figure 7.7 helps us understand Linda's influencing strategies and tactics in graphic terms because her primary efforts were to go outside the organization to the upper levels of other enterprises to develop both relationships and additional job possibilities. She also went up the organizational chain of command to both Walter and Max to manage the flow of information carefully, the conceptualization of her performance, and the public and private spin that the gossip and rumor channels of the organization produced. She also carefully reached up past Max to members of the board of directors with whom she had developed personal relationships to create additional lines of influence. Such moves above a superior are often the most delicate and dangerous influencing tactics because of the extreme responsiveness that most senior leaders feel and express when they believe that they are being maneuvered from below through potentially threatening or coercive efforts to use the chain of command above them.

Finally, she directed considerable energy and effort both across and up to the leaders of other major units in the company to solicit their support or to push them to take action that she believed would be helpful to her. Keeping this kind of topographic map in mind can be helpful in influencing situations because it is easy to become disoriented as the political and professional stakes and consequences rise and the associated levels of strong emotional responses expand. Remaining temperate, just, reverent, courageous, and wise in such circumstances requires the expenditure of enormous reserves of physical and psychic energy. I hope that this sequence of figures provides my readers with a conceptual and operational map that can help them to stay oriented to the wide variety of issues, structures and processes involved in building an influence strategy.

Additional Elements and Issues in the Exercise of Power and Influence

As I stated earlier, influencing processes and situations arise within the political and power structures of any organization. To be effective at the art of influence in any enterprise, leaders must accept the realities of power and politics, try to become an excellent student of how they operate in his or her institution, and simultaneously look for and create opportunities to shift these structures and processes. The references provided in this chapter offer a tremendous gateway to the history, science, and practice of power and politics. Three of the books to which I most constantly refer clients and colleagues to start this intellectual and professional journey are those by Cialdini (1993), Lasswell (1958), and Pfeffer (1992). Each of these books is steeped in the science and history of politics, power, and influence.

My earlier work (Kilburg, 2006) provided a conceptual framework with which to understand and conduct situational assessments as part of the constructing wisdom maps. A key component of such discernments involves the ability to explore and understand the long-standing and immediate political processes and field of forces inside organizations. Lasswell's (1958) treatment of politics provides a profoundly simple and elegant way of doing this by framing these processes as structures and methods through which the elites of societies and organizations tend to answer the key questions of who will get what, and how, when, and why they will do so. Once you understand that humans must come to grips with these essentials when more than two of them are present in any situation, it is easier to move past any distaste or disinclination to engage in political behavior. I often hear leaders say that they detest politics, and although this is often an accurate expression of their feelings, such emotions and thoughts nevertheless must be confronted directly. I believe strongly that anyone who aspires to lead human organizations can ill afford to deny the importance of politics or to believe that they can be avoided. Simply put, politics are pervasive and essential in human affairs. Without politics, virtually nothing gets accomplished. Therefore, they must be engaged and mastered for progress and performance to occur. It is also true that political processes and structures can be exceedingly delicate and that they have been misused, sometimes for horrendously evil and malign purposes, throughout human history.

In Kilburg (2006), I provided a specific methodology for promoting deconstructive political inquiry. It consisted of 40 interpenetrating questions designed to help a leader or a consultant explore the past and present political landscape within an organization and then construct an understanding of how it is working. In addition, it contained additional questions to help someone think creatively about how political situations could be changed creatively from different perspectives. The exercise included such practical and easy inquiries as who are the formal and informal leaders in an enterprise and how are they connected to each other, as well as extremely complex studies of the competitive and conflict landscapes in the institution. The more one understands about these variables, the better the diagnosis of the situation and the more nuanced and effective influencing strategies and tactics can become.

Any understanding of politics must incorporate a comprehensive understanding of how social power is distributed and expressed in organizations. French and Raven (1959) provided a simple taxonomy of six bases of social power that is still the most widely used in the literature. These include the following:

1. *Reward*—monetary, recognition, and other forms of positive reinforcement promised, threatened, or provided by an influencing agent to a target to achieve a result.

2. *Coercive*—punishments, criticisms, threats, and other negative behaviors applied to a target to reach an influencing goal.
3. *Legitimate*—usually position-based authority that enables an agent to require compliance or commitment from a target.
4. *Referent*—the ability of an agent to create an attraction to or respect for him, her, an organization, or a cause of some sort that will tend to engender support or positive responses from a target.
5. *Expert*—the belief by targets that influencing agents possess special knowledge, skills, abilities, and experience that are desirable or useful.
6. *Informational*—the ability to martial different forms of information including rational argument, rumor, gossip, persuasion, and qualitative and quantitative data in support of a position.

Virtually all leaders have an explicit understanding of their legitimate basis for power. It is contained in job descriptions and reinforced in the daily exchanges with superiors and subordinates. They also tend to have some comprehension of reward, coercion, and some aspects of informational power that they can exercise. However, they often misapprehend the nuances of these and the other sources of power, and as a result, they create influencing strategies and tactics that can be far less sophisticated and powerful than would be the case if a more comprehensive understanding were routinely available to them.

Exhibit 7.1 presents a fairly comprehensive listing of typical challenges that leaders often face as they try to acquire and use power. The issues span simple matters, such as learning where to find sources of information in and about the organization and its people, developing specific skills, and finding friends in an institution, to extraordinarily difficult problems, such as learning from failure, conducting overt and covert wars inside or between organizations, and giving and receiving gifts and favors. The first item on the list, developing a power base, begins with the awareness that such a foundation is essential for anyone in a leadership position or who desires such a job. The evolution of a strong base requires consistent effort applied over substantial periods of time. It can and often is aided by serendipity and spontaneous occurrences in which leaders meet and work with others, cocreate effective relationships to get a piece of work accomplished, and then recognizing afterward that those kinds of people and relationships can continue to be useful across a lifetime of leadership. Power bases can also be extended deliberately through the creation and deployment of influencing strategies and tactics of many sorts.

As executives gain experience and expertise in how to lead, they often create their own intuitive models for how to use power and influence in their lives and organizations. These are often idiosyncratic approaches nurtured in the heat and confusion of successes and failures along the pathway to senior positions. Some individuals develop an explicit code of practice in these

EXHIBIT 7.1
Typical Challenges in the Acquisition and Use of Power and Influence

1. Acquiring a power base.

2. Learning how to
   a. build relationships.
   b. perform effectively.
   c. behave virtuously (courage, temperance, justice, reverence, & wisdom).
   d. manage one's tendencies toward corruption and vice.
   e. make use of exchanges and favors.
   f. build alliances.
   g. challenge corruption.
   h. strategically use intemperance, irreverence, and injustice.
   i. use the processes of discernment, decision making, and taking action.
   j. compete effectively.
   k. manage conduct warfare—overt and covert.
   l. start, stop, and manage mutinous processes.
   m. become more emotionally intelligent.
   n. master communications skills (empathy, rhetoric, tact, listening, inquiry, advocacy, feedback).
   o. manage diversity in teams, work forces, organizations, social systems, communities.
   p. learn about targets of influence.
   q. let yourself be influenced strategically.
   r. manage emotions—anxiety, anger, shame, sadness, grief, loss, pain, suffering, joy, curiosity, compassion, love, kindness, surprise.
   s. overcome blind spots and gaps in knowledge, skill, abilities, experience, personal, group, and/or organizational culture, gender, race, ethnicity, other dimensions of diversity and community history.
   t. manage deadly management errors—hubris, narcissism, psychopathy, and sadomasochism.
   u. learn voraciously from success and failure.
   v. use the art of reflective engagement.

3. Managing the toxic or ineffective boss, subordinate, colleague, partner, peer, customer/client.

4. Acquiring and using effective and timely information channels.

5. Managing failure—fired, forced out, passed over, outmaneuvered, beaten.

6. Managing comebacks and rallies from disasters and failures.

7. Finding sponsors, mentors, and friends.

8. Developing and coaching others—allies, subordinates, colleagues, supporters.

9. Letting go, relinquishing power and influence—delegation and moving on.

10. Developing and using trust.

11. Managing change and innovation—knowing how much is enough, how to start, why/when to stop, why it is necessary.

12. Changing peoples' minds and feelings of others with varied or diverse interests, needs, or agendas.

13. Identifying and managing resistance.

(*continues*)

14. Identifying and managing domination and oppression dynamics.

15. Identifying and managing collusion dynamics.

16. Managing the repositioning and restructuring of an organization.

17. Constructing, deconstructing, and reconstructing the strategy and tactics of a leader for his/her organization—setting a new or different direction for the organization or group.

18. Leading strategic retreats and graceful exits.

19. Managing immovable objects and irresistible forces.

20. Managing the deadly sins of humanity.

21. Giving and granting voice to others.

22. Telling truth to power; making the unknown known, the unconscious conscious, the unsaid said, the undiscussable discussable.

23. Granting access to and giving gifts and loans of power and influence.

24. Uses of aggression—directing it; justification, modulation, containment, managing aftermaths—damage, wounds, emotional responses (anxiety, shame, sadness, rage, resentment, guilt, elation/joy).

25. Managing strengths as blind spots and preventing turns to weakness—the Aristotelian Tragedy.

26. Being seen and heard in the right places, right ways, right times, with the right people for the right reasons.

27. Managing conformity and obedience—ceding control, aligning with superiors, allies, and stronger competitors. When, where, how, how much, why, and with whom.

28. Managing deviance and disobedience—creative and destructive. When, where, how, how much, why, and with whom.

29. Introducing, changing, and managing methods of creating, interpreting, and enacting meaning for others and the organization—symbols, culture, values, beliefs, attitudes, ceremonies, rites, rituals—means and ends of defining reality; practicing the art of social construction.

30. Managing leadership, followership, and organizational implementation or performance.

31. Using organizational structures and processes to
    a. divide and conquer adversaries.
    b. expand one's domain.
    c. expand and consolidate one's power and influence.
    d. reduce or expand the domains of others.
    e. reduce or expand the power and influence of others.
    f. co-opt others, gain the support of allies.

32. Managing tests of loyalty.

33. Using power and influence too much, too soon, too fast, not enough, too late, too slow—problems of timing, diagnosis, and orchestration.

EXHIBIT 7.1
Typical Challenges in the Acquisition and Use of Power and Influence *(Continued)*

34.	Framing the use of power and influence correctly.
35.	Choosing the correct rhetoric.
36.	Staying in power too long.
37.	Removing someone who has stayed in power too long.
38.	Recognizing that anxiety, indecision, and confusion can be and often are a normal part of leadership and the management of change—the problem of the fog of war.
39.	The special problem of political will—the ability to conceive strategy and tactics and implement them in the face of opposition, resistance, hostility, significant risk, ambiguity, and uncertainty, the emotions of others and oneself, and anticipated negative impacts for those involved, including one's own death.
40.	Distinguishing and managing the distinctions between means and ends.
41.	Managing to reason morally under stressful and demanding conditions and avoiding the problems of amoral and immoral rationalization—developing and maintaining one's moral compass.
42.	Developing courageous curiosity.
43.	Constantly asking what you know, what you assume, hypothesize, do not know, fantasize, avoid, should know, need to know.
44.	Constantly trying to discover who knows what you need to know and cultivating their knowledge and support.

arenas. In my experience, most leaders gain an intuitive feel for how to proceed in their enterprises. They can tell you how to get something done, what to avoid, who to trust, and who is trouble and why, but they often have difficulty articulating these insights into a coherent model or theory of practice for themselves or others. Exhibit 7.2 presents a set of general principles in the use of power and influence that I have carved out of decades of experience in leadership positions; working for both skilled and completely inept or corrupt executives; and coaching, educating, and developing thousands of managers.

In a sense, the core elements of these principles are reflected in the chapters of this book. I believe strongly that leaders must focus on direction and strategy, the continued evolution and creation of the virtuous aspects of their characters, and the extremely careful management of their normal tendencies toward corrupt behavior. If on top of these components, executives understand the nature of the core tasks of management—discernment, decision making, and taking action—they have a powerful and deep foundation on which they can depend. From there they must become extraordinary students of power, politics, and influence. They need to deliberately practice the complete array of

EXHIBIT 7.2
General Principles in the Use of Power and Influence

1. Act virtuously through discernment, decision-making, taking action, and evaluating situations and responses.

2. Avoid the fundamental attribution error—the people involved and their actions and characteristics are most important; focus equally on the key variables in the situation.

3. Do not start with an effort to define the problem, instead start with the story that led to the situation.

4. Discern what the situation calls for—short or long-term interventions; accommodations, assimilations, or breaking frame; making gains or avoiding losses; compellance, deterrence, or engagement.

5. Discern carefully who the targets are for influencing efforts.

6. Discern and understand the motives of those involved in the influencing effort.

7. Decide what to do based on the strategic application of both analytic and intuitive approaches and use as many sources of information as you can develop in the time available.

8. To the extent possible, act with strategic aims in mind.

9. Develop and pursue common/super ordinate goals—directions and activities upon which everyone can agree.

10. Consciously construct your power base inside and outside of any given organization.

11. To the extent possible, gain control, power, and influence over critical resources in organizations and social systems (people, relationships, expertise, effort, jobs, budgets, facilities, legal resources, information, space); become invaluable.

12. Assist others in becoming dependent upon you and your resources.

13. Avoid becoming dependent upon others and their resources or abilities.

14. Search for unexploited resources, problems others cannot solve, jobs others cannot or will not do, and always work to reduce organizational and leadership risks and uncertainties—serve the organization and its leaders.

15. Do your job well and keep an eye on what your organization, boss, and CEO need—get things done.

16. Strive for consistency in perspective, effort, and the actions you take but be thoughtful about being seen as completely predictable.

17. Build relationships and alliances but be careful about whom you choose.

18. Look for opportunities to work with others interdependently, collaboratively, and cooperatively to establish relationships

19. Build trust, relationship, reputational, and favor capital with others—create a sense of obligation and commitment in others—carefully manage reciprocity.

20. Share credit, recognition, effort, and support with others in your relationship and alliance networks—meet their needs; fulfill their desires.

EXHIBIT 7.2
General Principles in the Use of Power and Influence *(Continued)*

21. Learn as much as you can about real or potential competitors, adversaries, and enemies.

22. Always be prepared for competition and warfare; it will sometimes come when you least expect it and often from whom or where you do not anticipate.

23. Study the networks in organizations and social systems—work, information, friendships, alliances, resource flows—and look to join or affiliate with those connected to power sources.

24. To the extent possible, gain access to and participate in groups that make decisions—use projects and task forces as opportunities to demonstrate your abilities, create relationships, and practice influencing strategy and skills.

25. Look to place yourself in a central physical location in organizations or social systems.

26. Look for winning issues; pick your battles carefully; fight for losers strategically with other gains and potential losses in mind; know when to submit and how to win and lose gracefully.

27. When offered a choice of a line or staff job, favor the line with budget, hiring, firing, and top and bottom line responsibilities.

28. Cultivate the virtues of reverence, temperance, justice, courage and wisdom; energy and stamina; the ability to engage sustained attention on stressful projects and long range challenges; interpersonal and environmental sensitivity; creativity; flexibility; and toughness (be prepared at all times to be in conflict and competitive situations).

29. Become an expert practitioner of reflective engagement.

30. Learn about and become a master of framing—how to describe and process problems, issues, challenges, opportunities, values, beliefs, attitudes, questions, assumptions, thoughts, feelings, and behaviors.
    a. Use compare and contrast methods.
    b. Enable and use the ability to enlist others in your efforts and obtain their commitment (free choice, public requests and offers, make the agreements explicit and irrevocable, escalate commitments, and offer the opportunity to be involved in something important).
    c. Attack the positions of others carefully, usually indirectly. If confronting, make it strategic not instinctual.
    d. Discern and exploit conditions of scarcity (the offer is available for a limited time).
    e. Be a superb storyteller.

31. Learn how and become a master of social construction.
    a. Develop consensus with those involved.
    b. Make your ideas, beliefs, values, and behaviors the norm for the group.
    c. Lead the creation of social proof—be, think, feel, and do what others want to be, think, feel, and do—the right way.
    d. Discern and exploit troupe/group awareness—where are they and where to they want to be (aspirations, vulnerabilities, and anxieties).
    e. To the extent possible take control of the story, how meaning is made, how events and reactions are interpreted and managed.

(continues)

32. Become a master of relationships and relating (share your interests; be aware of the interests of others and invest in them; empathize; pay attention to your and others' physical appearance; learn to recognize, compliment, and give feedback to others; develop a reputation for collaboration, cooperation, and being good company on difficult adventures; be positive even in bad times; make others feel special).

33. Become a master of emotional intelligence (emotional awareness, and understanding; resiliency; conveying/expressing the importance, urgency, threats, and opportunities in situations; the uses of empathy; a sense of humor and appropriate/strategic use of irreverence and intemperance).

34. Become a master of communications skills (see framing; empathy, rhetoric, inquiry, advocacy, listening, feedback).

35. Become a lifelong student of leadership, politics, power, and influence.

36. Become a master of timing (when to start an initiative—being first; when to delay an initiative—being second, late, last, a no show; when to stop; when and how to establish, meet, and beat deadlines; when to make announcements and take action; discern the "exact right moment").

37. Become a master of obtaining, analyzing, and using information (learn how to get others to tell their stories completely; when and how to use analytic tools and data; when and how to use intuitive information and intuitive methods; when to appear rational and irrational; when you need allies; when and how to spin—frame—to best advantage; getting and presenting facts; getting and using emotional responses; using outside experts/consultants; interpreting beliefs, attitudes, values, biases, thinking styles, group dynamics, covert processes, hidden agendas, cognitive distortions, unconscious conflicts and defenses; getting and using alternative perspectives and points of view; see social construction No. 30).

38. Learn voraciously from success and failure.

39. Be a master of managing diversity (be curious and empathic about the backgrounds, experiences, and expertise of others; learn to understand, value, and use the beliefs, values, attitudes, thoughts, feelings, habits, cultural norms, customs and practices of others in what you are trying to accomplish).

40. Become a master of moral reasoning—know your own moral compass intimately and where you may be at risk to reason or act amorally or immorally.

41. Be acutely aware of the seductive nature, pitfalls, and dark sides of the uses of power and influence—the invitation to abuse, corruption, vice, and failure (it is easy to lose your humanity as you accumulate power and influence).

42. Be astute in your assessments of means and ends.

influencing skills and methods outlined in this chapter. They must learn that virtually nothing happens in any organization without the mediation of human relationships. They should spend dedicated time and energy developing their own networks of relationships through which they can create and implement their experiments in power and influence. It helps tremendously if they have an understanding of the structures and processes that operate in social networks and how to diagnose and intervene in these elements of any enterprise. They can learn how to argue, make public presentations, develop and use data for the purposes of making gains or avoiding losses in power exchanges, manage their own thoughts and emotions (especially under conditions in which they may be deliberately provoked to act out in negative ways), and communicate in highly nuanced ways with widely varying audiences.

At the middle and most certainly at the top of organizations, they will find their performance greatly enhanced if they know how to deconstruct the efforts of others to influence them and to define how the world is to be approached. They also can aim to become experts in such meaning-making strategies and tactics themselves. They need to consider the timing in how they design and conduct any intervention based on power and influence. It is essential for leaders to develop and use the various channels of information available in every organization to help diagnose situations, create plans, make decisions, and take action. As the 21st century continues to unfold, it is clear that any executive will need to be able to move in, through, with, and against colleagues and organizations that have diverse backgrounds, cultures, and significant differences from those which he or she may derive the most personal comfort. Perhaps most important, when power and influence are engaged either overtly and deliberately or covertly and unconsciously, leaders must be able to apply highly nuanced systems of moral reasoning to what they are trying to do or what they see others initiating. In the end, any leader has only his or her own conscience to help discern what is virtuous and what is corrupt, to differentiate right from wrong, and to determine distinctions between means and ends that are implicit components of every use of power in human affairs.

Finally, with regard to the tactics and behaviors leaders can use to influence others, the range of possibilities can be extraordinarily large. The framework is always constrained if not determined by the external environment—the culture, history, membership, and managerial approaches of the organization in which an individual works and the dimensions of diversity of the executive, including age, gender, race, educational background, personality preferences, behavioral tendencies, knowledge, skills, abilities, and experience. As described earlier, influencing tactics are often differentiated in the literature into three major categories: hard, neutral, and soft. Hard tactics are often seen in the use of legitimate authority in directing others to perform tasks and the application of coercion to threaten others with punishment or other adverse consequences if they do not at least comply with demands and orders. Neutral tactics are engaged when leaders ask others for support, assistance, or task performance; when they try to rationally or emotionally persuade targets to follow them; when they create the conditions for collaboration and consultation by deliberately involving others in the tasks of problem identification, creating solutions, and implementing action plans; and finally, when they pursue exchanges of favors, information, resources, or political support. Soft tactics include inspirational appeals; appeals based on personal knowledge or relationships or triangulating with others with and through whom a target is encouraged to take a particular course of action; ingratiation through the use of compliments and emotional and professional support for key people; and laying the groundwork for potential influencing efforts, such as knowing someone well enough to determine the right time to make an appeal, ask for a favor, or even persuade a target to take action.

Exhibit 7.3 provides a summary of 189 identifiable methods and tactics that can be used in power and influencing engagements, including forms of pressure, assertiveness, sanctions, and aggression. Please note that some of the items on this list can be interpreted and experienced as corrupt, coercive, and even evil in the moral sense. It is important to realize that I am not advocating that anyone use these forms of influence in their roles as leaders. However, I do believe that it is vital that every executive know and understand how such approaches can be developed and deployed within and between organizations. In my experience, every leader must prepare for the possibility that other executives may well view the application of such tactics as being within what is permitted—yes, even expected—of senior leaders. Authors such as J. W. Davis (2000) and Greene (1998) have made it clear that such methods are both advocated and actually in wide use throughout the world. Of particular importance are the approaches that incorporate the strategic application of powerful, negative, human emotions such as rage, fear, shame, guilt, disgust, and contempt; the use of bribery of various types; and the adoption of positions involving threats, intimidation, and promises of various types. At their worst historically, we can see the expression of these hard tactics in political and military dictatorships such as Hitler's Third Reich, Stalin's communism, Mao's Cultural Revolution, and Pol Pot's wholesale extermination of millions of people. These methods of power and influence are in widespread practice by political elites in the 21st century within and between various countries. A close reading of human history and contemporary political and strategic analysis (Bobbitt, 2002, 2009) demonstrates clearly that these approaches have been in continuous use for millennia in human affairs. Anyone seeking an executive position must understand these realities and be prepared to confront such tactics during their terms of office.

EXHIBIT 7.3
Methods and Tactics of Power and Influence Pressure, Assertiveness, Sanctions, Aggression

1. Keep checking up on him or her.
2. Simply order him or her to do what is asked.
3. Demand that he or she do what I request.
4. Bawl him or her out.
5. Set a time deadline for him or her to do what I ask.
6. Tell him or her that the work must be done as ordered or he or she should propose a better way.
7. Become a nuisance (keep bugging him/her until he/she does what I want).
8. Repeatedly remind him or her about what I want.
9. Express my anger verbally.
10. Have a showdown in which I confront him or her face-to-face.
11. Point out that the rules require that he or she comply.
12. Blackmail someone.
13. Engage in overt or covert war or combat.
14. Attack someone's allies or protégés.
15. Defend your allies or protégés.
16. Isolate your enemies or competitors.
17. Plan and implement bids for power.
18. Plan and implement hostile takeovers. Sue them. Legislate them out of the business. Lobby them out of the deal.
19. Plan and make acquisitions.
20. Plan and implement mergers—be the lead partner.
21. Block takeovers, acquisitions, and mergers.
22. Stay independent.
23. Use bribes and rewards.
24. Make threats. Back them up.
25. Use punishments.
26. Make promises. Back them up. Keep them.
27. Spread disinformation.
28. Avoid the other, the problem, the decision, implementation.
29. Give direction.
30. Create confusion.
31. Throw hysterical bouts of rage.
32. Throw hysterical bouts of fear.
33. Give no salary increase or prevent the person from getting a pay raise.
34. Threaten his or her job security (e.g., hint of firing or getting him or her fired).
35. Promise (or give) a salary increase.
36. Threaten to give him or her an unsatisfactory performance evaluation.
37. Threaten him or her with loss of promotion.
38. Be apathetic deliberately.
39. Support or encourage deviance, insubordination, and rebellion.
40. Crush deviance, insubordination, and rebellion.
41. Refuse to appease.
42. Project despair deliberately.
43. Arouse pity or sympathy deliberately.
44. Disobey the rules.
45. Lie, cheat, steal, spy. Destroy safety and trust in the environment.
46. Divide and conquer.
47. Use public verbal or physical beatings.

(*continues*)

48. Use ritual verbal or physical beatings.
49. Test limits.
50. Encourage and create dependency.
51. Use bluffs.
52. Use public displays.
53. Engage in fight flight behavior.
54. Use stare downs.
55. Increase, gain, and use strength, information, wealth, allies, favors, intelligence, wisdom, temperance, justice, courage, reverence.
56. Use the vices—greed, lust, envy, etc.
57. Hide strengths, misdirect intentions.
58. Don't cooperate or collaborate.
59. Don't project confidence.
60. Detach, depersonalize.
61. Refuse to reconcile.
62. Avoid detection, don't leave tracks.
63. Deliberately miscommunicate and confuse people.
64. Deliberately provoke people.
65. Clarify rank or role in hierarchy.
66. Take rank or role away. Threaten to take it away.

Ingratiation
67. Make him or her feel important ("only you have the brains, talent to do this").
68. Act very humbly to him or her while making my request.
69. Act in a very friendly manner prior to asking for what I want.
70. Make him or her feel good about me before making my request.
71. Inflate the importance of what I want him or her to do.
72. Praise him or her in private or publicly.
73. Sympathize with him/her about the added problems that my request his or might cause.
74. Wait until he or she appears to be in a receptive mood before asking.
75. Show my need for their help.
76. Ask in a polite way.
77. Pretend I am leading him or her to decide to do what I want (act in a pseudo-democratic fashion).
78. Make promises in exchange for support or commitment.
79. Do favors for someone without being asked to do them. (Include someone, bring him or her to the table. Share private information with them. Share the booty.)
80. Trade favors with a positive attitude.
81. Be a cheerleader for someone without being asked to do so. Look for and create strength in others.
82. Sponsor or mentor someone who is connected to someone else with influence. Protect them.
83. Pay respects to someone in private or publicly.
84. Help someone's family. Protect them.
85. Be obedient. Follow the rules.
86. Sponsor or mentor someone who you think needs it or is an up and coming force in the organization.
87. Avoid provocations.
88. Avoid public displays of hot, negative emotion.

EXHIBIT 7.3

89. Ventilate privately with someone you trust or want to cultivate. Be conciliatory.
90. Avoid ventilating privately with someone you know doesn't like it.
91. Restore status, role, authority, resources, and dignity, to someone who has lost it.
92. Provide resources, information, support and privilege and don't ask for an exchange.

Rational Persuasion, Consultation
93. Write a detailed plan that justifies my ideas.
94. Present him or her with information/data/other influential opinions that support my point of view.
95. Engage in a dialogue or debate to clarify point of view.
96. Sit down to create joint solutions or do problem solving.
97. Explain the reasons for my request.
98. Use logic to convince him or her.
99. Write a memo, letter, or email that described what I want.
100. Offer to compromise over the issue (give in a little).
101. Demonstrate my competence to him or her before making my request.
102. Inquire systematically into the nature of a problem, perspective, and behavior.
103. Ask for and get the opinions, ideas, experience, and history of others before beginning to plan, finalizing a proposal, making a presentation, or executing a plan of action.
104. Engage in rigorous analysis and synthesis as you put together a proposal, seek allies, make a move.
105. Create rigorous theories of mind of others—allies, competitors, and enemies—before planning your own action.
106. Test your theories of mind of others.
107. Create scenarios, what if analyses of the future and test them before making proposals or developing and implementing plans.
108. Analyze the short and long term consequences of proposals, plans and actions before making and implementing them. (Ask the 150-year question.)
109. Create safety and trust in the environment.
110. Do what you promise to do.

Exchange
111. Offer an exchange (e.g., if you do this for me, I will do something for you).
112. Remind him or her of past favors that I did for them.
113. Offer to make a personal sacrifice if he or she would do what I wanted (e.g., work late, work harder, do his/her share of the work, etc.).
114. Do personal favors for him or her in anticipation of asking for something later.
115. Offer to help if he/she would do what I want.
116. Cooperate, collaborate, and reciprocate.
117. Draft and execute contracts, protocols, joint agreements, treaties, and agreements.
118. Be flexible in your deals.
119. Bargain.
120. Negotiate.
121. Agree to mediation or arbitration.
122. Compete fairly and openly.
123. Protect someone's reputation in exchange for similar protections.
124. Make trades.
125. Establish mutual norms, regulations, and laws.

(continues)

Legitimating, Upward Appeal
126. Make a formal appeal to higher levels to back up my request.
127. Obtain the informal support of higher ups.
128. File a report about the other person with higher ups (e.g., my superior).
129. Send him or her to my superior.
130. Discuss the situation with my superiors before taking action.
131. Use my supervisor's public support to generate respect, momentum, or suppress opposition.
132. Publicly align with the boss' position or initiatives.
133. Conduct intelligence operations to discover what positions will be taken.
134. Discover the boss' needs, desires, pet peeves, ideas, and use them to guide the positions you take.

Sanctions
135. Threaten to notify an outside agency if he or she does not give into my request.
136. Threaten to stop working with him or her until he or she gives in.
137. Engage in a work slowdown until he or she does what I want.
138. Ignore him or her and/or stop being friendly.
139. Threaten to or actually sue. Threaten to or actually call the media.
140. Actually inform authorities.
141. Withdraw support.
142. Be intolerant until you get your way.
143. Be rigid until you get your way.
144. Reverse policy or course of action to get your way.
145. Act on your prejudices and biases until you get your way.
146. Legislate the competition out of existence.

Coalition Formation
147. Obtain the support of coworkers or outsiders to back up my request.
148. Have him or her come to a formal conference with others at which I made my request.
149. Obtain the support of subordinates to back up my request.
150. Talk to someone else about the problem to vent or try to influence the other person.
151. Look for and obtain business partners, other sources of financial or political support.
152. Form subgroups.
153. Form or join alliances against stronger players or actors.
154. Pass the buck to stronger players to stop aggression on the part of others.
155. Destroy, undermine, or weaken alliances of others.
156. Send spies into other groups and alliances.
157. Examine how the coalition is or is not working.

Interpersonal and Personal Appeals
158. Recite the past history of favors and make a request.
159. Use rhetorical approaches and speeches to persuade others of the value of your ideas.
160. Make personal promises and keep them.
161. Make personal threats and keep them if you need to.
162. Appeal to others who have influence with the target or have favor balances with them.

EXHIBIT 7.3
Methods and Tactics of Power and Influence Pressure, Assertiveness, Sanctions, Aggression *(Continued)*

163. Use your theory of mind of the other to craft an acceptable approach or spin on a problem or issues.
164. Accept the personal appeal of another with the expectation of reciprocation
165. Appeal to reason, emotion, for war, for peace, for excellence, for partnership, for independence, for alliance, for merger, for compellence, for deterrence.
166. Take careful measure of your political capital with others. Do what you need to do to increase it.
167. Use your knowledge of the political landscape to form relationships with those who have influence. Socialize with them.
168. When in Rome, do as the Romans do.

Miscellaneous
169. Keep kidding or ragging him or her until he/she does what I wanted.
170. Ignore him or her and go ahead and do what I wanted.
171. Provide him or her with various benefits that they want.
172. Challenge his or her ability ("I bet you can't do that").
173. Pretend not to understand what needs to be done so that someone else would volunteer to do it for me.
174. Conceal some of my reasons for trying to influence him/her.
175. Embrace, hug or reassure someone.
176. Study politics, power, and influence.
177. Experiment with politics, power, and influence.
178. Distribute wealth to decrease animosity and motivation for rebellion.
179. Throw parties, circuses.
180. Give gifts.
181. Don't act on prejudice, isms.
182. Create healthy work environments.
183. Reinforce safety and trust.
184. Communicate clearly and honestly.
185. Don't retaliate or act out revenge.
186. Don't shoot messengers.
187. Get problems on the table.
188. Don't play the shame blame game.
189. Engage in great polyvocal, deconstructive discourse.

Exhibit 7.3 also implies that leaders must possess sufficient self-awareness and character to be able to discern, decide, and act in virtuous ways on behalf of their organizations. They must realize that when events or adversaries conspire to injure them and their institutions, they will need to respond vigorously. In the worst of these scenarios, executives must direct campaigns of overt or covert war against enemies. The exhibit also incorporates a wide variety of soft and neutral approaches, including interpersonal and personal appeals, the creation of alliances and coalitions, rational forms of persuasion, methods of exchange, legitimate upward appeal, and sanctions. Executives and their coaches must be well versed in the theory of influence and conversant with a variety of methods that they may be called on to use or to parry in their work. It often requires a hard-eyed assessment of what is happening to decide how to best prepare for, engage in, or respond to various influencing situations and scenarios.

If we examine the tactics and behaviors that Linda used in the case example we have studied in this chapter, it should be clear that over the course of her career, she had become an astute student and practitioner of politics, power, and influence. During the specific time in which she pursued the final components of her strategy to succeed Walter, she possessed both a rational and an intuitive understanding of the models and methods presented in this material. Our conversations rarely slowed down to discuss theory, except where she needed to clarify just what she was trying to accomplish with whom. Most of our exchanges emphasized the concrete, multidimensional, highly nuanced, overtly and covertly designed and implemented campaign of influence to achieve her goals. In the end, she was extremely successful. Max did move Walter aside and kept the organization's promise to Linda.

Max and the organization were rapidly rewarded for this action, as she moved quickly to staunch the losses that Walter and his cronies had been piling up and to restore organizational, political, and economic order in the subsidiary. Her new colleagues in the other subsidiaries discovered that they now had an extremely able collaborator who could see their challenges as well as hers and who worked hard to ensure their success as well as her own. Within a period of 12 months, Max began to describe himself as a "happy man" as Linda's leadership created a series of organizational and marketplace successes. Walter moved into retirement with a fair amount of grace as both Linda and Max worked to protect his dignity and reputation in the transition. The idiots were quietly removed from power and encouraged and supported to move on with their lives. These were expensive departures for the organization, but they were done in such a way that the individuals were protected against major economic losses. Linda quickly paid off her favors and promoted a group of highly capable colleagues to help her turn the organization around.

These kinds of coaching engagements are among the most challenging and rewarding. They are always difficult, sometimes excruciatingly so. The most difficult parts of any such assignment are creating a nuanced understanding of the whole organization, its environment, and the cast of major actors with only the information supplied by a client; developing an ethical stance toward all of the people involved, especially in the face of the knowledge that you are asked to work against others in an organization who probably view their own positions and behavior as virtuously motivated; and managing your emotions in response to the client's need for support in highly provocative, anxiety-arousing, and career- and personally threatening situations. Strategy, character, and influence are equally on call and display for any consultant or coach who works in these environments.

EPILOGUE

So we come to the end of this journey we have made together. I hope that as a reader, you now have a better understanding of why I have come to see strategy, character, and influence as perhaps the three most critical and consistently emphasized components of effective leadership. I also hope that you have learned something new and useful for yourself along the way. I have tried to provide ideas, case examples, succinct summaries of relevant research, and, above all, concrete methods and suggestions for developing more knowledge and skill in these arenas. Most of all, I wish that everyone who has had the determination to read the whole of this book now understands just how important I believe virtuous leadership is in our world and how we all suffer when it disappears in favor of the ever-available and infinitely easier to pursue pathways to corruption. Reading history, one would believe that humanity should have learned these lessons on a collective basis over the course of the past 4,000 years. Despite the ready availability of the experience of our ancestors, the contemporary research that solidifies our diagnostic understanding of what happened and why, and the enormous expansion of technologies that greatly support and aid leaders, the essentials of strategy, character, and influence appear to be as difficult if not more so to pursue and enact in the early 21st century as at any other time in human experience.

Albert Camus (1948) published his world-renowned novel *The Plague* shortly after World War II. It was a metaphoric examination of the human conflicts and processes he witnessed during the German occupation of France that he had experienced so personally as part of the underground Resistance movement. The novel stands as a testament to what I have identified as the seven deadly management errors and their associated problems in Chapter 3 of this book. The organized insanity and slaughter perpetrated by the Nazis and their French collaborators has been well chronicled, and Camus described it beautifully as a human plague. At the end of the story, the hero and first-person witness to what had happened, Dr. Rieux, made a decision to tell his tale as a precaution to humanity so that it might learn from what had happened. He took a completely philosophical stance toward the story, pointing out explicitly that it was not a tale of victory but rather a

> record of what had had to be done, and what assuredly would have to be done again in the never ending fight against terror and its relentless onslaughts, despite their personal afflictions, by all who, while unable to be saints but refusing to bow down to pestilences, strive their utmost to be healers. . . . He knew what those jubilant crowds did not know but could have learned from books: that the plague bacillus never dies or disappears for good; that it can lie dormant for years and years in furniture and linen chests; that it bides its time in bedrooms, cellars, trunks, and bookshelves; and that perhaps the day would come when, for the bane and enlighten-ment of men, it would rouse up its rats again and send them forth to die in a happy city. (p. 308)

Indeed, the inexorable advance of knowledge, skill, ability, experience, and technology driven by humanity's desire for progress, insatiable curiosity, and the need for power and mastery of the world in which we live have given us both more answers and a plague of problems to address. Environmental degradation, the wide availability and proliferation of weapons of mass destruction and the willingness of fanatic martyrs to use them, and the inexorable increases in the global population of *Homo sapiens* will require executives in the 21st century to face realities and threats that have only been imagined in science fiction. In our collective past, we have always been fortunate to benefit eventually from virtuous leaders who seem to present themselves when needed, even after centuries of darkness. If we are able to learn those lessons and incorporate them into how we prepare our colleagues for these most important positions in human affairs, we need not worry about whether we will have the leaders we need to help us solve the problems and challenges to come, to keep the plagues from our doors. After 4 decades of study and practice, I know that this is possible. After reading this book, it is my earnest belief that you may as well.

REFERENCES

Abdalla, I. A. H. (1987). Predictors of the effectiveness of supervisory social power. *Human Relations, 40,* 721–739. doi:10.1177/001872678704001102

Adizes, I. (1988). *Corporate life cycles.* Englewood Cliffs, NJ: Prentice Hall.

Aguinis, H., Nesler, M. S., Quigley, B. M., & Tedeschi, J. T. (1994). Perceptions of power: A cognitive perspective. *Social Behavior and Personality, 22,* 377–384. doi:10.2224/sbp.1994.22.4.377

Allen, R. W., Madison, D. L., Porter, L. W., Renwick, P. A., & Mayes, B. T. (1979). Organizational politics: Tactics and characteristics of its actors. *California Management Review, 22,* 77–83.

Allport, G. (1937). *Personality: A psychological interpretation.* New York, NY: Holt.

Alvesson, M. (1996). *Communication, power and organization.* Berlin, Germany: Walter de Gruyter.

American Psychiatric Association. (1994). *Quick reference to the diagnostic criteria from DSM–IV.* Washington, DC: Author.

Annis Hammond, S. (1996). *The thin book of appreciative inquiry.* Plano, TX: Kodiak Consulting.

Ansari, M. A., & Kapoor, A. (1987). Organizational context and upward influence tactics. *Organizational Behavior and Human Decision Processes, 40,* 39–49. doi:10.1016/0749-5978(87)90004-5

Ansari, M. A., Tandon, K., & Lakhtakia, U. (1989). Organizational context and leaders' use of influence strategies. *Psychological Studies, 34,* 29–38.

Archer, D. (2006). *Global warming: Understanding the forecast.* Malden, MA: Blackwell.

Argyris, C. (1990). *Overcoming organizational defenses.* Englewood Cliffs, NJ: Prentice Hall.

Argyris, C. (1993). *Knowledge for action: A guide to overcoming barriers to organizational change.* San Francisco, CA: Jossey-Bass.

Aristotle. (1908). *Nicomachean ethics* (W. D. Ross, Trans.). Oxford, England: Clarendon Press.

Ashforth, B. E., & Lee, R. T. (1990). Defensive behavior in organizations: A preliminary model. *Human Relations, 43,* 621–648. doi:10.1177/001872679004300702

Astley, W. G., & Sachdeva, P. S. (1984). Structural sources of interorganizational power: A theoretical synthesis. *Academy of Management Review, 9,* 104–113.

Atwater, L. E. (1995). The relationship between supervisory power and organizational characteristics. *Group & Organization Management, 20,* 460–485. doi:10.1177/1059601195204005

Atwater, L. E. (1988). The relative importance of situational and individual variables in predicting leader behavior: The surprising impact of subordinate trust. *Group & Organization Studies, 13,* 290–310. doi:10.1177/105960118801300304

Augustine. (2003). *The confessions of St. Augustine* (E. B. Pusey, Ed.). New York, NY: Barnes & Noble.

Avery, D. R. (2003). Personality as a predictor of the value of voice. *The Journal of Psychology, 137,* 435–446. doi:10.1080/00223980309600626

Bach, S. (1994). *The language of perversion and the language of love.* Northvale, NJ: Jason Aronson.

The Bhagavad-Gita. (1985). (E. Easwaran, Trans.). Petaluma, CA: Nilgiri Press.

Bandura, A. (1977). Self-efficacy: Toward a unifying theory of behavioral change. *Psychological Review, 84,* 191–215. doi:10.1037/0033-295X.84.2.191

Bandura, A. (1982). Self-efficacy mechanism in human agency. *American Psychologist, 37,* 122–147. doi:10.1037/0003-066X.37.2.122

Barry, B., & Bateman, T. S. (1992). Perceptions of influence in managerial dyads: The role of hierarchy, media, and tactics. *Human Relations, 45,* 555–574. doi:10.1177/001872679204500602

Barry, B., & Watson, M. R. (1996). Communication aspects of dyadic social influence in organizations: A review and integration of conceptual and empirical developments. In B. R. Burleson (Ed.), *Communication yearbook* (Vol. 19, pp. 269–317). Thousand Oaks, CA: Sage.

Bartram, D. (2005). The eight great competencies: A criterion-centric approach to validation. *Journal of Applied Psychology, 90,* 1185–1203. doi:10.1037/0021-9010.90.6.1185

Bartram, D., Robertson, I. T., & Callinan, M. (2002). Introduction: A framework for examining organizational effectiveness. In I. T. Robertson, M. Callinan, & D. Bartram (Eds.), *Organizational effectiveness: The role of psychology* (pp. 1–10). Chichester, England: Wiley. doi:10.1002/9780470696736.ch

Bazerman, M. H., & Lewicki, R. J. (1983). *Negotiating in organizations.* London, England: Sage.

Beck, A. T., Rush, A. J., Shaw, B. F., & Emery, G. (1979). *Cognitive therapy of depression.* New York, NY: Guilford Press.

Benedict, R. (1934). *Patterns of culture.* Boston, MA: Houghton Mifflin.

Bennett, J. B. (1988). Power and influence as distinct personality traits: Development and validation of a psychometric measure. *Journal of Research in Personality, 22,* 361–394. doi:10.1016/0092-6566(88)90036-0

Bennis, W. (2007). The challenges of leadership in the modern world: Introduction to the special issue. *American Psychologist, 62,* 2–5. doi:10.1037/0003-066X.62.1.2

Benson, P. G., & Hornsby, J. S. (1988). The politics of pay: The use of influence tactics in job evaluation committees. *Group & Organization Studies, 13,* 208–224. doi:10.1177/105960118801300207

Berridge, G. R. (2002). *Diplomacy: Theory and practice* (2nd ed.). New York, NY: Palgrave.

Bhal, K. T. (2006). LMX-citizenship behavior relationship: Justice as a mediator. *Leadership & Organization Development Journal, 27,* 106–117. doi:10.1108/01437730610646615

Blau, P. M. (1964). *Exchange and power in social life.* New York, NY: Wiley.

Bobbitt, P. (2002). *The shield of Achilles: War, peace, and the course of history.* New York, NY: Anchor Books.

Bobbitt, P. (2009). *Terror and consent: The wars for the twenty-first century.* New York, NY: Anchor Books.

Bohra, K. A., & Pandey, J. (1984). Ingratiation toward strangers, friends, and bosses. *The Journal of Social Psychology, 122,* 217–222. doi:10.1080/00224545.1984.9713483

Bono, J. E., & Anderson, M. H. (2005). The advice and influence networks of transformational leaders. *Journal of Applied Psychology, 90,* 1306–1314. doi:10.1037/0021-9010.90.6.1306

Booth, R. Z., Vinograd-Bausell, C. R., & Harper, D. C. (1984). Social power need and gender among college students. *Psychological Reports, 55,* 243–246.

Booth, W. J. (1994). On the idea of the moral economy. *The American Political Science Review, 88,* 653–667. doi:10.2307/2944801

Boss, R. W. (1978). Trust and managerial problem solving revisited. *Group & Organization Studies, 3,* 331–342. doi:10.1177/105960117800300306

Bossidy, L., & Charan, R. (2002). *Execution: The discipline of getting things done.* New York, NY: Crown Business.

Boyatzis, R., & McKee, A. (2005). *Resonant leadership.* Boston, MA: Harvard Business School Press.

Boyle, B. A., & Dwyer, F. R. (1995). Power, bureaucracy, influence, and performance: Their relationships in industrial distribution channels. *Journal of Business Research, 32,* 189–200. doi:10.1016/0148-2963(94)00045-G

Boyle, B., Dwyer, F. R., Robicheaux, R. A., & Simpson, J. T. (1992). Influence strategies in marketing channels: Measures and use in different relationship structures. *Journal of Marketing Research, 29,* 462–473. doi:10.2307/3172712

Bradford, D. L., & Cohen, A. R. (1998). *Power up: Transforming organizations through shared leadership.* New York, NY: Wiley.

Bremmer, I. (2010). *The end of the free market: Who wins the war between states and corporations?* New York, NY: Portfolio.

Broom, M. F. (2002). *The infinite organization: Celebrating the positive use of power in organizations.* Palo Alto, CA: Davies-Black.

Burns, J. M. (1978). *Leadership.* New York, NY: Harper & Row.

Buss, D. M. (2005). *Handbook of evolutionary psychology.* Hoboken, NJ: Wiley.

Byrne, J. (2002, August 12). Fall from grace. *Business Week,* 50–56.

Caldwell, D. F., & Burger, J. M. (1997). Personality and social influence strategies in the workplace. *Personality and Social Psychology Bulletin, 23,* 1003–1012. doi:10.1177/01461672972310001

Campbell, J. P. (1990). Modeling the performance prediction problem in industrial and organizational psychology. In M. D. Dunnette & L. M. Hough (Eds.), *Handbook of industrial and organizational psychology* (2nd ed., Vol. 1, pp. 687–732). Palo Alto, CA: Consulting Psychologists Press.

Camus, A. (1948). *The plague* (S. Gilbert, Trans.). New York, NY: Vintage Books.

Carlyle, T. (1907). *On heroes, hero-worship, and the heroic in history.* Boston, MA: Houghton Mifflin. (Original work published 1849)

Carver, C. S., & Scheier, M. F. (1998). *On the self-regulation of behavior.* Cambridge, England: Cambridge University Press.

Case, T., Dosier, L., Murkison, G., & Keys, B. (1988). How managers influence superiors: A study of upward influence tactics. *Leadership and Organization Development Journal, 9,* 25–31. doi:10.1108/eb053641

Cateora, P. R., Gilly, M. C., & Graham, J. L. (2009). *International marketing* (14th ed.). New York, NY: McGraw-Hill Irwin.

Cialdini, R. B. (1993). *Influence: The psychology of persuasion.* New York, NY: Quill.

Ciulla, J. B. (2003). *The ethics of leadership.* London, England: Thomson Wadsworth.

Cocivera, T. (1998). *How to get what you want: Using influence, power, and previous experiences in organizations.* Unpublished master's thesis, University of Guelph, Ontario, Canada.

Cocivera, T. (2002). *Influence in organizations: Testing an integrative model of agents' decision-making processes for selecting tactics.* Unpublished doctoral dissertation, University of Guelph, Ontario, Canada.

Cohen, A. R., & Bradford, D. L. (1989). Influence without authority: The uses of alliances, reciprocity, and exchange to accomplish work. *Organizational Dynamics, 17,* 5–17. doi:10.1016/0090-2616(89)90033-8

Cohen, A. R., & Bradford, D. L. (1991). Influence without authority: The uses of alliances, reciprocity, and exchange to accomplish work. In B. M. Shaw (Ed.), *Psychological dimensions of organizational behavior* (pp. 378–402). Toronto, Ontario, Canada: Macmillan.

Coleman, G., & Jinpa, T. (Eds.). (2005). *The Tibetan book of the dead* (G. Dorje, Trans.). New York, NY: Penguin Books.

Coles, R. (2000). *Lives of moral leadership.* New York, NY: Random House.

Collins, J. C., & Porras, J. I. (1994). *Built to last: Successful habits of visionary companies.* New York, NY: HarperCollins.

Collins, J. C. (2001). *Good to great: Why some companies make the leap and others don't.* New York, NY: HarperCollins.

Colquitt, J. A., Conlon, D. E., Wesson, M. J., Porter, C. O., & Ng, K. Y. (2001). Justice at the millennium: A meta-analytic review of 25 years of organizational justice research. *Journal of Applied Psychology, 86*(3), 425–445. doi:10.1037/0021-9010.86.3.425

Confucius. (1989). *The analects of Confucius* (A. Waley, Ed. & Trans.). New York, NY: Vintage Books.

Conger, J. A. (1998). The necessary art of persuasion. *Harvard Business Review, 76,* 84–95.

Côté, S., & Miners, C. T. H. (2006). Emotional intelligence, cognitive intelligence, and job performance. *Administrative Science Quarterly, 51,* 1–28.

Cropanzano, R., Byrne, Z. S., Bobocel, D. R., & Rupp, D. E. (2001). Moral virtues, fairness heuristics, social entities, and other denizens of organizational justice. *Journal of Vocational Behavior, 58,* 164–209. doi:10.1006/jvbe.2001.1791

Crosby, L. A., Evans, K. R., & Cowles, D. (1990). Relationship quality in services selling: An interpersonal influence perspective. *Journal of Marketing, 54,* 68–81. doi:10.2307/1251817

Daniels, T., & Ivey, A. (2007). *Microcounseling: Making skills training work in a multicultural world.* Springfield, IL: Charles C Thomas.

Davis, J. W., Jr. (2000). *Threats and promises: The pursuit of international influence.* Baltimore, MD: The Johns Hopkins University Press.

Davis, M. H. (1996). *Empathy: A psychological approach.* Boulder, CO: Westview Press.

Dawood, N. J. (Ed. & Trans.). (1990). *The Koran.* New York, NY: Penguin Books.

De Cremer, D. (2006). When authorities influence followers' affect: The interactive effect of procedural justice and transformational leadership. *European Journal of Work and Organizational Psychology, 15,* 322–351. doi:10.1080/13594320600627662

De Cremer, D. (2007). Emotional effects of distributive justice as a function of autocratic leader behavior. *Journal of Applied Social Psychology, 37,* 1385–1404. doi:10.1111/j.1559-1816.2007.00217.x

Deluga, R. J. (1991). The relationship of upward-influencing behavior with subordinate-impression management characteristics. *Journal of Applied Social Psychology, 21,* 1145–1160. doi:10.1111/j.1559-1816.1991.tb00463.x

Diedrich, R. C., & Kilburg, R. R. (Eds.). (2001). Further consideration of executive coaching as an emerging competency [Special issue]. *Consulting Psychology Journal: Practice and Research, 53*(4). doi:10.1037/1061-4087.53.4.203

Dillard, J. P., Kinney, T. A., & Cruz, M. G. (1996). Influence, appraisals, and emotions in close relationships. *Communication Monographs, 63,* 105–130. doi:10.1080/03637759609376382

Dosier, L., Case, T., & Keys, B. (1988). How managers influence subordinates: An empirical study of downward influence tactics. *Leadership & Organization Development Journal, 9,* 22–31. doi:10.1108/eb053645

Dotlich, D. L., & Cairo, P. C. (2003). *Why CEOs fail: The 11 behaviors that can derail your climb to the top—and how to manage them.* San Francisco, CA: Jossey-Bass.

Emerson, R. M. (1962). Power–dependence relations. *American Sociological Review, 27,* 31–40. doi:10.2307/2089716

Erez, M., Rim, Y., & Keider, I. (1986). The two sides of the tactics of influence: Agent vs. target. *Journal of Occupational Psychology, 59,* 25–39.

Ericsson, K. A. (Ed.). (1996). *The road to excellence: The acquisition of expert performance in the arts and sciences, sports and games.* Mahwah, NJ: Erlbaum.

Erikson, E. (1962). *Young man Luther: A study in psychoanalysis and history.* New York, NY: Norton.

Erikson, E. (1969). *Gandhi's truth: On the origins of militant nonviolence.* New York, NY: Norton.

Etzioni, A. (1975). *A comparative analysis of complex organizations: On power, involvement, and their correlates.* New York, NY: Free Press.

Falbo, T., & Peplau, L. A. (1980). Power strategies in intimate relationships. *Journal of Personality and Social Psychology, 38,* 618–628. doi:10.1037/0022-3514.38.4.618

Farris, P. W., Bendle, N. T., Pfeifer, P. E., & Reibstein, D. J. (2006). *Marketing metrics: 50+ metrics every executive should master.* Upper Saddle River, NJ: Wharton School Publishing.

Finkel, N. J., & Moghaddam, F. M. (Eds.). (2005). *The psychology of rights and duties: Empirical contributions and normative commentaries.* Washington, DC: American Psychological Association. doi:10.1037/10872-000

Finkelstein, S. (2003). *Why smart executives fail and what you can learn from their mistakes.* New York, NY: Portfolio.

Flick, D. L. (1998). *From debate to dialogue: Using the understanding process to transform our conversations.* Boulder, CO: Orchid.

Folkes, V. S., & Whang, Y. (2003). Account-giving for a corporate transgression influences moral judgment: When those who "Spin" condone harm-doing. *Journal of Applied Psychology, 88,* 79–86. doi:10.1037/0021-9010.88.1.79

Folkman, J. (1996). *Turning feedback into change!* Provo, UT: Publishers Press.

Fowers, B. J. (2005). *Virtue and psychology: Pursuing excellence in ordinary practices.* Washington, DC: American Psychological Association. doi:10.1037/11219-000

Franklin, J. L. (1975). Down the organization: Influence processes across levels of hierarchy. *Administrative Science Quarterly, 20,* 153–164. doi:10.2307/2391691

Fredrickson, B. L. (1998). What good are positive emotions? *Review of General Psychology, 2,* 300–319. doi:10.1037/1089-2680.2.3.300

Fredrickson, B. L. (2009). *Positivity.* New York, NY: Crown.

Freeman, C. W. (1997). *Arts of power: Statecraft and diplomacy.* Washington, DC: U.S. Institute of Peace Press.

Frenay, R. (2006). *Pulse: The coming age of systems and things inspired by living things.* New York, NY: Farrar, Straus & Giroux.

French, J. P., & Raven, B. (1959). The bases of social power. In D. Cartwright & A. Zander (Eds.), *Group dynamics* (pp. 150–167). New York, NY: Harper & Row.

Freud, S. (1973a). Analysis terminable and interminable. In J. Strachey (Ed.), *The standard edition of the complete psychological works of Sigmund Freud* (Vol. 23, pp. 216–237). London, England: Hogarth Press. (Original work published 1937)

Freud, S. (1973b). A child is being beaten. In J. Strachey (Ed.), *The standard edition of the complete psychological works of Sigmund Freud* (Vol. 17, pp. 175–204). London, England: Hogarth Press. (Original work published 1919)

Freud, S. (1973c). The economic problem of masochism. In J. Strachey (Ed.), *The standard edition of the complete psychological works of Sigmund Freud* (Vol. 19, pp. 155–170). London, England: Hogarth Press. (Original work published 1924)

Freud, S. (1973d). The ego and the id. In J. Strachey (Ed.), *The standard edition of the complete psychological works of Sigmund Freud* (Vol. 19, pp. 1–66). London, England: Hogarth Press. (Original work published 1923)

Freud, S. (1973e). Introductory lectures on psychoanalysis. In J. Strachey (Ed.), *The standard edition of the complete psychological works of Sigmund Freud* (Vol. 16, pp. 431–463). London, England: Hogarth Press. (Original work published 1916)

Freud, S. (1973f). New introductory lectures on psychoanalysis. In J. Strachey (Ed.), *The standard edition of the complete psychological works of Sigmund Freud* (Vol. 22, pp. 1–182). London, England: Hogarth Press. (Original work published 1933)

Gaski, J. F. (1986). Interrelations among a channel entity's power sources: Impact of the exercise of reward and coercion on expert, reference, and legitimate power sources. *Journal of Marketing Research, 23,* 62–77. doi:10.2307/3151777

Gergen, K. J. (1999). *An invitation to social construction.* London, England: Sage.

Gerstner, L. V., Jr. (2002). *Who says elephants can't dance?* New York, NY: Harper Business.

Golding, W. (1954). *Lord of the flies.* New York, NY: Perigee.

Goldstein, M., & Henry, D. (2008, July 7). Bear scandal: A widening probe. *Business Week,* 22–23.

Goleman, D. (1995). *Emotional intelligence: Why it can matter more than IQ.* New York, NY: Bantam Books.

Goleman, D. (2006). *Social intelligence: The new science of human relationships.* New York, NY: Bantam Books.

Goleman, D. (2009). *Ecological intelligence: How knowing the hidden impacts of what we buy can change everything.* New York, NY: Broadway Books.

Goleman, D., Boyatzis, R., & McKee, A. (2002). *Primal leadership: Realizing the power of emotional intelligence.* Boston, MA: Harvard Business School Press.

Gordon, T. (1975). *Parent effectiveness training: The tested new way to raise responsible children.* New York, NY: Peter H. Wyden.

Grams, W. C., & Rogers, R. W. (1990). Power and personality: Effects of Machiavellianism, need for approval, and motivation on use of influence tactics. *Journal of General Psychology, 117,* 71–82. doi:10.1080/00221309.1990.9917774

Gray, P. (1994). *The ego and analysis of defense.* Washington, DC: American Psychological Association.

Greenberg, J. (1990). Organizational justice: Yesterday, today, and tomorrow. *Journal of Management, 16,* 399–432. doi:10.1177/014920639001600208

Greenberg, J. (1993). The intellectual adolescence of organizational justice: You've come a long way baby. *Social Justice Research, 6,* 135–148. doi:10.1007/BF01048736

Greene, R. (1998). *The 48 laws of power.* New York, NY: Penguin Books.

Gurtman, M. B. (1992). Trust, distrust, and interpersonal problems: A circumplex analysis. *Journal of Personality and Social Psychology, 62,* 989–1002. doi:10.1037/0022-3514.62.6.989

Hadot, P. (1995). *Philosophy as a way of life.* Malden, MA: Blackwell.

Hagberg, J. O. (2003). *Real power: The stages of personal power in organizations* (3rd ed.). Salem, WI: Sheffield.

Hammett, P. (2007). *Unbalanced influence: Recognizing and resolving the impact of myth and paradox in executive performance.* Mountain View, CA: Davis-Black.

Hanh, T. N. (1975). *The miracle of mindfulness: An introduction to the practice of meditation.* Boston, MA: Beacon Press.

Hargie, O. (2006). *Handbook of communication skills* (3rd ed.). New York, NY: Routledge.

Hargrove, R. (1995). *Masterful coaching: Extraordinary results by impacting people and the way they think and work together.* San Francisco, CA: Pfeiffer.

Harris, H. (2001, May 11). *Courage: Management virtue or dangerous excess?* Paper prepared for Caring for Country: Workshop on Environmental Ethics and the Virtue of Courage in Today's Business World, Angaston, Australia. Retrieved from http://www.unisa.edu.au/hawkeinstitute/gig/documents/courage-dangerous.pdf

Hartley, R. F. (2003). *Management mistakes and successes* (7th ed.). Hoboken, NJ: Wiley.

Hartmann, H. (1958). *Ego psychology and the problem of adaptation.* New York, NY: International Universities Press. doi:10.1037/13180-000

Heifetz, R. A. (1994). *Leadership without easy answers.* Cambridge, MA: Harvard University Press.

Henry, J. P., & Stephens, P. M. (1977). *Stress, health, and the social environment: A sociobiologic approach to medicine.* New York, NY: Springer-Verlag.

Herman, J. (1992). *Trauma and recovery: The aftermath of violence—from domestic abuse to political terror.* New York, NY: Basic Books.

Hobbes, T. (1962). *Leviathan.* New York, NY: Simon & Schuster. (Original work published 1651)

Hogan, R., Curphy, G., & Hogan, J. (1994). What we know about leadership: Effectiveness and personality. *American Psychologist, 49,* 493–504. doi:10.1037/0003-066X.51.5.469

Hornstein, H. A. (1986). *Managerial courage: Revitalizing your company without sacrificing your job.* New York, NY: Wiley.

Hussey, D., & Jenster, P. (2000). *Competitor analysis: Turning intelligence into success.* New York, NY: Wiley.

Hyatt, C., & Gottlieb, L. (1987). *When smart people fail: Rebuilding yourself for success.* New York, NY: Penguin Books.

Ickes, H. (1997). *Empathic accuracy.* New York, NY: Guilford Press.

Imai, Y. (1993). Perceived social power and power motive in interpersonal relationships. *Journal of Social Behavior & Personality, 8,* 687–702.

James, W. (1961). *The varieties of religious experience.* New York, NY: Collier Books. (Original work published 1902)

Jaspers, K. (1957). *Socrates, Buddha, Confucius, Jesus: The paradigmatic individuals.* New York, NY: Harcourt Brace Jovanovich.

Kaeuper, R. W. (1999). *Chivalry and violence in medieval Europe.* New York, NY: Oxford University Press.

Kaiser, R. B., Hogan, R., & Craig, S. B. (2008). Leadership and the fate of organizations. *American Psychologist, 63,* 96–110. doi:10.1037/0003-066X.63.2.96

Kant, I. (1993). *Grounding for the metaphysics of morals* (W. James, Trans.). Indianapolis, IN: Hackett. (Original work published 1785)

Kanter, R. M. (1979). Power failure in management circuits. *Harvard Business Review, 57,* 65–75.

Kaplan, R. S., & Norton, D. P. (2005). The balanced scorecard: Measures that drive performance. *Harvard Business Review, 83,* 172–180.

Katzenbach, J. R. (1998). *Teams at the top: Unleashing the potential of both teams and individual leaders.* Boston, MA: Harvard Business School Press.

Katzenbach, J. R., & Smith, D. K. (1994). *The wisdom of teams: Creating the high-performance organization.* New York, NY: Harper Business.

Kaufman, R., Oakley-Browne, H., Watkins, R., & Leigh, D. (2003). *Strategic planning for success: Aligning people, performance, and payoffs.* San Francisco, CA: Jossey-Bass/Pfeiffer.

Kegan, R., & Lahey, L. L. (2001). *How the way we talk can change the way we work: Seven languages for transformation.* San Francisco, CA: Jossey-Bass.

Kellerman, B. (2004). *Bad leadership: What it is, how it happens, why it matters.* Boston, MA: Harvard Business School Press.

Keys, B., Case, T., Curran, K. E., Miller, T., & Jones, C. (1987). Lateral influence in organizations. *International Journal of Management, 4,* 425–431.

Kilborne, B. (2002). *Disappearing persons: Shame and appearance.* Albany: State University of New York Press.

Kilburg, R. R. (1996). Toward a conceptual understanding and definition of executive coaching. *Consulting Psychology Journal: Practice and Research, 48,* 134–144. doi:10.1037/1061-4087.48.2.134

Kilburg, R. R. (1997). Coaching and executive character: Core problems and basic approaches. *Consulting Psychology Journal: Practice and Research, 49,* 281–299. doi:10.1037/1061-4087.49.4.281

Kilburg, R. R. (2000). *Executive coaching: Developing managerial wisdom in a world of chaos.* Washington, DC: American Psychological Association. doi:10.1037/10355-000

Kilburg, R. R. (2002). Failure and negative outcomes: The taboo topic in executive coaching. In C. Fitzgerald & J. B. Berger (Eds.), *Executive coaching: Practices and perspectives* (pp. 283–301). Palo Alto, CA: Davies-Black.

Kilburg, R. R. (2004). When shadows fall: Using psychodynamic approaches in executive coaching. *Consulting Psychology Journal: Practice and Research, 56,* 246–268. doi:10.1037/1065-9293.56.4.246

Kilburg, R. R. (2006). *Executive wisdom: Coaching and the emergence of virtuous leaders.* Washington, DC: American Psychological Association. doi:10.1037/11464-000

Kilburg, R. R., & Diedrich, R. C. (Eds.). (2007). *The wisdom of coaching.* Washington, DC: American Psychological Association.

Kilburg, R. R., & Donohue, M. D. (2011). Toward a grand unifying theory of leadership: Implications for consulting psychology. *Consulting Psychology Journal: Research and Practice, 63,* 6–25. doi:10.1037/a0023053

Kimble, G. A. (1961). *Hilgard & Marquis' conditioning and learning* (2nd ed.). New York, NY: Appleton-Century-Crofts.

Kipnis, D. (1976). *The powerholders.* Chicago: University of Chicago Press.

Kipnis, D., & Schmidt, S. M. (1985). The language of persuasion. *Psychology Today, 4,* 40–46.

Kipnis, D., Schmidt, S. M., Swaffin-Smith, C., & Wilkinson, I. (1984). Patterns of managerial influence: Shotgun managers, tacticians, and bystanders. *Organizational Dynamics, 12,* 58–67. doi:10.1016/0090-2616(84)90025-1

Kipnis, D., Schmidt, S. M., & Wilkinson, I. (1980). Intraorganizational influence tactics: Explorations in getting one's way. *Journal of Applied Psychology, 65,* 440–452. doi:10.1037/0021-9010.65.4.440

Kipnis, D., Silverman, A., & Copeland, C. (1973). Effects of emotional arousal on the use of supervised coercion with black and union employees. *Journal of Applied Psychology, 57,* 38–43. doi:10.1037/h0034191

Klein, G. (1999). *Sources of power: How people make decisions.* Cambridge, MA: MIT Press.

Klein, G. (2003). *Intuition at work.* New York, NY: Doubleday.

Kohlberg, L. (1981). *Essays on moral development: Vol. 1. The philosophy of moral development.* New York, NY: Harper & Row.

Korda, M. (1975). *Power.* New York, NY: Ballantine Books.

Kotter, J. P. (1977, July/August). Power, dependence, and effective management. *Organizational Dynamics,* 125–136.

Kotter, J. P. (1985). *Power and influence.* New York, NY: Free Press.

Kramer, R. M., & Baron, R. A. (1999). Organizational politics: The state of the field, links to related processes, and an agenda for future research. *Research in Personnel and Human Resources Management, 17,* 1–39.

Kurzweil, R. (1999). *The age of spiritual machines: When computers exceed human intelligence*. New York, NY: Penguin.

Lachapelle, E. (2005). Morality, ethics, and globalization: Lessons from Kant, Hegel, Rawls, and Habermas. *Perspectives on Global Development and Technology, 4*, 603–644. doi:10.1163/156915005775093296

Lao-Tzu. (1989). *Te-tao ching: A new translation based on the recently discovered Ma-wang texts* (R. G. Henricks, Trans.). New York, NY: Ballantine.

Lapsley, D. K. (1996). *Moral psychology*. Boulder, CO: Westview Press.

Lasswell, H. (1958). *Politics: Who gets what, when, and how*. New York, NY: Meridian Books.

Lebacqz, K. (1986). *Six theories of justice: Perspectives from philosophical and theological ethics*. Minneapolis, MN: Augsburg.

Leffert, N., Benson, P. L., Scales, P. C., Sharma, A. R., Drake, D. R., & Dale, A. B. (1998). Developmental assets: Measurement and prediction of risk behaviors among adolescents. *Applied Developmental Science, 2*, 209–230. doi:10.1207/s1532480xads0204_4

Lehmann, D. R., & Winer, R. S. (1994). *Analysis for marketing planning* (3rd ed.). Burr Ridge, IL: Irwin.

Leventhal, G. S. (1980). What should be done with equity theory? New approaches to the study of fairness in social relationships. In L. Berkowitz & W. Walster (Eds.), *Advances in experimental social psychology* (Vol. 9, pp. 91–131). New York, NY: Academic Press.

Leventhal, G. S., Karuza, J., & Fry, W. R. (1980). Beyond fairness: A theory of allocation preferences. In G. Mikula (Ed.), *Social exchange: Advances in theory and research* (pp. 27–55). New York, NY: Springer-Verlag.

Lewicki, R. J., & Litterer, J. A. (1985). *Negotiation: Readings, exercises, and cases*. Homewood, IL: Richard D. Irwin.

Lind, E. A., & Tyler, T. R. (1988). *The social psychology of procedural justice*. New York, NY: Plenum Press.

Lindgren, M., & Bandhold, H. (2009). *Scenario planning: The link between future and strategy* (2nd ed.). New York, NY: Palgrave.

Lipman-Blumen, J. (2005). *The allure of toxic leaders: Why we follow destructive bosses and corrupt politicians and how we can survive them*. New York, NY: Oxford University Press.

Little, J. (2002). *Will Durant: The greatest minds and ideas of all time*. New York, NY: Simon & Schuster.

Lombardo, M. M., & Eichinger, R. W. (2001). *The leadership machine: Architecture to develop leaders for any future*. Minneapolis, MN: Lominger.

Losada, M. (1999). The complex dynamics of high performance teams. *Mathematical and Computer Modelling, 30*, 179–192. doi:10.1016/S0895-7177(99)00189-2

Losada, M., & Heaphy, E. (2004). The role of positivity and connectivity in the performance of business teams. *American Behavioral Scientist, 47*, 740–765. doi:10.1177/0002764203260208

Lubinski, D., & Benbow, C. P. (2000). States of excellence. *American Psychologist, 55*, 137–150. doi:10.1037/0003-066X.55.1.137

Maccoby, M. (2003). *The productive narcissist: The promise and peril of visionary leadership*. New York, NY: Broadway Books.

Machiavelli, N. (1964). *The prince*. New York, NY: Washington Square Press. (Original work published 1582)

MacIntyre, A. (2008). *After virtue* (3rd ed.). Notre Dame, IN: University of Notre Dame Press.

Maimonides, M. (1956). *The guide for the perplexed* (M. Friedländer, Trans.). Mineola, NY: Dover.

March, J. G. (1962). The business firm as a political coalition. *The Journal of Politics, 24*, 662–678. doi:10.2307/2128040

Mayer, J. D., Salovey, P., & Caruso, D. R. (2004a). Emotional intelligence: Theory, findings, and implications. *Psychological Inquiry, 15*, 197–215. doi:10.1207/s15327965pli1503_02

Mayer, J. D., Salovey, P., & Caruso, D. R. (2004b). A further consideration of the issues of emotional intelligence. *Psychological Inquiry, 15*, 249–255. doi:10.1207/s15327965pli1503_05

McClelland, D., & Burnham, D. (1976, March/April). Power is the great motivator. *Harvard Business Review, 54*, 100–110.

McLean, B., & Elkind, P. (2003). *The smartest guys in the room: The amazing rise and scandalous fall of Enron*. London, England: Portfolio.

Meara, N. M. (2001). Response: Just and virtuous leaders and organizations. *Journal of Vocational Behavior, 58*, 227–234. doi:10.1006/jvbe.2001.1794

Mearsheimer, J. J. (2001). *The tragedy of great power politics*. New York, NY: Norton.

Mechanic, D. (1962). Sources of power of lower participants in complex organizations. *Administrative Science Quarterly, 7*, 349–364. doi:10.2307/2390947

Mill, J. S., & Bentham, J. (1987). *Utilitarianism and other essays* (A. Ryan, Ed.). New York, NY: Penguin Books.

Miller, A. G. (2004). *The social psychology of good and evil*. New York, NY: Guilford Press.

Miller, W. I. (2000). *The mystery of courage*. Cambridge, MA: Harvard University Press.

Mintzberg, H. (1983). *Power in and around organizations*. Englewood Cliffs, NJ: Prentice Hall.

Mintzberg, H., Ahlstrand, B., & Lampel, J. (1998). *Strategy safari: A guided tour through the wilds of strategic management*. New York, NY: Free Press.

Mumby, D. K. (1988). *Communication and power in organizations: Discourse, ideology, domination*. Norwood, NJ: Ablex.

Murphy, L. R., Hurrell, J. J., Jr., Sauter, S. L., & Puryear Keita, G. (Eds.). (1995). *Job stress interventions*. Washington, DC: American Psychological Association. doi:10.1037/10183-000

Newman, J. W. (1996). *Asian thought and culture: Disciplines of attention: Buddhist insight meditation, Ignatian spiritual exercises, and classical psychoanalysis*. New York, NY: Peter Lang.

Newton, D. A., & Burgoon, J. K. (1990). The use and consequence of verbal influence strategies during interpersonal disagreements. *Human Communication Research, 16*, 477–518. doi:10.1111/j.1468-2958.1990.tb00220.x

Nicolson, P. (1996). *Gender, power and organization: A psychological perspective*. London, England: Routledge. doi:10.4324/9780203359877

Nietzsche, F. (1993). *Thus spake Zarathustra*. Amherst, NY: Prometheus Books. (Original work published 1883–1885)

Northouse, P. G. (2010). *Leadership: Theory & practice* (5th ed.). Los Angeles, CA: Sage.

Novick, J., & Novick, K. K. (1996). *Fearful symmetry: The development and treatment of sadomasochism*. Northvale, NJ: Jason Aronson.

Oxford Dictionary of English. (1998). New York, NY: Oxford University Press.

Patterson, K., Grenny, J., Maxfield, D., McMillan, R., & Switzler, A. (2008). *Influencer: The power to change anything*. New York, NY: McGraw-Hill.

Patterson, K., Grenny, J., McMillan, R., & Switzler, A. (2002). *Crucial conversations: Tools for talking when stakes are high*. New York, NY: McGraw-Hill.

Pearce, J. A., II, & Robinson, R. B., Jr. (1997). *Formulation, implementation, and control of competitive strategy* (6th ed.). New York: McGraw-Hill/Irwin.

Pearce, W. B., & Littlejohn, S. W. (1997). *Moral conflict: When social worlds collide*. Thousand Oaks, CA: Sage.

Peng, M. W. (2009). *Global strategy* (2nd ed.). Mason, OH: South-Western Cengage Learning.

Personnel Decisions. (1991). *The profiler*. Minneapolis, MN: Author.

Peters, T. (1992). *Liberation management: Necessary disorganization for the nanosecond nineties*. New York, NY: Knopf.

Peterson, C., & Seligman, M. E. (2004). *Character strengths and virtues: A handbook and classification*. New York, NY, and Washington, DC: Oxford University Press and American Psychological Association.

Pfeffer, J. (1981). *Power in organizations*. Marshield, MA: Pittman.

Pfeffer, J. (1992). *Managing with power: Politics and influence in organizations*. Boston, MA: Harvard Business School Press.

Phillips, J. M., Doiuthitt, E. A., & Hyland, M. M. (2001). The role of justice in team member satisfaction with the leader and attachment to the team. *Journal of Applied Psychology, 86*, 316–325. doi:10.1037/0021-9010.86.2.316

Piaget, J. (1965). *The moral judgment of the child* (M. Gabain, Trans.). New York, NY: Free Press.

Picken, J. C., & Dess, G. C. (1997). *Mission critical: The 7 strategic traps that derail even the smartest companies*. Chicago, IL: Irwin Professional.

Pieper, J. (1966). *The four cardinal virtues*. Notre Dame, IN: University of Notre Dame Press.

Plato. (1999). *The republic*. London, England: Everyman.

Porter, M. E. (1980a). *Competitive advantage*. New York, NY: Free Press.

Porter, M. E. (1980b). *Competitive strategy: Techniques for analyzing industries and competitors*. New York, NY: Free Press.

Porter, M. E. (1990a). *The competitive advantage of nations*. New York, NY: Free Press.

Porter, M. E. (1990b, March/April). The competitive advantage of nations. *Harvard Business Review, 89,* 73–93.

Porter, M. E. (1996, November/December). What is strategy? *Harvard Business Review, 74,* 61–78.

Porter, M. E. (2008, January). The five competitive forces that shape strategy. *Harvard Business Review, 93,* 79–93.

Prahalad, C. K., & Hamel, G. (1990, May/June). The core competence of the corporation. *Harvard Business Review, 68,* 79–91.

Price, T. L. (2006). *Understanding ethical failures in leadership*. New York, NY: Cambridge University Press.

Pury, C. L. S., & Lopez, S. J. (Eds.). (2010). *The psychology of courage: Modern research on an ancient virtue*. Washington, DC: American Psychological Association. doi:10.1037/12168-000

Puryear Keita, G., & Sauter, S. L. (Eds.). (1992). *Work and well-being: An agenda for the 1990s*. Washington, DC: American Psychological Association. doi:10.1037/10108-000

Putman, D. (2004). *Psychological courage*. Lanham, MD: University Press of America.

Putman, D. (2010). Philosophical roots of the concept of courage. In C. L. S. Pury & S. L. Lopez (Eds.), *The psychology of courage: Modern research on an ancient virtue* (pp. 9–22). Washington, DC: American Psychological Association. doi:10.1037/12168-001

Quick, J. C., Quick, J. D., Nelson, D., & Hurrell, J. J., Jr. (1997). *Preventive stress management in organizations*. Washington, DC: American Psychological Association. doi:10.1037/10238-000

Radhakrishnan, S., & Moore, C. A. (1967). *Source book in Indian philosophy*. Princeton, NJ: Princeton University Press.

Ralston, B., & Wilson, I. (2006). *The scenario planning handbook: Developing strategies in uncertain times*. Mason, OH: Thomson Higher Education.

Randall, L. (2005). *Warped passages: Unraveling the mysteries of the universe's hidden dimensions*. New York, NY: HarperCollins.

Rate, C. R. (2010). Defining the features of courage: A search for meaning. In C. L. S. Pury & S. L. Lopez (Eds.), *The psychology of courage: Modern research on an ancient virtue* (pp. 47–66). Washington, DC: American Psychological Association. doi:10.1037/12168-003

Raven, B. H. (1992). A power/interaction model of interpersonal influence: French and Raven thirty years later. *Journal of Social Behavior & Personality, 7*, 217–244.

Raven, B. H. (1993). The bases of power: Origins and recent developments. *Journal of Social Issues, 49*, 227–251. doi:10.1111/j.1540-4560.1993.tb01191.x

Raven, B. H. (1999). Kurt Lewin address: Influence, power, religion, and the mechanisms of social control. *Journal of Social Issues, 55*, 161–186. doi:10.1111/0022-4537.00111

Rawls, J. (1971). *A theory of justice*. Cambridge, MA: Harvard University Press.

Reivich, K., & Shatté, A. (2002). *The resilience factor: 7 essential skills for overcoming life's inevitable obstacles*. New York, NY: Broadway Books.

Rogers, G. L. (1996). *Benjamin Franklin's "The art of virtue"* (3rd ed.). Midvale, UT: ChoiceSkills.

Rorty, A. O. (1988). *Mind in action: Essays in the philosophy of mind*. Boston, MA: Beacon Press.

Rosenbluth, S. C., & Steil, J. M. (1995). Predictors of intimacy for women in heterosexual and homosexual couples. *Journal of Social and Personal Relationships, 12*, 163–175. doi:10.1177/0265407595122001

Roskies, E. (1987). *Stress management for the healthy Type A: Theory and practice*. New York: Guilford Press.

Rotter, J. B. (1980). Interpersonal trust, trustworthiness, and gullibility. *American Psychologist, 35*, 1–7. doi:10.1037/0003-066X.35.1.1

Rotundo, M., & Sackett, P. R. (2002). The relative importance of task, citizenship, and counterproductive performance to global ratings of job performance: A policy-capturing approach. *Journal of Applied Psychology, 87*, 66–80. doi:10.1037/0021-9010.87.1.66

Rowling, M. (1979). *Life in medieval times*. New York, NY: Perigee Books.

Salancik, G. R., & Pfeffer, J. (1977). Who gets power and how they hold on to it: A strategic-contingency model of power. *Organizational Dynamics, 5*, 3–21. doi:10.1016/0090-2616(77)90028-6

Schilit, W. K., & Locke, E. (1982). A study of upward influence in organizations. *Administrative Science Quarterly, 27*, 304–316. doi:10.2307/2392305

Schimmel, S. (1997). *The seven deadly sins: Jewish, Christian, and classical reflections on human psychology*. New York, NY: Oxford University Press.

Schön, D. A. (1987). *Educating the reflective practitioner*. San Francisco, CA: Jossey-Bass.

Schumpeter, J. A. (2009). *Can capitalism survive? Creative destruction and the global economy*. New York, NY: HarperCollins.

Schunk, D. H., & Zimmerman, B. J. (Eds.). (1998). *Self-regulated learning: From teaching to self-reflective practice*. New York, NY: Guilford Press.

Seligman, M. E. P., & Csikszentmihalyi, M. (2000). Positive psychology: An introduction. *American Psychologist, 55*, 5–14. doi:10.1037/0003-066X.55.1.5

Sennet, R. (1998). *The corrosion of character*. New York, NY: Norton.

Shengold, L. (1989). *Soul murder: The effects of childhood abuse and deprivation*. New Haven, CT: Yale University Press.

Shotter, J. (1993). *Conversational realities: Constructing life through language*. London, England: Sage.

Siebert, K. W., & Daudelin, M. W. (1999). *The role of reflection in managerial learning*. Westport, CT: Quorum.

Siu, R. G. H. (1979). *The craft of power*. New York, NY: Wiley.

Skolnick, J., Dulberg, N., & Maestre, T. (1999). *Through other eyes: Developing empathy and multicultural perspectives in the social studies*. Toronto, Ontario, Canada: Pippin.

Smith, R., & Emshwiller, J. R. (2003). *24 days: How two* Wall Street Journal *reporters uncovered the lies that destroyed faith in corporate America*. New York, NY: Harper Business.

Snyder, C. R., & Lopez, S. J. (Eds.). (2002). *Handbook of positive psychology*. New York, NY: Oxford University Press.

Spencer, R. (2010). *The great global warming blunder: How mother nature fooled the world's top climate scientists*. New York, NY: Encounter Books.

Stacey, R. D. (1992). *Managing the unknowable: Strategic boundaries between order and chaos in organizations*. San Francisco, CA: Jossey-Bass.

Stacey, R. D. (1996). *Complexity and creativity in organizations*. San Francisco, CA: Berret-Koehler.

Stacey, R. D. (2007). *Strategic management and organizational dynamics: The challenges of complexity* (5th ed.). Harlow, England: Financial Times/Prentice Hall.

Stevens, R. E., Sherwood, P. K., Dunn, J. P., & Loudon, D. L. (2006). *Market opportunity analysis: Text and cases*. New York, NY: Best Business Books.

Strebel, P., & Ohlsson, A.-V. (2006). The art of making smart big moves. *Sloan Management Review, 47*, 72–83.

Swartz, M., & Watkins, S. (2003). *Power failure: The inside story of the collapse of Enron*. New York, NY: Doubleday.

Tandon, K., Ansari, M. A., & Kapoor, A. (1991). Attributing upward influence attempts in organizations. *The Journal of Psychology, 125*, 59–63.

Tedlow, R. S. (2001). *Giants of enterprise: Seven business innovators and the empires they built*. New York, NY: Harper Business.

Tepper, B. J., Eisenbach, R. J., Kirby, S. L., & Potter, P. W. (1998). Test of a justice-based model of subordinates' resistance to downward influence attempts. *Group & Organization Management, 23*, 144–160. doi:10.1177/1059601198232004

Thayer, L. (1988). Leadership/communication: A critical view and a modest proposal. In G. M. Goldhaber & G. A. Barnett (Eds.), *Handbook of organizational communication* (pp. 231–263). Norwood, NJ: Ablex.

Thibaut, J., & Walker, L. (1975). *Procedural justice: A psychological analysis*. Hillsdale, NJ: Erlbaum.

Thompson, L. (2006). *The moral compass: Leadership for a free world*. Baltimore, MD: Johns Hopkins University Press.

Tjosvold, D., Andrews, I. R., & Struthers, J. T. (1992). Leadership influence: Goal interdependence and power. *The Journal of Social Psychology, 132,* 39–50. doi:10.1080/00224545.1992.9924686

Tjosvold, D., Johnson, D. W., & Johnson, R. (1984). Influence strategy, perspective-taking, and relationships between high- and low-power individuals in cooperative and competitive contexts. *The Journal of Psychology, 116,* 187–202. doi:10.1080/00223980.1984.9923636

Treacy, M., & Wiersema, F. (1993, January/February). Customer intimacy and other value disciplines. *Harvard Business Review, 71,* 84–93.

Tugade, M. M., & Frederickson, B. L. (2004). Resilient individuals use positive emotions to bounce back from negative emotional experiences. *Journal of Personality and Social Psychology, 86,* 320–333. doi:10.1037/0022-3514.86.2.320

Tugade, M. M., Frederickson, B. L., & Barrett, L. F. (2004). Psychological resilience and positive emotional granularity: Examining the benefits of positive emotions on coping and health. *Journal of Personality, 72,* 1161–1190. doi:10.1111/j.1467-6494.2004.00294.x

Turner, N., Barling, J., Epitropaki, O., Butcher, V., & Milner, C. (2002). Transformational leadership and moral reasoning. *Journal of Applied Psychology, 87,* 304–311. doi:10.1037/0021-9010.87.2.304

Tushman, M. L. (1977). A political approach to organizations: A review and rationale. *Academy of Management Review, 2,* 206–216.

Van der Heijden, D. (2005). *Scenarios: The art of strategic conversation* (2nd ed.). New York, NY: Wiley.

Velasquez, M. G. (1992). *Business ethics: Concepts and cases* (3rd ed.). Englewood Cliffs, NJ: Prentice Hall.

von Bertalanffy, L. (1968). *General systems theory*. New York, NY: Braziller.

Wack, P. A. (1985a). Scenarios: Shooting the rapids. *Harvard Business Review, 63,* 139–150.

Wack, P. A. (1985b). Scenarios: Uncharted waters ahead. *Harvard Business Review, 63,* 72–79.

Washington, G. (1988). *George Washington's rules of civility and decent behavior in company and conversation*. Bedford, MA: Applewood Books.

Watson, J. D., & Crick, F. H. C. (1953). A structure for deoxyribose nucleic acid. *Nature, 171,* 737–738.

Weber, M. (1975). *The theory of social and economic organization* (T. Parsons, Ed., & A. M. Anderson, Trans.). New York, NY: Simon & Schuster. (Original work published c. 1915)

Weick, K. E. (1995). *Sensemaking in organizations.* Thousand Oaks, CA: Sage.

Weisinger, H. (1998). *Emotional intelligence at work.* San Francisco, CA: Jossey-Bass.

Wheelen, T. L., & Hunger, J. D. (2008). *Strategic management and business policy: Concepts & cases* (11th ed.). Upper Saddle River, NJ: Pearson Prentice Hall.

Whetten, D. A., & Cameron, K. S. (1993). *Developing management skills: Communicating supportively.* New York, NY: HarperCollins.

Wilkinson, I., & Kipnis, D. (1978). Interfirm use of power. *Journal of Applied Psychology, 63*(3), 315–320. doi:10.1037/0021-9010.63.3.315

Woodruff, P. (2001). *Reverence: Renewing a forgotten virtue.* New York, NY: Oxford University Press.

Wurmser, L. (2000). *The power of the inner judge: Psychodynamic treatment of the severe neuroses.* New York, NY: Jason Aronson.

Wurmser, L. (2007). *Torment me, but don't abandon me: Psychoanalysis of the severe neuroses in a new key.* New York, NY: Jason Aronson.

Yates, D., Jr. (1985). *The politics of management.* San Francisco, CA: Jossey-Bass.

Yukl, G. (2010). *Leadership in organizations* (7th ed.). Upper Saddle River, NJ: Prentice Hall.

Yukl, G., & Falbe, C. M. (1990). Influence tactics and objectives in upward, downward, and lateral influence attempts. *Journal of Applied Psychology, 75,* 132–140. doi:10.1037/0021-9010.75.2.132

Yukl, G., & Falbe, C. M. (1991). The importance of different power sources in downward and lateral relations. *Journal of Applied Psychology, 76,* 416–423. doi:10.1037/0021-9010.76.3.416

Yukl, G., Falbe, C. M., & Youn, J. Y. (1993). Patterns of influence behavior for managers. *Group & Organization Management, 18,* 5–28. doi:10.1177/1059601193181002

Yukl, G., Guinan, P. J., & Sottolano, D. (1995). Influence tactics used for different objectives with subordinates, peers, and superiors. *Group & Organization Management, 20,* 272–296. doi:10.1177/1059601195203003

Yukl, G., Kim, H., & Falbe, C. M. (1996). Antecedents of influence outcomes. *Journal of Applied Psychology, 81,* 309–317. doi:10.1037/0021-9010.81.3.309

Yukl, G., & Tracey, B. (1992). Consequences of influence tactics used with subordinates, peers, and the boss. *Journal of Applied Psychology, 77,* 525–535. doi:10.1037/0021-9010.77.4.525

Zhang, T., & Meaney, M. J. (2010). Epigenetics and the environmental regulation of the genome and its function. In S. T. Fiske, D. L. Schacter, & R. J. Sternberg (Eds.), *Annual Review of Psychology* (pp. 439–466). Palo Alto, CA: Annual Reviews.

INDEX

Freud, S., 55, 65
Fry, W. R., 172
Future leaders, 6–11, 20–21

Gains, 204
Gandhi, M., 152
Gaski, J. F., 193
General Electric, 73–74
Geopolitical cycles
    of global population, 224
    recent and current, 3–6
    in strategy formation, 24
GEP (global economic product), 5
Gergen, K. J., 47
Gerstner, Louis, 17–21, 37, 39, 50, 68
Global economic product (GEP), 5
Global economy
    current situation of, 150
    development of, 3–6
    morality in, 174–175
    strategy in, 22–28
Global population, 224
God's laws, 171
Golden rule, 169
Golding, W., 65, 66
Goleman, D., 9–10, 48, 121, 122,
    130, 192
Good opinion approach, 119
Governments, 5–7
Gray, P., 55
Greek models, 13, 83, 103
Greenberg, J., 172–173
Greene, R., 216
Greenhouse gases, 10
Grounding for the Metaphysics of Morals
    (I. Kant), 165
The Guide for the Perplexed
    (M. Maimonides), 164

Hamel, G., 28
Hard tactics, 215–216
Heaphy, E., 123–124, 127
Hedgehog Concept, 118–119
Heifetz, R. A., 21
Herman, J., 55
Heroic executives, 49–50
Hierarchy, administrative, 190–191
Historical context
    geopolitics in, 3–6
    hard tactics of influence in, 216

justice theories in, 163–169
leaders in, 3–6
moral reasoning in, 161–162,
    169–171
problem behavior in, 46–47
severely neurotic leaders in, 63, 68
Hitler, Adolf, 68
Hobbes, Thomas, 165
Hogan, J., 48, 175
Hogan, R., 21, 48, 175
Hornsby, J. S., 195
Hot buttons, 146–147
Human genome project, 9
Humanity, 82
Human resources, 25–26
Hyland, M. M., 174

IBM, 17–21, 39, 50, 73
Identity, 11–12, 27
Incontinence, emotional, 48
Individual leaders, 57–64
Inflated expectations, 48–49
Influence, 185–222
    acquisition and use of, 209–211
    behaviors of, 215–222
    in case study, 185–190, 222
    conceptual model of, 195–206
    core elements of, 195–198
    essential components of, 190–195
    general principles in use of, 211–214
    mutual processes of, 198–203
    power and politics in, 206–222
    strategies for, 203–206
    tactics of, 215–222
    targets of, 200–206
Informational power, 208
Information industries, 8
Integrity, 48
Intelligence
    cognitive, 122
    emotional, 48, 121–122
    social, 121–123, 130
Interaction processes, 195–198
The Internet, 5, 8
Intrapsychic structures, 58–59, 62–63
Intuition
    in influencing processes, 199
    in strategy, 25
    in use of power, 208, 211
iPhone, 8

James, William, 117
Judeo-Christian-Islamic tradition, 46–47
Justice
    communication skills in, 178, 182
    as core virtue, 83
    in executive work model, 84
    organizational case examples of, 183
    in organizational systems, 171–176
    principles of, 161–162, 169–171
    theories of, 163–169
    in virtuous leadership model, 124–127

Kaiser, R. B., 21
Kant, Immanuel, 165
Kanter, R. M., 193
Kaplan, R. S., 27–28
Kapoor, A., 193
Karuza, J., 172
Keider, I., 195
Kellerman, B., 175
Kilborne, B., 64
Kilburg, R. R., 48, 59, 83, 86, 88, 90,
    101, 121, 128, 174, 195, 207
Kinney, T. A., 194
Kipnis, D., 192, 193
Kirby, S. L., 195
Klein, G., 56, 127
Knowledge, 50, 82
Kohlberg, Lawrence, 168
Kotter, J. P., 192, 195
Kramer, R. M., 193
Kurzweil, R., 8

Lachapelle, E., 174
Lakhtakia, U., 193
Lampel, J., 25
Lao Tzu, 163
Lapsley, D. K., 174
Large-scale influence, 203–206
Lasswell, H., 204, 206, 207
Laws, 171
Lay, Ken, 86, 88, 154–161
Leaders, 3–15. *See also* Virtuous leaders
    comprehension skills of, 175
    core functions of, 21–22
    creation of societal dynamics by, 176
    effective, 11–13
    in future, 6–11
    heroic, 49–50
    in historical context, 3–6

intrapsychic structures of, 58–59
    moral point of view of, 177–180
    omnipotent fantasies of, 51–52
    personal characteristics of, 176
    psychopathology of, 62–68
    sacrifice and traumas of, 175–176
    vulnerabilities of, 49–51
Leadership
    amoral, 151, 153–161
    in ancient world, 103
    circular flow models of, 61–62
    as emergent, 59–62
    failure of, 175–176
    measures for, 81–82
    seven deadly errors of, 48–52, 56–57,
        69, 161
    temperate, 120–121
    virtuous leadership model of,
        124–133
Leadership (J. M. Burns), 168–169
The Leadership Architect, 81, 85
Leadership team, 144–145
Learning patterns, 53–57
Legitimate power, 208
Level Five Leaders, 120–121
Leventhal, G. S., 172
Leviathan (T. Hobbes), 165
Lewicki, R. J., 192
Literacy, emotional, 121
Littlejohn, S. W., 174
Lominger's The Leadership Architect,
    81, 85
Long War, 7
Lord of the Flies (W. Golding), 65, 66
Losada, M., 123–124, 127
Losses, 204

Maccoby, M., 48
Machiavelli, Niccoló, 164–165
Madison, D. L., 193
Madoff, Bernie, 48
Maimonides, Moses, 164
Management errors, 41–71
    adaptive world of leaders in, 57–64
    in case study, 41–45, 52–53, 67–68
    correction of, 68–70
    in executive derailment, 45–53
    learning patterns in, 53–57
    psychodynamic foundations of, 53–68
    sadomasochistic patterns in, 64–68

Role-modeling behavior, 56
Roosevelt, Teddy, 4
Rosenbluth, S. C., 194
Rotundo, M., 81
Rules of Civility and Decent Behavior (G. Washington), 117

Sachdeva, P. S., 193
Sackett, P. R., 81
Sacrifice, 175–176
Sadomasochistic patterns, 64–68
Salancik, G. R., 195
Sanctions, 216–222
Sarbanes–Oxley Act, 149, 154
Scenario planning, 38–39
Schön, D. A., 56
Schumpeter, J. A., 51
Scientific community, 5
Secrecy, 49
Securities trading, 50, 155
Self-awareness, 128–129, 221
Self-reflection, 98–100, 121
Self-regulation, 121
Self-restraint, 114
Seligman, M. E., 82–85, 88, 96, 98, 117, 120
Sensitivity, moral and ethical, 178–180
Seven deadly leadership errors
    descriptions of, 48–52
    in Enron case study, 161
    learning patterns in, 56–57
    prevention of, 69
Seven deadly sins, 47
Severe neuroses, 62–68
Shadow structure, 66
Shengold, L., 63
SHL Group's Universal Competency Framework, 81, 85
Shotter, 26–27
Siebert, K. W., 56
Simplicity, 19–20
Simpson, J. T., 193
Sins, 47
Situational assessment, 199–200, 207–208
Skilling, Jeffrey, 154–161
Social control, 46–47
Social intelligence, 121–123, 130
Social Intelligence (D. Goleman), 122
Social networking, 8

Societal dynamics, 176
Socrates, 13, 47, 83, 94, 103, 115–116, 121, 122, 163
Socratic virtues, 85
Soft tactics, 216
South Boston High School, 151–153, 161
Southwest Airlines, 22
Speed, 50
Stacey, R. D., 12
Standard Oil Trust, 4
State capitalism, 7–8
Steil, J. M., 194
Strategy(-ies), 17–39
    in case study, 17–21
    and direction, 21–28
    formation of, 28–39
    for influence, 203–206, 215–222
    for reverence and temperance, 124–145
Strategy formation, 24
Strengths, weaknesses, opportunities, and threats (SWOT) analysis, 28–36, 38
Stress, 182–183
Structured inquiries
    on courage and cowardice, 98–100
    for moral and ethical sensitivity, 178–180
    for reverence, 131–136, 140
    for situational assessment, 207
    for temperance, 140
SWOT (strengths, weaknesses, opportunities, and threats) analysis, 28–36, 38
System theory, 88

Taft, William Howard, 4
Talent management programs, 74
Tandon, K., 193
Tao Te Ching (Lao Tzu), 163
Targets of influence, 200–206
Technological advancements, 3–6, 8–11
Tedeschi, J. T., 193
Telecommunication industries, 8
Temperance, 83, 84. *See also* Reverence and temperance
Temperate leadership, 120–121
Tepper, B. J., 195

ABOUT THE AUTHOR

Richard R. Kilburg received his PhD in clinical psychology from the University of Pittsburgh, Pennsylvania, in 1972. He attended a postgraduate program in mental health administration at the Community Psychiatry Laboratory at Harvard University, Cambridge, Massachusetts, in 1976–1977 and obtained a master's degree in professional writing from Towson University, Baltimore, Maryland, in 1992. He has held positions in the Department of Psychiatry of the University of Pittsburgh as an assistant professor; as the director of the Champlain Valley Mental Health Council, a community mental health center in Burlington, Vermont; the American Psychological Association's (APA's) offices of Professional Affairs and Public Affairs; and the Human Resources Department of the Johns Hopkins University, Baltimore, Maryland, where he directed the human resources development programs. Dr. Kilburg has also been in private practice as a clinician and consultant. He was an associate professor and director of the Master's in Business Administration/ Organization Development Program in the Carey Business School at the Johns Hopkins University 2007–2010. He is the CEO of RRK Coaching and Executive Development, a consulting firm based in Baltimore, Maryland. He has published widely in the fields of management, professional impairment, and executive coaching. He has published five previous books with APA: *Professionals in Distress: Issues, Syndromes, and Solutions in Psychology; How to Manage Your Career in Psychology; Executive Coaching: Developing Managerial Wisdom in a World of Chaos; Executive Wisdom: Coaching and the Emergence of Virtuous Leaders;* and *The Wisdom of Coaching,* coedited with Richard Dietrich. He was the founding president of the Society of Psychologists in Management, and he is a fellow of APA Division 13 (Consulting Psychology). He is the recipient of the 2002 Distinguished Contribution to Psychology in Management Award given by the Society of Psychologists in Management and the 2005 Harry and Miriam Levinson Award for Outstanding Contributions to Consulting Organizational Psychology given by APA. Dr. Kilburg has one son, Benjamin, and currently lives in Towson, Maryland, with his wife, Joy Moore.